The Family Canoe Trip

D1606200

Dear Eric,

Thank you so very much for all of your encouragement and support while I've been at Duke. I always enjoy your tales of adventure, and hope this one of mine will entertain you.

with love and thanks,

Tina

NEW... VT. L.CHAMPLAIN MONTREAL OTTAWA MATTAWA NORTHERN CHURCH...

SANDERS, '85 ©

The Family Canoe Trip

A
unique approach
to canoeing ...

Carl Shepardson

ICS BOOKS, INC.
MERRILLVILLE, INDIANA

THE FAMILY CANOE TRIP

Copyright © 1985 by Carl Shepardson

10 9 8 7 6 5 4 3 2 1

All rights reserved, including the right to reproduce this book or portions thereof in any form or by any means, electronic or mechanical, including photocopying and recording, unless authorization, in writing, is obtained from the publisher. All inquiries should be addressed to Stackpole Books, Cameron and Kelker Streets, Harrisburg, Pennsylvania 17105.

Printed in U.S.A.

Published by:
ICS Books, Inc.
1000 E. 80th Place
Merrillville, IN 46410

Distributed by:
Stackpole Books
Cameron and Kelker Street
Harrisburg, PA 17105

Library of Congress Cataloging in Publication Data

Shepardson, Carl.
   A family canoe trip.

   1. Canoes and canoeing--Canada.   2. Canoes and canoeing--United States.   3. Family recreation--United States.   4. Camping--Canada.   5. Camping--United States.   I. Title.
GV776.15.A2S53   1985   797.1'22'0971   85-2400
ISBN 0-934802-15-7

Table of Contents

PREFACE

One hundred seventy-five years ago the northern portion of this continent was the far-flung empire of a hardy breed of men, the fur-trading voyageurs. The great canoe routes extended west and north from Montreal and each spring's thaw heralded the movement of the annual fur brigades. Covering incredible distances with immense loads, the brigades would sweep back and forth across the continent before the onset of winter. Those days have passed but the canoe routes remain, to a large extent, unchanged.

Each decade has brought forth a few determined adventurers seeking to experience the great canoe journeys of the past. In many ways this is just the story of another such canoe trip but in other ways it is unique. Never before has a family with 2 young children set out to follow the old routes in their entirety. In fact, there are scarcely a handful of men alive today who have completed the adventure we have undertaken. Starting from our home in southern New Hampshire we set out to reach Alaska, a distance of some 6,000 miles, in 3 summers. Setting out in mid-May of 1980, travelling in a 20-foot family canoe, we reached Lake of the Woods in late August of the first year. The next year saw us up to the Northwest Territories and then, in August of 1982, we reached Fort Yukon in Alaska.

We hope our story will appeal to everyone who enjoys the outdoors but family campers and especially canoeists should identify most strongly with our experiences. Although historical allusions and camp-craft lore are sprinkled throughout, this is foremost a daily journal. It was written by 2 tired co-journalists who alternated nights of record keeping, each cajoling the other to write the log before dropping off to sleep. Much of it was hastily scrawled during the last murky moments of twilight in a darkening tent. Exhaustion bares the soul and at times we were consumed by transient difficulties. The vagaries of daily travel are soon forgotten, however. Illusive memory softens the harsh realities of bugs, portages, rain, cold, and wracking stints against wind and current. In retrospect we now recall the panoramic vistas, the evening fires and people met. Remembered best, however, is the supreme contentment of life well-lived. Tripping is not so much a vacation as a way of life. Prepare to travel with us as we get set to leave. As strangers first met we begin by adopting a pleasant custom of the north. We stop to boil the kettle and make acquaintance.

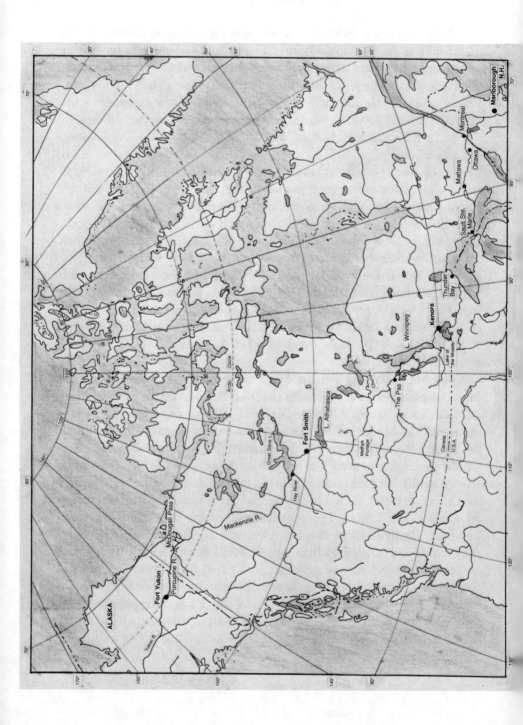

INTRODUCTION

A family with two young children does not normally set out to ensnare itself in a 6,000-mile multi-year canoeing extravaganza. How did we get to this point? The answer, at least in part, is that canoeing is insidiously addictive.

For us it began in the middle 60's when Margie and I took our first 3-day trip together. We paddled down the Delaware from Delhi to Port Jervis late one March. It snowed hard, 15 inches in one day, but we were not even smart enough to pull over. Cold and wet, we survived our first bout with hypothermia -- two dumb college kids.

In August of '68 we realized a boyhood dream of mine by taking a longer 2-week trip through the Boundary Waters of Minnesota. Another less than roaring success. We had enough packs, paddles, duffel and miscellany to require 4 round trip carries on each portage, and Minnesota is mostly portages. For the uninitiated, and that was us, portaging is a form of hiking (particularly popular in Minnesota) in which the poor canoeist seizes his entire outfit and lugs it overland. It is not uncommon for native Minnesotans to come jogging by carrying their entire outfit tucked in a single knapsack beneath their canoe; a sight we found less than refreshing.

In June of '69 we were married and that summer found us on the Allagash in Maine. At 8:00 each morning the Churchill flood gates open and the waters swirl down the 8-mile Chase "Rips" (Yankee for rapids). The extra water covers the worst of the rocks and obstructions and makes the entire route moderately passable. Ignorant of this procedure, we started out at 6:00 and commenced to bang our way down an almost empty river bed. The only other untoward event that trip as I recall was an unfortunate bout with appendicitis (survived, thank you).

The first 2 years of marriage we lived and worked as teachers in Syracuse, New York. These summers we were free to indulge in races and short trips around the state. The Black, Hudson, Genesee, Susquehanna, Delaware and Fulton chain of lakes were all grist for our mill. Flushed with confidence, we visited my folks in March '71 and gave my poor mother a lesson in white water canoeing she'll never forget on Connecticut's Farmington River. In less than an hour we were all 3 swimming with the ice and snow. Bout 2 with hypothermia. This was our first and, hopefully, last swamping.

In '71 we returned to the Boundary Waters / Quetico Region for a

3-week trip in which we proudly covered 375 miles and 115 portages. The Minnesota one-trip style of portaging had been mastered. At that time we were long on brute strength and endurance but rather short on experience. The idea of bushwhacking portages and camping without grills, latrines and picnic tables still dismayed us. Canoeing was still a "vacation"; fishing was for fun, not food.

In January '72 Tina was born and then in December of '74 along came Randy. By then we were living in north central Maine, and were spending spring weekends and summers on its rock-strewn streams and windy lakes. Unknowingly, we were honing the rock picking, wind cheating, canoe poling, rapid running skills that would come in so handy later on. By '75 our attention was turning to Canada and the northern fur trading routes. It was not without some apprehension though that the 4 of us got off the train at Dog Lake in mid-July of '76 and headed down the Missinabie to James Bay -- 1 canoe, 2 kids, 2 adults, 4 weeks of food and 3 dozen diapers.

By the time Randy was 3 the children had reached Hudson Bay 3 times. The second time we paddled the 750 miles from Sioux Lookout to Fort Albany via the Albany River. Then in '78, we travelled the 800 miles from The Pas to York Factory via Lake Winnipeg and the Hayes. Each trip had its lessons. Never again will I stand stranded by an outgoing tide on the mud flats of Hudson Bay facing a polar bear with nothing but a camp axe in one hand and an emergency rescue flare in the other. In '79 we took a breather and contented ourselves with the leisurely 2-week paddle down Labrador's wonderful Moisie River from Lac de Mille.

And now the present; every long canoe trip is the subject of much discussion beforehand and this year's is no exception. We have thought for years about the possibility of crossing the country by canoe and finally we decided the time was right. It would be easier without children of course, but we weren't ready to go before having them and we don't want to wait till they have grown up. Really the time is fairly ideal as we can still all fit in one good sized canoe. We'd hardly hung up our paddles from the Moisie trip before we began to organize.

The first real excitement of a new trip though is when the maps arrive. One cold, snowy day they finally came; we spread them all over the living room floor and began to plan in detail. We looked for the best route, for towns to resupply, and made a rough schedule. And now, well now we are sitting in our front yard perched above the small town of Marlborough in southern New Hampshire. Come along with us as we shoulder our gear and swing down the hill to the Minnewawa Brook on the first leg of a 3-summer trip to Alaska. It is 9:00 a.m., May 17, 1980.

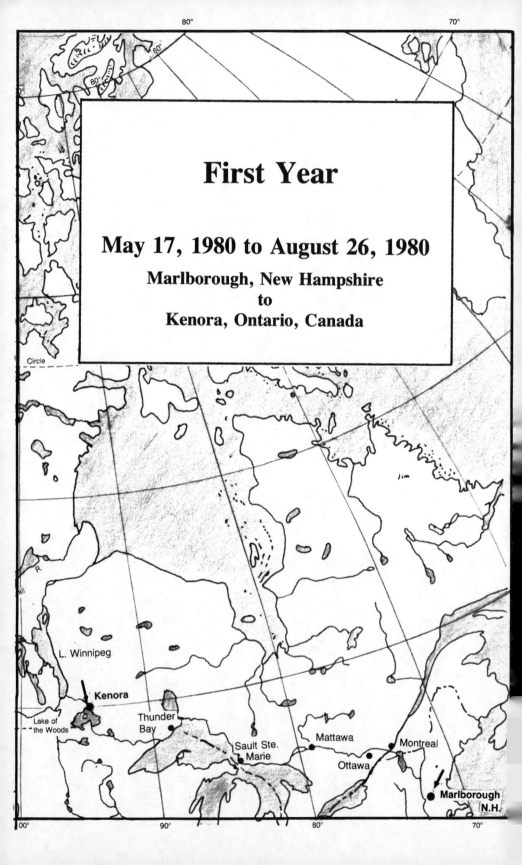

First Year

May 17, 1980 to August 26, 1980

Marlborough, New Hampshire
to
Kenora, Ontario, Canada

MAY 17: DEPARTURE

Well, we did it. Today, after all those weeks of anticipation, we finally put the canoe in the water. Several relatives came up last night to sleep over and see us off this morning so the house was really bustling at breakfast. We got up early and enjoyed a leisurely "last meal" of pancakes and bacon to fortify us for our first day on the river. Then we went clumping around the house in our boots and camping gear, feeling out of place, as we began to sever the ties -- one last drink of water from the faucet, a final trip to the bathroom, a look around (for the hundredth time) to make sure nothing was left behind. It felt strange to be leaving from our house, to just walk down the familiar driveway and know we wouldn't be back for three months. Already we began to disassociate ourselves from the familiar surroundings. Our aunt and uncle were going to be living in the house over the summer and we had already mentally turned the place over to them. It didn't matter if someone put dishes away in the wrong cabinet or brought in some plants to redecorate. We wouldn't be around to live with the changes.

A parade of friends and relatives left the house with us shortly after 9:00. The children, Tina (8) and Randy (5), accompanied us on the half-mile walk down the hill to the brook. It was their first portage of the summer, and their only one for a while since they are not starting with us. It is strange starting off without the kids, but we can't let Tina miss a whole month of school. The neighbors will board her for the next two weeks and the grandparents are taking care of Randy. The plan is for them to drive the children up to Mooer's Forks in upstate New York to join us, two weeks from today. This means we can use our small 16-foot, 67-pound ABS canoe to cross New England and won't have to put the children through the ordeal of the upcoming 5 and 10-mile carries across Vermont.

Months ago we arbitrarily chose 10:00 a.m., May 17 as our departure date and we were right on time. By 9:30 the canoe was loaded and in we popped, poised for the good-bye pictures. It was a glorious morning,

1

crisp blue sky, Margie with her corsage, a bunch of balloons, an Alaska flag -- all in all a very proper start -- except there was no water. It's been a dry spring and it's hard to float even an empty canoe, much less a loaded one, on the Minnewawa Brook these days. Once pictures were taken we had to hop right out and start hauling down over the rocky streambed. Everybody was there to see us go, lunging down the polluted stream, dragging the canoe behind us. Neither of us felt very clever, but it was still a relief to be off. We have both felt a self-imposed burden of expectations the last few days. Everybody knows our plans and they seemed to bubble to the surface of every conversation lately. Our time of departure was no secret and I believe we would have felt compelled to leave even if it was snowing. Fortunately the weather was beautiful.

I suppose technically the trip started last night. It is a half-mile carry down to the brook at the bottom of our hill and neither of us wished to look too foolish by being unable to portage our stuff that far. Instead we carried everything half way yesterday, down to where the minister lives, and then spent a relaxing evening with him and his family. They had invited us for supper, and for dessert there was a chocolate cake with a paper canoe and two little paddles on top. "Alaska, here we come," it said.

Well, it was a slow start -- we are not fast draggers. It took an hour or so to do the half mile before our first portage, a short one through Beauregard's Lumber Yard on the far side of town.

At 1:00 we reached the town line and by 2:00 we had zoomed out of sight. Immediately we stopped for lunch and a chance to wiggle our toes in the sun and dry out. The first 4 hours were enough wading and dragging for the entire summer. Although the stream was too shallow and rocky to float the canoe it was deep enough between the rocks to go over our boots. Then too, the tireder we became, the slipperier the rocks got. Of course we fell in that smelly water more than once and both acquired small scrapes and bangs. Really the only ones who enjoyed that section were the town dogs. They splashed and barked uproariously as they accompanied us down the stream, romping in and out of the shallow pools ahead of us.

Things picked up after lunch though and by 5:30 we reached West Swanzey on the Ashuelot. We have set up camp by the falls below the old covered bridge. This appears to be the local trysting place. The highschool prom is tonight and several couples have been out already to practice their necking. My nephew has been by to say there will be a beer drinking party nearby later on but we are too tired to continue downriver out of their way.

The Ashuelot is terribly, disgustingly polluted (and smells worse than the Minnewawa) but at least there is enough water to paddle. It is a shame though to see the way that even a small city like Keene can destroy what should be a beautiful river. We did manage to take pictures of ducks, muskrats and a beaver dam today. In all we did 5 portages, none long. The next time I go to Alaska, however, I shall not start in Marlborough. I pass this observation on as sound advice to future travellers: you can't get there from here.

MAY 18: FIRST CHEAT

Well, we are feeling some remorse tonight. In all our weeks of planning we never discussed the possibility of accepting a ride part way. Then it happened so fast. There we were a mile or so into our sixth portage of the day. It was late afternoon and a cold steady spring rain had been falling since 6:30 in the morning. A truck stopped to offer us a lift and that was it. The next moment we were inside the cab, heater on, rain drumming loudly, wipers swishing on the window. Mercifully it was over soon. Five minutes and we were standing in the rain again but something momentous had happened. We had been assuming that we would do this trip entirely on our own and had even refused a friend's offer to drive us down our hill yesterday. Now only a day later we had spoiled it, or so it seemed. It is hours later now though and we have finally reconciled the event to our satisfaction. We haven't talked it out but it is clear that while neither of us would try to hitch a ride we are both prepared to accept one if the chance should ever come up again. A faint aura of guilt still persists but it is dissipating rapidly.

The canoeing was a little more interesting today although it was cool (52 degrees) and wet. We set out about 6:30 and travelled pretty steadily till 5:00. The lower portions of the Ashuelot were far more exciting than yesterday and we ran many fine rapids, choosing to portage only the dams and worst sets of white water. Although there was no way to keep our gear completely dry, we did manage to warm up once at a paper mill this afternoon. Even though it is Sunday the steam generators were going and the watchman invited us inside to chat and steam dry. The noise was tremendous.

3

Once by the Vernon Dam on the Connecticut we were able to zoom along against the negligible current with a wind at our backs. An hour of such travel brought us to a beautiful campsite high on the east bank and we set up an elaborate shelter using tent, tarps and canoe. It is very homey and towards sundown the rain stopped and the sun came out. Tomorrow should be a beautiful day.

Of course we are not drinking the water. We have brought a plastic gallon milk bottle with us and plan to refill it with fresh water at people's houses a couple of times a day. So far there has been no trouble. People have been more than willing to let us fill it up.

Although we had a sandy place to set up last night neither of us slept well. No surprise. We never do sleep much on the first night of a trip regardless of the terrain. Perhaps we aren't tired enough so early in the journey. Most years we take small pads to spread beneath our sleeping bags but this time we have regretfully left them at home. We decided that:

1) travelling so far south we really didn't need them for warmth and

2) the space they occupied could be better utilized. There are a lot of carries between here and Mooer's Forks and we wanted to make them all one-trip-portages. The pads will arrive there with the children and we shall have a second chance then to decide whether we need them. As for the one-trip-portages, disregarding the slip up with the truck, things are going well. We have done over ten in two days. Margie staggers along with a huge 85-pound pack while I carry the 67-lb. canoe and a relatively light pack. The rain of course tends to soak in and make her load even heavier and surprisingly enough I am observing the same phenomenon. While the ABS canoe is impervious to water afloat, I have recently noticed that it appears to soak up considerable weight by the end of a long carry.

MAY 19: ONE WAY STREET

It has been a hard day and we are both tired. We thought that we might reach Bellows Falls but we seem to have fallen some seven miles short. The Connecticut is a pretty river and we travelled from 7:30 till 6:00 but the current is tiresomely strong. In places it was hard to hold our own, much less progress. As the nations's natural highways the rivers seem to be pretty much one-way streets.

The day was cloudy with only a few sprinkles here and there. We saw several large hawks but the most intriguing sights were the large colonies of cliff swallows. Many of the large sand-mud cliffs have literally hundreds of dwellings and we could see the residents popping in and out of their holes like so many condominium dwellers. The holes appeared to have no particular pattern but I believe they have the "broken stick" distribution familiar to statisticians.

Tonight we are camped on Taylor Island just south of Walpole. The river has been deserted all day except for an occasional fisherman.

Last night's bannock was a little too salty but hopefully today's is better. It usually takes a few days before they start coming out perfect. The evening bannock baking is the last of our daily chores before we pick up for the evening and retire. It is practically a nightly ritual. Everybody has his own techniques and recipes of course but there is no harm in detailing ours.

First, melt 1 heaping tablespoon of shortening in a large frying pan. The pan now greased, pour the excess drippings into a mixture of two and half to three cups of flour, one teaspoon of salt, one tablespoon of baking powder and one tablespoon of sugar. You may add milk powder and extra sugar if you like. Then pour in one cup of water and mix well, adding more flour if necessary until it is not too sticky to pick up in a ball. If the dough is too stiff it won't cook through easily. If too soft you will have trouble propping up the pan. A couple of day's practice is usually enough to master the procedure.

The whole mixture can be prepared right in the top of a flour bag but, since we frequently carry flour in gallon plastic milk bottles, this approach is not practical for us. (We use a pan for mixing instead and have found that the children love to pick and lick it clean afterwards which is very convenient as bannock pans can be a devil to wash.) Be warned though, that these milk bottles can burst even when placed deep inside a pack and the resulting mess can spoil an entire evening. However, by and large, the bottles prove dry and secure and one bottle holds five pounds. Sending flour (or powdered milk) through a blender beforehand will save space but is not really worth the trouble.

There are at least two more efficient approaches to making bannock:

1) Use bisquick (unfortunately it does not seem to taste quite as good and is expensive).

2) Premix the ingredients at home. This is probably the most sensible ploy. It saves a lot of packing and unpacking of ingredients when you are tired. On rainy nights it is particularly helpful. Every year we solemnly agree that we shall do this for our next trip, but we never do.

5

For a special treat add blueberries, cinnamon and extra brown sugar.

Once mixed, spread your bannock out to cover the frying pan to a depth of about an inch. Then place the pan on the grill several inches above the coals (or hold it above the fire for about ten minutes). In either case it should be allowed to rise and brown on the bottom. Allowing the bottom to brown will give your bannock the extra stiffness necessary to prevent its sagging into a heap on the ground in the next step.

Once the bottom is browned, remove it and kick off the grill (the grill is hot). You should have your bannock boulder and kindling at hand now. Take a stick and place it crosswise horizontally above the coals near the front of your fire. Now stand your kindling vertically, picket fence wise, against this horizontal support. The boulder goes out front about a foot away. Now lean the frying pan straight up against the rock facing the hot wall of kindling flames. It should be only minutes 'til you have a delicious golden brown bannock (you will probably need to rotate the pan for even cooking). It should be two to three inches thick and practically irresistible. We always cook one for the next day's lunch and occasionally an extra just to demolish on the spot, steamy hot with butter and strawberry jam. Once you have tried this you will never again use bread, rye crisp, pilot biscuits, cold pancakes or whatever on your excursions.

NOTE. When travelling with others be very careful of your campanion's bannocks. Some people are very possessive and we were once accused of filching a still warm bannock. Fortunately, the owner found it down at the bottom of his own pack some days later and so we were eventually forgiven.

MAY 20: FORT NUMBER 4

This morning dawned a beautiful hazy peach color everywhere. I changed the film and took a picture: "Dawn on the Connecticut" looking north towards the Walpole Bridge. It turns out we camped about one mile below it last night. We suspected as much once we noticed the blinking light high on the east shore at dusk.

We left at our usual time of 7:30 after eating breakfast and washing clothes. The current flowing off the tip of our campsite island was such that we had to leap into the canoe and paddle off at a furious pace to avoid being swept downstream. We headed right for the east bank where we hoped to gain at least some shelter from the current. Once there we crept along a few feet (or even inches) at a time, hugging the shore and rejoicing in each little indentation that offered easier paddling. Occasionally there would be an eddy where the water would actually flow in our direction. At other times, however, we would come to a fallen tree or a gravel bar which would force us out into the current. We would dash out there, turn the canoe so it was facing straight upstream, then paddle madly to hold our own and eventually inch ahead of the obstruction. Then we'd zip back to the relative calm of the bank. A couple of times we even managed to paddle up riffles, one of which had small standing waves. Then at 9:30 we rounded a corner and came in sight of Bellows Falls. It was still a mile or so off but we hadn't expected to see it quite so soon. We paddled up right into the narrow rocky chasm there. The walls appeared to be at least 75 feet straight up. There was no convenient landing place but we soon settled for a spot below the stone arched bridge. From there we tried to scale the cliffs to the road. It was the kind of place that even a mountain goat would have to get down on all eights to negotiate but somehow we hauled the canoe and gear up to the bridge. From there it was about a two-thirds mile carry to get around the dam. It was after 12:00 by then and we collapsed in the shade to enjoy our lunch. It used to take about three days of travel to harden us into shape but this is the fourth already and I believe we are still deteriorating. Fortunately, however, the current above the dam was almost nonexistent and we were able to do the next ten miles to the mouth of the Black River in about 3 hours.

Just before reaching the Black we saw a reconstructed fort on the east bank of the Connecticut. We scrambled up the mud bank and crossed the little field to learn that it is "Fort Number 4" originally built in 1746. There are 13 buildings inside the stockade but not all are reconstructed yet. The fort's most interesting feature is the stockade itself, a spaced out "Indian Fence". The pickets are all several inches apart so that the colonists can see any Indians approaching the fort. An interesting idea but one which is apparently ineffective. No one saw us sneaking up from the river until we were well inside the fort itself.

Tonight we are camped on an island at the mouth of the Black River. It is a cozy spot amongst some trees and the weather is perfect now that it has finally cooled off a bit. We are both well sunburned. Across from us is a public boat ramp and the place has been really hopping. Fishermen have been buzzing in and out all evening, although it is starting to quiet down now.

7

The Connecticut has cleaner water than the Ashuelot but it is very muddy and still not drinkable. At least now instead of smelling the polluted water and exposed mud flats of the Ashuelot we can scent fields and flowers as we paddle along. There are lots of birds around making cheerful noises. Redwing blackbirds chirp from the tree branches and cattails along the shore while cliff swallows dart in and out of their sandy holes. It is still early enough that the trees have their beautiful bright spring green. The hills too are all shades of green, almost as colorful as in the fall. The flowering trees and shrubs make bright splashes of white and pink. Earlier we saw Mt. Ascutney in the distance. We should close to within a few miles of it in the next day or two. We are happy to be at the junction with the Black but we are dreading the next few days of steep upstream travel. It has been hard going on the Connecticut but we expect the Black to be worse, as we start our cut across Vermont.

MAY 21: WE TRACK THE BLACK

There might well be conditions under which tracking a canoe upriver could be enjoyable. In theory it seems so simple. Just tie a line to the canoe and then go hiking along the bank, the canoe docilely rippling its way upstream behind you like a well-trained puppy on its leash. Actually, even in theory, there is somewhat more to the process than this. The first trick is to use two ropes, one tied to each end of the canoe. If the sternman then keeps his end in close to shore, comparatively speaking, the current will catch the canoe obliquely and push it out into the middle away from the shallows and any obstructions. A well-coordinated couple working as a team can have the canoe nimbly darting in and out amongst rocks lying many yards off shore while they stride with good-natured nonchalance along the beach. So much for theory.

In practice you will discover several things. First there is no such thing as a well-coordinated team. Your partner is always fouling things up. As a corollary trackers rarely experience good-naturedness. In fact, tracking is the most trying experience a couple can have with a canoe. Furthermore, the existence of good tracking terrain is a myth. Your normal options appear to be:

a) a boulder garden of a shore line along which you must stagger. Usually it is raining and the rocks are slippery. The idea is to stumble along the rocks at an even pace maintaining your balance while you keep

8

your eyes on the canoe and keep the rope taut in your hand, not tangled in your feet.

b) mud. We spent several days once, forcing our way up the muddy shores of the Nelson River from Hudson Bay. The consistency of the mud was such that you always sank in above your ankles and were in continual danger of losing your boots. The authorities have dammed the Nelson, allowing them to maintain the uniform quality of their mud which they do by raising and lowering the water level four feet twice a day.

c) alder bushes. These are a real curse. They usually overhang the water and the idea is to stumble along the edge of the bank pushing the branches aside with your free arm. Inevitably, however, you will find yourself either tripped up by the lower lying branches or else deliberately pushed into the drink by the whippy upper boughs (there is nothing more irritating than this). In the same class with alder bushes are the trees and bushes which have slid down steep banks into swift water. You can't quite flip those ropes over the tiptop branches so you have to either climb out along the branches over the water with attendant difficulties or else give up, plunge in and wade around.

The Black, however, added a new twist to tracking, at least for us. There was the usual tedious hanging up of the ropes on bushes and the canoe on rocks. There were also the steep banks and overhanging branches which forced us down on our bellies snaking the ropes along as we crawled upstream. But then in addition there was a special New England touch; spanking fresh poison ivy plants crowding the shoreline everywhere you looked.

Overall then the day was a hard one with many types of travel. At 3:00 we took a break though, when we reached a newly erected sign on the north bank saying "Welcome, Shepardsons." Some friends from Keene have been expecting us and we stopped for a visit. Afterwards we forged our way upstream till 6:00. Tonight we are camped at a beautiful spot, scenic and sandy, at a broken dam and falls about a mile below Perkinsville. At times today we had to paddle hard against the current, at others we got out and waded, dragging the canoe upriver rock by rock, or scrambled tracking along the banks. Finally there were three good portages, the most amusing being a three-quarters mile trek through downtown Springfield around the 6 dams and falls there. We drew a curious crowd of shoppers and storekeepers, most of whom seemed to voice the opinion that we were "going the wrong way". We were both hot and tired by then, however, and such good humor fell upon deaf ears.

9

MAY 22: THE PACE SLOWS

This morning started off hazy and cool. Right after breakfast we portaged up around the dam and were off. We had finally eaten enough so that everything fit pretty easily into our packs. After paddling about a mile we reached the next dam which we also portaged. By then the sun was bright and the day growing warm. The current picked up but still we were able to paddle and wade the next two miles to the covered bridge at Downers. Two deer came down to the stream and crossed nimbly ahead of us. The next three miles were all pretty much class three rapids so we climbed up to the road and started carrying.

The portaging was along the highway, good walking but very hot and tiring. We must have looked a sight as we struggled on with our loads and trotted off down the road. Being thin, it feels as if the center thwart of the canoe rests directly on my neck vertebrae and the load quickly becomes a nagging nuisance. I realize that padded canoe yokes and shoulder pads exist but I find them aesthetically wrong. Then too, having grown up without them, they strike me as a little effete. At any rate, not having them is a good excuse to set the canoe down for frequent rests. On a long carry, however, you find yourself using little tricks to prolong the distance between stops. One is to keep switching the canoe from one shoulder to the other. Along this line it helps to place one hand in your hip pocket. This bunches the shoulder muscle, lifting the canoe off of your bones. Of course if you are carrying a pack, the straps too will absorb some of the canoe's weight. The second trick is to try trotting when the terrain permits. Margie just jogs along but I use a gliding stride so as to keep the shoulders level and prevent the canoe's jouncing. Years ago I simply let the canoe bounce but this eventually broke the center thwart. It happened in the middle of a long carry. I was jogging through a swamp when the thwart parted with a heart-rending snap, dropping the boat about my ears and pitching me forward into the bog. Luckily I was also carrying a large pack which absorbed the shock of the descending canoe, although the weight did drive me pretty deeply into the muck. Fortunately, it was the pack with the axe and the tackle box (it carries the spare nails) and so in short order I had fashioned temporary repairs and was on my way. Since then, however, I have always run gently.

Well, anyway we hadn't done more than two miles before a truck stopped and gave us a lift to a rest area at the end of the carry. We ate lunch and had a long rest. Then we faced two more miles of wading and dragging. We decided to take turns. One dragged while the other walked a half mile along the highway to wait for the canoe to arrive. It was pleasant waiting there barefoot, drying out in the sun while the other stumbled, sloshed and swam their way upstream. We switched off twice each, finally reaching Whitesville. It was slow work, about one mile an hour, but easier than portaging and much pleasanter on a hot day (the temperature was 85 degrees in the shade). There was a quarter mile carry at Whitesville, then another mile of wading to Cavendish Gorge. A quarter mile vertical carry there brought us to the top, where we are camped tonight. Water is still somewhat of a problem. We are using river water to do the dishes but even so our gallon jug does not seem to hold enough for the supper-breakfast combination. The bugs are out in force tonight.

MAY 23: CROSSING THE GREEN MOUNTAINS

We got up about 6:00 this morning and while Margie cooked breakfast I tried three times to take a picture of a beaver working down below. The lighting was poor and I suspect I snapped the last picture a little late. Oh well, one more photo of concentric ripples to add to our collection of "just dived" pictures.

Today was the second hot day in a row. We waded, tracked, paddled, and portaged till about 4:00, when we finally reached the golf course at the top of the Black River where Route 103 goes west and 100 north. Those were agonizing miles and as I have not yet detailed the vicissitudes of wading, I shall try to do so now.

Wading is often done when a shallow river is too rocky to track (or line). Usually you are continually slipping off of or stumbling into submerged boulders. It is generally not possible to see where you are placing your feet so your toes keep stabbing into the rocks and your feet get twisted in the crevices. Your boots fill up with water and every step becomes an effort. Soon the fronts of your thighs ache and your legs are quivering with exhaustion. You can't walk erect, hold the canoe, and maintain your balance all at the same time, so you are continually hunched over clinging to the stems of the canoe. Soon your back begins to ache. You and your partner naturally proceed at different speeds. Thus the bowman is forever in danger of either having the stem pushed up his backside as he dances around the front end to get on the shallow side of the boat, or else having the canoe yanked backwards out of his grasp.

11

the PORTAGE

SANDERS '84

Meanwhile the sternman continually finds the boat snatched forward just as he attempts to lean on it to maintain his balance or to ride over a particularly deep spot. A good wading match quickly degenerates into a conniving tug of war.

Anyway, we finally reached the golf course and it was still an hour to supper time so we decided to pick up and start the 10 mile carry west over Mount Holly to the Mill River. People are so nice. We hadn't gone more than a mile when a pickup truck stopped and gave us a lift halfway across. We started hiking again and in about a mile a second truck stopped and took us the rest of the way. You hear how hard it is to hitchhike these days and yet here were people falling all over themselves to offer us unsolicited rides. We were awfully grateful but it is hard to thank people adequately.

Anyway here we are on the bank of the Mill River, a mile or so below East Wallingford. Frankly things do not look good. The river is extremely rocky and almost dry (much like the Minnewawa -- except steeper) so tomorrow will begin with a portage of indefinite length. We are both a little tired and have agreed that the next time we "walk" to Alaska we shall leave the canoe at home. It is an awkward burden. We rarely second guess our actions but we can't help wondering how our alternate route would have worked. Earlier this spring we had given some thought to turning left on the Connecticut and proceeding downstream to Long Island Sound. Then we could have visited New York City and come up the Hudson to Lake Champlain. It would have been a lot further, but there would have been a good deal less carrying. Well, it is about 10 miles to Otter Creek where we hope things will begin to pick up. Maybe we won't have to walk all the way.

We have enjoyed passing under the large deciduous trees this spring. This is an experience northern travellers rarely have as the north is mostly pines. We especially like the apple and cherry trees all in bloom; they really make the air smell sweet. And now the violets and lilacs are also out. We passed by several attractive old stone houses in Cavendish this morning. Spring in New England is so beautiful.

We seem to have acquired a case of poison ivy on our hands.

MAY 24: PIT STOP

This was another hot sunny day. We got up at 5:30 and portaged from 6 till 7 in the cool of the day, carrying the one and a half miles to Cuttingsville. There we rested by the bridge and ate breakfast. Soon the people across the street were awake and we went over to get some water. The river still looked too rocky and shallow to canoe or wade, and besides portaging is faster than dragging. Also it was still a little cool to be getting wet so, sufficiently refreshed, we picked up and carried another mile out of town to the next bridge. It was 9:00 by then and getting warmer and so were we. Anxious to get in the water, we plunged in and started wading and dragging and continued on this way till we reached Clarendon Gorge at noon. The last mile was absolutely miserable, practically a continual descent down small falls, and the gorge was impassable. That did it, we decided to pick up and carry the long miles to Otter Creek. The Long Trail crosses at the gorge and we used it to hike up to the road.

The hiking trail had been freshly relocated and blazed but was still poorly chosen for the canoeist. It seemed to go unnecessarily high above the highway and then steeply down to the road. The trees had been cleverly situated in such a way as to make almost impossible the passage of a boat. It was 80 degrees by then -- too hot for hiking -- and Margie writes: "The trail was impossibly steep and muddy. I couldn't step up onto the log steps since my pants were wet from wading, making it hard to bend and lift my knees, and because of the pack I could hardly raise my head high enough to see up the slope. Then every time I tried to step up I slipped on the mud, nearly losing my balance with my heavy unwieldy pack. Up on the trail the paddles (which were strapped sideways on top of the pack) kept getting caught between the trees and had to be removed. To top it off a hiker in for the day breezed by with a cheery 'Nice day, isn't it?' I wasn't inclined to agree with him." Finally however, we did reach the road.

We persevered and, despite blistered feet, eventually finished portaging all the way to Otter Creek (three more miles) with a lunch stop in East Clarendon. From East Clarendon it was less than a mile out of our way to visit the airport and a public phone so Margie jogged over to call Karen, a friend who lives in Rutland, and say hello. I lay under a purple lilac bush and ate gorp (good ol' raisins and peanuts). Sometime I shall write more on menus but gorp, bannock and water is a popular lunch with us. For variety we occasionally add mixed nuts, currants or gaily colored M&M's.

Margie returned to say Karen was going to meet us at Otter Creek and drive us into Rutland for a meal and a good night's sleep at her place.

14

Heaven! We hustled through lunch and sped down the road towards the river. An hour later we staggered down to the shoreline and there was Karen. We cached the canoe and threw the gear into her trunk. We then spent a wonderful afternoon cleaning ourselves up and eating fresh food.

We have been driven around to see Otter Creek from several different vantages and can hardly wait till tomorrow -- the creek is so nice and deep, no rocks! Margie hopes she still remembers how to paddle. It will certainly give our feet a chance to rest -- this is the first time they have ever gotten blisters on a canoe trip. The hot pavement and excessive portaging have been too much for us. We saw a dead diamond back rattlesnake on the road as we hiked along today. Quite a surprise this far north.

It was with some hesitation that I left my setting pole at home this year. I have a nice light aluminum one and normally I don't get into a canoe without it. In view of the terrain, however, I finally decided not to bring it. There have been a few places that I could have used it these past few days but by and large it would have been far more problem than it was worth. A pole is good for swift, shallow streams and rivers. An experienced user easily goes up and down rapids where a paddle is useless. This spring, however, the streams have just been too dry and rock studded for such maneuverings.

MAY 25: STRAINERS

We had a good time at Karen's yesterday. We ate hamburgers for supper and then went out to the ice-cream store for sundaes. Margie visited a laundromat, then we phoned my folks and talked to the kids. Only one more week and they'll be joining us. Today we also heard that the simmering Washington volcano, Mount St. Helens, had finally blown its top. Funny how soon the affairs of the world have ceased to be of interest. The canoe traveller's attention is focused on his immediate surroundings and the outside world quickly pales to insignificance.

We had a wonderful breakfast of fresh food. We weighed ourselves before we left and discovered nothing had changed -- Margie 105 and me 132. Then Karen drove us back to Clarendon where we had left the canoe.

Today was a little disappointing. In the miles before Rutland, Otter Creek meanders with an idle laziness, back and forth with many oxbows.

15

Beautiful old trees line the sides of the steeply sloping ten-foot banks and you pass comfortably beneath their arching boughs, but they can create a problem. All too often a big old tree has fallen down the bank and toppled crosswise into the water. The stream is narrow enough that the branches reach clear across, blocking the way. These strainers are not dangerous, the current is not sufficiently strong for that, but they are an obstacle. Floating debris (logs, decaying dead animals, etc.) gradually accumulates up against them and soon an impenetrable screen is formed. Most we fought our way through, occasionally chopping a clear passage with the axe, but there were the annoying few we had to portage around. Unload the canoe, haul it up the steep muddy bank, drag through the meadow, slide down the bank, dump in the packs, and tumble in after them. What a muddy, debilitating procedure just to pass a slid-down tree! It was not so much the obstacle itself as the "unfairness" of the situation that offended us. How dare they place such picayune and unsuspected impediments in our path? This river should have been clear sailing -- or so we thought! At the very least, the trees could have the decency to fall obliquely leaving the canoeist passageway on the far side.

Gradually, however, the miles passed and the river widened. We saw a large turtle sunning himself on the bank. Over the bank we could see the Green Mountains rising above the fields. We were west of them now and our problems ought to have been over. It was bright, crisp and clear, and we longed to whiz downstream enjoying the current. Instead we had to struggle for every mile. The wind blew strongly out of the north, directly in our face. Such are the vicissitudes of canoe travel. We took out the wind gauge and recorded winds from 10 to 25 miles per hour with higher gusts. Fortunately the high banks protected us somewhat.

The most notable carry of the day came at Proctor. They have a beautiful marble bridge there and below it is a dam and falls. There is no trail on either side of the canyon and no one could offer any information as to how we could proceed downstream. The only suggestion was to drive several miles along the road; just one variation of, "You can't get there from here," a refrain we have heard many times before. I ended up carrying the canoe straight down the 75-foot rock wall beside the falls. The wind tried valiantly to whip the canoe away from me as I descended but in the end I triumphed. Margie paid a short visit to the marble museum there and then we were off. Tonight we are embedded deep in the Brandon Swamp perched on a little mud knoll between the main stream and a slough. Hopefully it won't rain. Steak for supper -- yum, yum!

16

We saw a lot of owls today. One poor fellow was being hounded unmercifully by a flock of crows. We also passed lots of cows and horses close to the river. Cows are definitely not impressed by my animal imitations but the horses are. All the animals stare silently as we go by -- our admiring crowd cheers us on!

MAY 26: FIRE

We left our mud pinnacle at 5:45 this morning and paddled through a freezing mist until 7:30. By then the sun was warm up on the banks. We beached the canoe and climbed up to enjoy a cold cereal breakfast in the sun and a chance to warm our hands and feet. Margie kept her winter jacket on, most of the morning and part of the afternoon. Although it warmed up in the 60's eventually, the strong north wind, continuing for a second day, kept us well chilled.

Shortly before noon we began to smell fire and soon heavy clouds of smoke were scudding by. The pall continued for several hours and we worried some about the possibility of a forest fire but we never did see flames -- just lots of smoke.

Life along the river has been peaceful and slow to change from one day to the next. We have been seeing raccoon tracks for several days and today we finally saw one as he ambled up the bank from the river. We still have dirt banks and muddy water but by afternoon we were finally starting to see a few rocks.

It was 5:00 when we reached Middlebury. We'd been looking forward all day to arriving since we both have fond memories of our college days there. We portaged across the road where the dam is and then had a pizza from the local pizzaria for supper. Several people warned us about the upcoming gorge and we thanked them before starting off. I know the next 20 miles like the back of my hand thanks to 4 years of college here, and I'm weighing their admonitions accordingly. To be truthful the "you can't go there" syndrome is one we are beginning to tire of. At every town we have been direly warned of upcoming death-dealing obstacles. Still, you have to be grateful for their concern. We paddled a mile downstream to the next carry, a dam, and stopped for the night. We have a nice grassy spot but there are lots of mosquitoes. When they stab their stickers through the roof of the tent to get at us I have been clinching them off inside. Now when they all flutter their wings at once it nearly lifts us off the ground. The experienced traveller of course never hesitates to deal in hyperbole when detailing encounters with insects. You dare not be too specific lest someone in the audience offer up a competing worse experience. Still in a day or two I may describe some of the problems we have been having with blackflies and mosquitoes.

Well, this was a long day and we are both tired. The two easy days that we had looked forward to have turned into long tiring marathons against the wind. Yet, we can't complain. We did 34 miles today and are only a little behind our schedule to meet the kids. Perhaps tomorrow the wind will shift.

MAY 27: THE INFAMOUS GORGE

It was in the 1960's when I first started to get serious about white water. Going to school in central Vermont, I had plenty of places to practice during spring runoff, but my favorite was the gorge below Middlebury. It is a challenging (nearly impossible) run for an open canoe at high water and I would strenuously discourage anyone from attempting it under such conditions, but at the time I loved it. It is short, narrow and tumultuous and immediately preceded by a set of rapids in which you dare not make a mistake for fear of being swept through the gorge unprepared. Many is the time I was flushed out of the gorge trailing my pinwheeling canoe into the huge eddy below, there to climb ashore and build the ritual drying out bonfire. I shudder now to recall the close bouts that I had in my ignorance with hypothermia.

Today, however, we were not particularly worried. The river was low and the sun brightly warm although the wind was still annoyingly steady out of the north. Still, as we began to draw closer an inevitable tingle of anticipation began to surface. We reached the dam above the gorge by 8:00 and as we stood there looking ahead down the rapids the excitement was clearly mounting. We carried down to the powerhouse and set the canoe in at the edge. A moment later we were bobbing downstream through the waves towards the gorge mouth, but it was all anticlimax. We passed through with no real difficulty, camera clicking, and really shipped only a few drops of water. We played in the eddy below a few minutes, recalling old times and laughing out of our systems the momentary anxiety that had built. Then we were off to Vergennes which, on account of the wind, we did not reach till nearly 3:00.

The Adirondacks could be clearly seen now out beyond Lake Champlain and we were eager to continue. It has been eleven days since we started though and our food has been running low so we stopped long enough to shop. On northern trips we carry mostly staples and are able to pack about 4 weeks' food into the canoe each stop. This summer, however, with towns occurring so frequently, we are carrying "normal" food (nothing that needs refrigeration of course) and plan to stop about every ten days.

We left town hoping to get out to the lake in time for sunset, but the wind was so strong that we finally had to give up and stop to cook supper. Afterwards we raced down the river as fast as we could, but failed to reach the lake until about a half hour after the sun had gone down behind the Adirondacks. Still it was beautiful. The wind was down and the lake had subsided to big gentle swells. The mountains run down both sides of the lake (Camel's Hump is particularly conspicuous on the east) and the whole scene was postcard picturesque in the purpling twilight. The opposite shore of the lake appeared steeply formidable in the darkening light but we decided to cross anyway while we could. By the time we got over there though it was night and the shore every bit as steep and rocky as we had feared. There was no place for a tent so we emptied the canoe, turned it over, found the flashlight and began to improvise. The sleeping pads are at home of course but by using our life jackets, clothes, fifty foot lines, tarps and sleeping bags we were able to construct a fairly comfortable mattress. It was a clear night with almost a full moon and it was late enough that most of the mosquitoes had already retired. We flopped down under the stars and went right to sleep.

Although the gorge was the highlight of the day we did get some wonderful pictures of geese in the swamp below Vergennes. One big mother goose with her young family was in the grass on shore. They allowed us to walk right up to them before finally shuffling off in haughty grandeur. We did four portages around dams today.

MAY 28: WINDBOUND ON CHAMPLAIN

That darn wind. The prevailing direction is out of the south but for four straight days now it has come whistling out of the north. On a long north-south lake like Champlain, hemmed in by mountains, such a wind is no joke. We got up fairly early and left a few minutes later at 6:00

(perhaps the improvised mattress was not really all that comfortable). The wind was already blowing some and quickly picking up force. After about a mile we realized we had to get off the lake and so backtracked to a nice little sheltered rocky cove. When the wind blows you off at 6:30 in the morning you know you are in for a long day. We spent the time catching up on sewing, washing, writing postcards and napping.

We have always been ambivalent in our feelings about windbound days. On the one hand we kind of look forward to them. They are a chance to catch up on all the little things. Then too, while travelling hard, we can't help thinking how nice it might be to just lie in the sun for a day. However, when they finally do come, we soon find ourselves fretting to leave. We have had scheduled rest days in the past, but have nowadays pretty much given them up. They seem to drag on so. We have tried fishing, swimming, berrying, cooking, playing, napping etc. but by mid-afternoon we always find ourselves wishing to be out paddling. The psychology of travelling is such that when the weather is uniformly good you are afraid to stop for fear it will change and you will lose your chance to progress. On the other hand when it is adverse you soon begin to think it will always be so and are anxious to take advantage of any little break. Thus when the wind let up at about three this afternoon, we were quick to pack up and take off. It turned out to be only a temporary respite however, and in little more than an hour we were blown off again, this time at Essex.

We hung around the town for a while and then built a secret insignificant fire behind a rock near the "No Picnicking" sign, to heat a can of beans for supper. As often happens the wind died down about 7:00, so we set out rested and well fed, for a peaceful moonlight paddle. The lake gradually grew quite calm and we passed Port Douglas around 11:00. The full moon rising over the blue-purple mountains was really beautiful. Soon after that we found a nice pebble beach shining in the moonlight and pulled over for the night. It was cold once we stopped paddling and we went right to bed, not bothering to erect the tent.

MAY 29: POSTED

Private Property, Posted, Keep Off, No Trespassing. How many of these signs have we seen in the last 12 days? Truly I begin to believe that the waterways from Marlborough to Alaska will be posted every 100 feet with these annoying bits of paper. It is so irritating that people living many miles away can lock up hundreds of acres for their occasional use. And yet the people themselves are invariably pleasant. Several times we have had to stop and cook a meal or sleep over on private land and the owners, when present, have always accommodated us in the friendliest way. Still, the tacking of all those little scraps of paper to trees in the wilderness somehow bothers us. We can't help wishing to turn the clock back to when the environment was clean and the landowners and cities were still a thing of the future. Yesterday, Burlington was uniquely pretty, blazing in the night across the lake as we paddled by, but it further served to remind us that it is we, passing silently, who are so sadly out of place now.

Anyway, we woke up this morning about 7:00 with the sun already shining in our eyes. We were a little surprised to discover we had spent the night flaked out on fist-sized boulders but I guess, despite appearances, they were really fairly smooth and comfy.

The day was hot and still, no wind, the kind of day we have been waiting so long for and we wasted no time taking advantage of it. We passed by Plattsburgh about noon. The outstanding feature of the area was the seemingly endless stream of planes and jets. Almost by the minute they came swooping up and down from a nearby airport and out over the lake. There must be a big Air Force training base nearby. Monster after monster would come thundering overhead, exhaust cloud trailing out behind. The fumes, gray and billowy, would hang in the calmness, slowly drifting apart. I worked two summers in a pea cannery and the smell was appalling to the casual passerby. Yet we workers soon became oblivious to the noxious stench and noise. Surely it is this way in the cities today. The noise and the pallid sky are invisible screens to the deadened senses of those living within.

We stoppped for lunch on an island in the middle of the lake and thought about skinny-dipping. Reluctantly we concluded that there were too many sailboats around. We were tired today and wanted to stop early but were forced to continue on. Everyplace we looked was posted (hence my earlier outburst) but finally, with the sun setting and darkness coming, we started asking people for permission to sleep on their land. We were soon successful and have set up camp in the bushes just inshore of a rocky point. We are now just a couple of miles short of Chazy Landing on the Great Chazy River. The sunsets have been beautiful lately. The mountains are behind us now but we can still see them in the background.

21

By the way, I have continued to pass each night when it comes to describing the bugs for lack of suitable words. However, they have not disappeared. In fact, just going to the bathroom is a miserable problem. You know the mosquitoes are thick when your toilet paper comes away smeared with their blood.

Well tomorrow we begin our deviation from the accepted route. Starting with Champlain's trip in 1609, visitors to the lake passing to and from Montreal all chose to make their way via the Richelieu River. I grew up on the Richelieu (St. Johns) and am not particularly anxious to go that way down to Sorel and then up the St. Lawrence to Montreal. Instead we have chosen an alternate route which will, in addition, bypass the Lachine Rapids above Montreal and let us out directly onto Lake St. Louis. The plan is to go up the Great Chazy to Mooer's Forks and then to portage over to the English River where we shall meet the kids. From there we will pass down the Chateauguay and so on to the lake. This will be many miles shorter.

I suppose in one sense it is handy to have towns nearby. One can be so needlessly profligate. It is less than two weeks now and we are already starting our second roll of toilet paper.

Margie has been measuring today's accomplishment and reports that we have now totaled a distance of 255 miles.

MAY 30: PORTAGING THE CHAZY

Perhaps the Indians and early travellers knew what they were doing after all. The upper reaches of the Chazy are not navigable in any sense of the word. The day began well enough. We didn't want to build a cooking fire on private property so it was a quick start. We were up early and left before 6:00 planning to have breakfast later. The wind was out there waiting for us, but, pleasant surprise, today it was from the south. Too bad we had so few miles left to take advantage of it. It was already strong at our backs as we pushed off and so we zipped right along. In fact if it had been much stronger we might well have begun to have difficulty. As it was though we breezed up the river to Champlain where we stopped to phone the Shepardsons and confirm our rendezvous with the children at 3:00 tomorrow afternoon. It was still mid-morning and we had only 15 miles left to go. With the strong wind and negligible current the situation was certainly rosy.

Ha, ha. The river runs dry above Champlain. There was only one thing to do. We picked up and started walking. The land is flat here and we were proceeding along open highway. That was part of the problem. The unobstructed wind blew havoc with the canoe and I found it nearly impossible to maintain my balance, much less walk with it on my shoulders. Margie was forced to come along behind me holding the stern as we proceeded west. Even so it was all we could do to keep from being blown north into Canada. We weren't jogging. Teeth clenched, we were barely staggering along. Three and a half miles and several hours later a truck took pity on us and carried us the next seven miles. We took a long rest and then started walking again. Blisters developed quickly and we only got a few more miles before giving up for the night. We stopped at a farmhouse to get water. Margie said we were hiking by and was given permission to set up a tent in their neighbor's yard. They never questioned the canoe. So here we sit, miles from any river, camping alongside the road with our canoe. It has been very warm and buggy today with light showers this afternoon. Neither the farmhouse nor any passersby have commented on our situation. Perhaps more people hike the highways with canoes than I suspect. Still we feel conspicuous. We need a bath, too.

Margie had an interesting experience today. While looking for a telephone in Champlain, she wandered into an old shambles of a hotel. It was full of seedy-looking patrons who gave her a good once-over before turning back to their drinks. We later learned that the place is renowned for hundreds of miles. All the truckers make a big effort to stop there to date the local prostitutes. Needless to say they were a little disappointed.

MAY 31: RENDEZVOUS

Because of the rain we were in the tent by 6:00 yesterday and so had a good night's sleep. It began to taper off about 7:00 this morning when we got up to have breakfast. It was very buggy, the kind of day when you speak through clenched teeth to avoid inhaling the black flies. We jogged back and forth on the shoulder of the road while eating our cereal, so as to outrun the worst of them. Traffic was light but a couple of times we were drenched by passing motorists who dodged into the puddles to give us a good splashing.

Once fed, we packed up quickly and started portaging down the road

DILEMMA

SANDERS, '85 ©

24

towards Canada and our river. Today is Saturday and as we hiked by the rural homes huffing and puffing we saw many families out planting their gardens and mowing their lawns. Occasionally they would stop work to call off their dogs but for the most part they averted their eyes and studiously ignored us. Many of them had probably driven by us on their way home yesterday.

Each half mile we would stop for a rest and a chance to look at the map. Following behind us, at a discreet distance, were the local children -- a crowd of bicycles and tricycles. After six such breaks we reached our destination. We threw down our gear and tumbled into the ditch beside it to rest. The river was less than 100 yards away and it was only 10:00. We were five hours early. We lay there recovering and soon the family across the road could stand it no longer. They had seen us portaging yesterday through Champlain 15 miles back and in Mooer's five miles back and now here we were still portaging! They came over to talk and a small crowd quickly gathered. We were invited in for a delicious snack of milk and donuts.

Later we went down to take a bath in the river (I use the term loosely). It is clear that we have a problem in so far as the water is concerned. The stream is small enough in places that one can easily hop across without wetting any toes. The more serious problem though will be the fences; every few hundred feet a barbed wire fence crosses the stream. Everybody was amused by the idea that we might try to canoe in it. We were warned that the next farm alone had three fences and the owner generally shot trespassers. Fortunately we soon met the owner and he was very nice, only he repeatedly cautioned us not to touch a strand of his fences. Anyways we started down to take a quick skinny dip in a gravelly spot between two cow-plopped fields and promply met the border patrol. We had forgotten about customs and they reminded us. The road we hiked up ends at the border and the actual customs people were five miles back the way we had come. We absorbed this information as we watched them drive away. Then we climbed under a fence and splashed around in the shallow pool with our bar of soap. Everyone stayed discreetly nearly out of sight so as not to embarrass us. After bathing we changed into cleaner clothes and went up to sit by the canoe for lunch. The sky was cloudy and threatening with lots of bugs and it sprinkled some.

We are anxious to get the kids of course but in a way it will be a shame. With just the two of us and the light canoe, portaging and hard travel are no big deal. Once our big yellow 20-foot canoe (the big banana) arrives, however, everything will change. It is awkward to carry (it weighs over a hundred pounds) and we will have three 75-pound packs besides. Every little carry will be an ordeal; just loading and unloading the canoe will be a chore. It is fun to look forward to the days when the kids are a little older and we shall be able to go back to a permanent life of easy travelling. Reluctantly we decided to continue for the rest of the summer without sleeping pads to save space in the packs.

The kids arrived at two and my folks had brought some varnish as we requested. Our paddles have taken a real beating coming upstream through New England and we took a few minutes to refurbish them. First we cut off the splinters and fuzzies with a knife, sanded, and then spread a little varnish over the blades. It was quick drying and they were ready to use (just a little sticky) in an hour. By 3:30 we were packed and pushing off across the Canadian Border. We had been warned about the electric eye there but did not see it. The river was slow going and it took us over an hour to get about a mile. We had to lift over a lot of rocks or where possible kick them aside to deepen the channel. We also passed under and through several barbed wire fences doing no real damage, although the big heavy canoe did have a little too much momentum for one feeble old strand. Hopefully conditions will improve tomorrow. Shortly after 5:00 we found an old abandoned cow meadow and set up camp in the lush green grass. What fun to have the big tent! We relegated the kids to the two-man tent that we have been using the past couple of weeks, and took over for ourselves the four-man tent my folks brought up. It is extra work to bring two tents, of course, but the extra space and privacy is well worth the trouble for such a long trip.

The kids were able to go swimming tonight (the river is only a little over knee deep) and had a grand time. They ran around trying to build the fire, cook the bannock, set up the tent, etc. and generally had a ball. It was very buggy and thundering though, and now we are all in bed by 7:30. It is starting to rain.

JUNE 1: BULLS

It rained a great deal last night after we went to bed. It is too bad the kids have to start out with such poor weather. Last year Margie and I switched to the relatively new fiber filled sleeping bags. They are not waterproof but at least if they get wet they still provide some warmth and, in fact, dry out very quickly. The children are not quite so fortunate as they have inherited our old down bags, which must of course be kept dry. The problem is basically that their tent has a mosquito netting roof, covered by a rainproof fly. When the wind blows and it rains a lot as it did last night the water tends to whip in around the edges of their fly and get things wet. Thus they were a little damp this morning. Still they braved the storm very well. There was lots of thunder and lightning but they didn't make a peep (that we could hear) all night.

We got up at 5:30 this morning to a cold grey day and quickly started a breakfast fire. Fortunately I had put a couple of dry sticks under the canoe for safekeeping before going to bed and there was no trouble getting a blaze going. It was a nice fire and it sure would have felt good to warm up by it but we never got to use it. We had hardly turned around before a herd of bulls ambled out of the bushes into our campsite. The meadow was no longer abandoned. Somewhere back in the bushes a farmer was probably laughing himself silly. We certainly made a sight. These were not the shy retiring sort of bulls and we decided to postpone breakfast. Apparently there is not too much truth to the idea that bulls are inflamed by the sight of red. I was wearing my bright red rain suit and scurrying backwards around the site saying "nice bull" and generally trying to act reassuring. A big one started to lick our green tent vigorously so I rushed over and crawled between his legs to empty the tent out and start taking it down. He didn't step on me. In fact, he looked sort of noncommittal as I knelt there in front of him blithering soothingly and folding things up. Some of the others went over to inspect our packs. The big red tarp (10 feet by 12) was all spread out and before they could stand on it we whisked it out from under them, popping it by their noses. In general we were rolling, dragging, and shoving all our gear at once across the grass. The bulls followed tight behind us as we bundled everything down to the water's edge and threw it into the canoe. Usually I am meticulous about extinguishing fires but by this time there were too many bulls pawing around between me and it. It wasn't a very big fire anyway. We jumped into the canoe and paddled off with a sigh of relief. It wasn't a splendid packing job but then it had only taken us a few minutes. It wasn't even 6:00 yet. We went around the corner out of sight and practiced our cow-mooing imitations. Then we put in a couple of hours paddling.

We came to a burnt out house about 8:00 and stopped for breakfast. All wood was wet and hard to light and we had to hunker down out of the bitter wind to stay warm. Still we got a fire going and had hot oatmeal.

Well, we spent the entire day till 4:00 overcoming one obstacle after another. It was cold, cloudy and windy all day long and we worked hard bypassing blown down trees, shallow rocky riffles and numerous barbed wire fences. At times we would have to unload the canoe, then stand deep in the water to lift it over a fence. Next we would lift over the packs and reload. Very discouraging. We were forced to revive the Shepardson Water Ballet, a technique which we had last practiced 2 weeks ago on the Black. In this delightful "pas de deux" each wader tips one foot at a time high in the air so as to empty the water out of his boot before stepping into the canoe. Very entertaining for the children. While wading under a bridge on the Black a few days back an old spike embedded in a concrete block pierced my left boot. I walk without limping now but that foot is almost always wet on account of the leak. One of Margie's boots leaks also.

The kids are being a big help. They do a lot of paddling and help get firewood and set up camp. At one point today we sent them out to hike along a road and meet us below while we portaged through a long combination of rapids and falls. A couple of years ago they could never have managed it alone.

Tonight the river is still a narrow rocky little stream. We are camped in another field, a plowed one this time so everything should be okay. We have talked to the farmer and all the cows are safely across the river behind a fence. It is hard to communicate well with the farmer, who speaks only French. He is a little nonplussed by these strange people in his field but we believe he said that the river improves rapidly in a few more miles. Right here though the canoe still dwarfs the stream, which looks more like a drainage ditch.

JUNE 2: THE CHATEAUGUAY

We still have not reached Montreal. Today was pretty much a repeat of yesterday and it is clear now that we made a mistake. We should have gone down the Richelieu rather than pick our way portaging up and down all these miserable little streams the last four days. We are off the English River at last though and on the Chateauguay. I really believe the worst is behind us at least and tomorrow we should reach the St. Lawrence.

We had breakfast about 6:00 and then pushed off and travelled fairly steadily until 4:00. There were no bulls today but otherwise conditions continued poor. There was some wading, some portaging and a fence to negotiate. As we continued downstream the water became increasingly sewery. There was a little rain in the morning and a few drips later but mostly just cloudy and warm. The problem was the wind -- there wasn't any; and the mosquitoes were out in force. With the warm dampness and the swampy country the mosquitoes have multiplied to a hysteria-inducing thickness. At such times they can quickly reduce a person to tears or frenzied helplessness. All you can do is retreat inside yourself and wade down the middle of the stream as far from the buggy banks as you can get. The last thing you want to do is slow down, so the harder the travelling becomes the more determinedly you push on. You lift and drag until your legs are unsteady and then you lie resting draped over the ends of your canoe. Perhaps it would have been more pleasant if the dirty water hadn't smelled so. Fortunately a few minutes rest and a chocolate bar are usually enough to send us whistling on our way again.

Tonight we are camped on a mud bank at the edge of someone's backyard. The country is very civilized. Randy fell out of a tree earlier but seems to be okay now. He and Tina are off watching a couple of French lads fish. They are not catching anything and probably wouldn't dare eat it even if they did.

JUNE 3: THE GRAND KNIGHT

Last night was very still and we could hear a lot of big carp jumping and splashing, and they were still at it this morning when we got up. The poor things are probably desperate to get out of the awful water. Even with our boots on neither of us enjoys stepping into the foul water or the disgusting ooziness of the mud banks. Yesterday we laid down a mat of broken boards and branches on which to unload the canoe.

From the map it appeared that we would have as many as four or five portages to reach the St. Lawrence today, so we decided to leave early and have breakfast on the first carry. As a general rule, we prefer to eat and camp at portage sites. Such a procedure is usually efficient timewise since you have to get out and unload the canoe anyway. Also such respites are a delightful break in the brutal exercise of unload, carry and load. Today though we were pleasantly surprised to learn that what looked like dams on the map were in fact only bridges. Hallelujah! We got water from a house near the first bridge and then ate a cold breakfast out in the middle of the river as we drifted along in the canoe (fewer bugs that way).

We had two drops to line and portage around during the morning but aside from that we were able to run all the riffles -- no wading! The kids are getting good at walking around to the bottom of a rapids to wait for us. Yesterday while doing that they each found some money on the ground, twenty-one cents in all. Now they can hardly wait to get out and scrounge around for more. Randy is a great collector and he is inexorably filling the canoe with muddy bottle tops.

This is an Olympic year and when we reached the St. Lawrence we stopped in at the Chateauguay canoe club. The kids played in the playground there while we talked to a couple of people who were training to race. They had beautiful racing canoe/kayaks.

It was nearly noon by then and fairly foggy. We could not see across Lake St. Louis but were able to make out a couple of islets in the middle. Everything was calm so we started out to cross the two miles to the islands where we planned to eat lunch. Once there, however, we decided that the safest course was to finish crossing the lake while conditions were good. The crossing was uneventful except for a large freighter-like shape which appeared to be bearing down on us out of the fog. We paddled hard and so successfully outmaneuvered it that now we are not sure that we really saw it. At the very least it was a well imagined hallucination. In any case it took about an hour and a half to cross the lake. We stopped for lunch and then continued on. It is a very exciting area with the big boats and Montreal so near by, and the kids couldn't wait to get back in the canoe to continue.

By 4:00 we had reached the Ottawa River and were battling our way up the small rapids under the bridge at St. Anne de Belleville at the tip of Montreal's Island. The water here is a great improvement, not drinkable but quite clear. In the brown jello of the Chateauguay we weren't even able to see the blades of our paddles. It was hard going under the bridge and Tina pitched in to help paddle. Randy who had counted out 1000 strokes earlier in the day insisted on resting. Actually he was engrossed in counting the 100-plus-cars of a nearby train. We stopped to rest at the top and discovered that we had paddled right by a little canal and lock beside the rapids. The men working there were very friendly and told us that we could have used the lock for free. They were closing for the night in a few minutes, but it was too rare an opportunity to pass up. We quickly twirled the canoe around and whizzed back downstream to come around again at the lock entrance. It was a little silly but we all enjoyed locking through.

By now it was getting late and we were starting to get concerned about finding a place to sleep. The area right around Montreal is fairly well built up. Fortunately the lock master was the local Grand Knight and he invited us to just paddle around the corner and sleep on the Knights of Columbus' property. He escorted us over, got out a table and chairs and was very helpful. We built a little fire down on the rock beach while the children went off to play at a nearby park. It was sort of like camping in our own backyard, but we were grateful for the spot. We debated whether to buy bread but I finally made a bannock while Margie went off to play with the kids.

It feels so good to have finally reached the Ottawa. Tomorrow we set out from Montreal much as the voyageurs of old did, heading for Grand Portage. To be sure there are some differences. They used to travel 8 or 10 in a canoe and would start a month earlier than we are. Travelling in brigades of several canoes, paddling almost night and day in their heavily loaded 36-foot "Canots de Maitre", they would reach Grand Portage at the west end of Lake Superior in as little as 6 to 8 weeks. It shall be sometime in August before we arrive. Still from here on the route is steeped in history and we shall be following in their footsteps. Stroke for stroke, carry for carry we shall face the very obstacles they knew so well.

For the record we have now come 329 miles in 18 days.

JUNE 4: LAKE OF TWO MOUNTAINS

We had showers between 5:00 and 6:00 this morning and then it gradually cleared to a cloudy, windy day. The Grand Knight came by to warn us of the dangers of the Lake of Two Mountains, our first obstacle on the Ottawa River, and we thanked him again before pushing off. We paddled hard into the wind for an hour or so before coming out onto the lake but then we had to give up for the day. The wind was a steady 10-15 mph with gusts up to 25 and the water was just too rough. The waves were marching directly toward us and we took shelter in the lee of a bridge.

It was time to buy food again so Margie hitchhiked into town to go shopping. We were hoping that we were in Ontario by now but she learned to our disappointment that this is still Quebec. We have been planning to get an Ontario fishing license but I guess we shall have to wait another day. Randy can hardly wait now to start fishing.

At home we take so many things for granted. When you are on the trail, however, even a little thing like washing clothes requires planning. Every few days it is time to wash out underwear and the bigger items get done every two weeks. Of course it depends more on the weather than on any schedule of ours. Margie prefers to keep the laundry bag as empty as possible but it doesn't always work out that way. You don't want to wash when it is raining or when you have lots of portages coming up. At other times you are travelling hard to reach a certain place and there is no time to fuss with dirty clothes. Our favorite place to wash is over the side of the canoe as we travel along. It is comfortable and the water is cleaner than on shore. It is particularly fun to swish out the clothes as you go bobbing through some little rapids. The best thing for the environment however would be to wash in a pot of water which you dump out on the shore. Biodegradable soap is a good idea too. Anyway today was a perfect wash day -- breezy and sunny, with nowhere to go. We changed into our last clean clothes and gave everything else a good scrubbing. Clothes will dry on a bush, clothesline or best of all a warm rock facing the sun. If they are weighted down with little rocks you don't need to worry about them blowing away when dry. There are also plenty of places to lay out clothes in the canoe to dry things as you paddle along. Just make sure they are firmly secured. If you are travelling with a baby bring 12 to 18 cloth diapers, the gauze ones that need to be folded. We found they dry the fastest and you won't be burdened with the problem of disposing of the "disposable" diapers. Of course in bad weather you may end up with a heavy pack of wet diapers.

This afternoon we wrote letters and then, after a light shower, we pushed off and paddled on another 100 yards to the lee of an island where we cooked supper and are now sitting. It is 6:00 and still windy, but letting up, and we have not made camp as we may be able to travel soon. The kids are watching little sailboats capsize, sometimes two and three at a time, in a nearby bay and cheering them on. Although the lake has been too rough for us today I'm sure that the big voyageur canoes could have somehow pushed upstream against this wind. They were determined travellers and not easily denied. Still, we shall get there too.

At 7:00 we left and started out through the middle of a 37-sailboat race. The wind had died some but it never went to zero. It was a beautiful sunset, and we planned to paddle late, but gradually the wind increased again and by 10:00 we were forced to stop. We pulled the canoe up on a sandy beach and flopped down our sleeping bags. The kids were already asleep in the boat so we just left them there, covered with a ground cloth, and went to bed ourselves on the beach beside them.

JUNE 5 CARILLON

We woke to a fairly calm morning so we jumped back in the canoe and paddled off at 5:00. It was easy to leave -- no tent to take down and the kids were still sleeping in the canoe. In fact they awoke later and never even realized that we had stopped for a few hours in the night.

Soon we started stalking great blue herons. There were a lot of them around, and we wasted 5 or 6 pictures trying to get the definitive portrait. They are not hard to hunt down as they only fly a few hundred yards when alarmed. Just before takeoff they dip their necks uncertainly and crouch down. Then with a jump and a big flap they are off. Best of all they always go in the direction you are heading rather than circling around behind. This way you get several chances at each one. At any rate we finally succeeded and can now relax. For the rest of the summer we can just enjoy the herons without getting out the camera. We stopped at 7:30 for breakfast.

Today we have even outpaced the old time voyageurs. First the weather was excellent. The day grew calmer instead of windier. Then at noon we had a wonderful surprise, Carillon Dam. There we got a free vertical 65-foot ride in the huge lock. We learned that the single dam and lock there have replaced 3 old small ones along the river. Of course, before that there were only the rapids and current which the voyageurs had to face. One break for us. Apparently the next serious obstacle will be all the rapids at Ottawa, 68 miles away.

An hour of paddling past Carillon brought us to a nice campgound on the north shore with picnic tables, grills, water faucets and toilets. It wasn't open yet for the summer (nothing is perfect), but we stopped anyway and spent a leisurely three and a half hours playing and cooking before the caretaker came down to chase us off. He was very nice and let us stay to finish our pea soup and cornbread, which we have just done. Now we plan to paddle on for a few hours in the cool calm evening. The children are looking forward to sleeping in the canoe again. The river is finally narrowing down after the backed-up lake at Carillon and

33

we can detect some current. The water is still not clean enough to drink.

We paddled from 7:00 to 9:30 through the sunset and gathering twilight. The early morning and late evening hours are often the most pleasant for travelling. Going west as we are though, the setting sun is blinding and Margie sometimes paddles with her eyes closed. Just before dark we stopped for the night at a nice level spot beneath the Grenville Bridge. It was a bit noisy with heavy traffic, but quite private. The mosquitoes were pretty thick so we set up the big tent and bundled the four of us in. Today was long, commencing as it did at 5:00.

JUNE 6: NOTHING SPECIAL

Today was fairly easy but even so the past few days and the hot sun have tired us. Nothing memorable happened. We started off about 6:00 and went for an hour and a half before coming to a provincial park. We had breakfast there while the kids played on the swing set and jungle gym.

Lunch was at Lefaivre where we mailed the kids' postcards, bought a fishing license (at last), and took a swim. By and large the wind was with us all day, offsetting the current nicely. We even tried sailing (not too successfully) with the big red tarp raised. Margie stood up in the bow and held it out. Anyway we breezed along with the wind at our backs and didn't stop until nearly 5:00 in what appears to be a farmer's overgrown ex-(we hope) cow pasture. It has been clouding up all day and surely looks like rain tomorrow which should give us a nice excuse to take it easy.

The river was sort of pretty today, although a little monotonous. If it weren't for the church steeples rising out of the wooded hillsides it would be easy to miss the towns. As it is though you can see the spires marking their little hamlets as much as five miles away. They make nice goals and give you something to aim for when paddling.

Tonight is our first in Ontario. It is 7:00 now, the kids are already in bed, and in another half hour we shall be too. Margie is already starting the pre-bedtime chores. Each night at dusk we:

a) read the kids a story and all brush our teeth

b) fish out the next day's breakfast, lunch and snacks

c) place the paddles, packs and firewood beneath the tarp and tip the canoe over it all

d) decide whether we are leaving before breakfast. This last decision must be made now because to postpone it is to guarantee that we shall sleep in and stay for breakfast.

34

JUNE 7: ANNIVERSARY

This morning was warm, buggy and overcast, but still there was no rain. We expected it at any moment but instead the sky gradually cleared off and it began to get hot. We had breakfast at camp and then paddled from 7:15 till 12:00 with a short snack break around 10:00. We continue to mark our progress by church spires and occasional ferry boats (the river is too wide for bridges).

At lunchtime we took a swim and the children made a slide on a huge sandpile. Unfortunately Randy lost one of his matchbox cars in the sand there and I don't imagine that we shall hear the last of it for quite some time. The children were only allowed to bring a few toys on the trip and it was with great agony that Randy winnowed his matchbox collection down to his best four. Now he had lost his tank and was temporarily inconsolable.

Today was Saturday and in the afternoon we met an RCMP speedboat down from Ottawa. They were stopping all the weekend boats to check for life preservers, etc. and came over to talk with us. The gist of their conversation was that we can go no farther. They claim the river is impassable at Ottawa because of all the rapids and dams and that it is regretfully not possible to portage through the town. It was a pretty familiar conversation ("you can't get there from here") and they were very earnest. We stopped shortly afterwards for another swim, it was so hot, and then continued on to a roadside picnic area for supper.

We fished a little there, used the bathroom and talked to a couple from Ottawa. They too tried to help us out with information about the dams and portage possibilities in the city. Most people know very little about the rivers that pass through their towns, however, and they were no exception.

For the amount of time we are putting in, we don't seem to cover an awful lot of distance. The canoe is heavy and the river current is a continual nuisance ready to drag us steadily backwards at our slightest letup. Still, we managed 20 miles today, thanks in part to a light tailwind, and tomorrow we are confidently hoping to breeze into Ottawa. Today was our eleventh wedding anniversary but we have decided to postpone the celebration till tomorrow and go out for a big dinner in the city. We are lying here in the tent now planning the ideal menu.

Tina paddled 3000 strokes today. I feel a little sorry for her now though. She is in the same tent with Randy and he is being really obnoxious. Of course he learned most of his tricks from her. Everyone is sunburned.

JUNE 8: AARGH!

JUNE 9: FAT ALBERTS

Yesterday was a little disappointing. It rained some in the night and the last shower didn't finish till about 6:00 when we were getting up. We set off without breakfast and decided to go back across the river since the other side seemed to be more protected from the wind. With the river so wide and the current so strong in the center, it is a major decision each time we decide to cross. Once over we paddled pretty directly into an increasing wind for about an hour. We were surely within no more than 50 feet of the island we had picked for breakfast when a tremendous gust blew us backwards, perhaps 100 yards. This was an unheard of event. We have a heavy load and a low silhouette and I take some pride in being able to control the canoe. Still it happened -- nearly a hundred yards straight backwards. We dug in and really began to paddle in earnest. By sideslipping further into the lee of the shore, and getting Tina to paddle, we eventually prevailed and landed to cook breakfast. Afterwards, we paddled in the lee of the island to its very tip and then that was it. Done for the day at 10:00. It was cold and overcast all day long although by 4:00 it had warmed up to 53 degrees. That was the day we were going to visit Ottawa. At least the kids had some fun there playing in a field of ferns that was higher than their heads. The wind continued strong until at least 7:30 when we gave up waiting and went to bed. I was too disgusted to even write the log. Aargh.

Rested and determined to reach Ottawa, we got up at 4:30 this morning. We popped the kids, still in their sleeping bags, into the canoe to sleep some more, and then we paddled off in the predawn stillness. It was quite calm and we were able to get out around the tip of our island and recross the river to the Quebec side. We had been told that our best chance to portage lay on the north shore.

It was very cold. At breakfast it had warmed up to 43 degrees but the rising sun didn't help much as it was immediately blocked out by a bank of clouds. Margie was wearing work gloves but she was wishing that she had brought her wool mittens.

The wind increased during the morning and the current got quite strong. Soon we passed some paper mills. They had giant wide escalator type ramps on which the logs would go spinning and banging up from the river to disappear high into the side of the mill. Occasionally the sticks would lose their balance and tumble back down, but the general trend was for the logs to be forced kicking and rolling willy nilly into the building. There were guards with long spiked poles to prod the stragglers on. The smell was unpleasant, especially down below where the polluted remains were piped back into the river. The current and wind were strong enough now that it was taking us 10 strokes (me 4 and Margie 6) to progress a single log length.

The real fun began though about 11:00 when we reached Ottawa and had a snack. As advised, we planned to portage the first obstacle (a dam) on the Quebec side. It turned out that we were on Eddy Company's property however, and I was soon picked up by their security force and escorted to headquarters. There I was issued a visitor's pass but was persuaded not to use it. Instead they suggested a landing spot on the other side of the river where conditions were better. Properly grateful, I returned to the canoe and we started across, contending with what was at this point a very strong current. Landing successfully, we unloaded the canoe and got the gear up the steep bank. Ha,ha, the joke was on us -- we were on an island. To make things worse, it was starting to rain. We reloaded the canoe and crossed the last channel to the Ontario side. Once more we carted everything up a steep muddy bank, this time in a cold rain. It was 1:00 now and still only 52 degrees. We placed everything under the tarp and started out in search of food. It was time for our anniversary dinner. We seemed to be in a non-dining section of town, however, and the kids tired quickly of tramping around the streets in the rain. After a careful search, we settled for Fat Albert's and all went in to enjoy a hot meatball sub. Dressed as we were we felt a little conspicuous for downtown Ottawa but we were cordially received and seated by ourselves behind a little partition at the rear of the room.

It was pouring hard when we emerged and we hurried back to begin the portage. The carry was roughly a mile and in about an hour we had bundled everything across. The kids each carried their own pack plus some little things in their hands which helped a lot. We were already pretty wet by then and so decided to avoid the next two portages by wading and tracking up the rapids. The rain was letting up some but it was still cold. By 4:30 though, the sun peeked out and we crossed the river to set up camp about 2 miles upstream of Ottawa on the Quebec side. Another obstacle overcome! We ate supper and went to bed.

JUNE 10: CELEBRITIES

It was bright and sunny when we got up at 6:00 this morning. There had been a hard frost which persistently refused to melt, and the canoe and tarp were caked white. Once on our way, we found the two mile paddle up to the last of the Ottawa city rapids was fairly calm and surprisingly enough we saw a deer standing there at the water's edge. The rapids themselves were extremely fast and powerful -- the kind of death dealing obstacle that only a really big river can generate. There were no thoughts of tracking up these. We portaged half a mile (on the Quebec side) to the south end of Lac Deschenes and then paddled near to Aylmer. It was overcast by now and still very cold.

Aylmer is set back some miles from the lake. Margie hitchhiked in to visit a laundromat and do some food shopping while the kids and I built a fire to stay warm. It rained intermittently and Margie returned at noon accompanied by an excited reporter. He had chanced to give her a lift as she was hitchhiking back to the lake and he was anxious to interview us. He made us promise to stay right there while he went off to finish his current assignment. We were still eating lunch when he returned and he sat down around the fire with us. We all had fun taking turns at being celebrities. Before going he took a few pictures including some posed snapshots of us leaving. We shall try to get a copy of the paper in a few days even though it will all be in French.

Once he had left we settled down to the miserable task at hand. It was 1:00 now and as warm as the day was going to get, 51 degrees. There was a strong wind in our faces and travelling conditions were borderline. Three separate times in the next few hours we were blown ashore and forced to take cover during violent rain squalls. They would come marching down the river tossing the narrow lake into a frenzy. Finally at 4:00 we just gave up for the day. Rarely have we experienced such consistently adverse weather as we have seen the last three days, unseasonable cold, very strong winds, and persistent rain. Fortunately, when conditions are worst, the children are at their best. We have always noticed that during times of extreme stress they tend to fall asleep. Be it

38

prolonged rapids, wavy lakes or miserable weather, they tend to just lie down and close their eyes.

We huddled around a scrubby little fire and roasted hotdogs on sticks. Then we set up our tents and climbed into bed. On days like today our minds tend to fixate on the pleasures of luxuriating in a soft puffy sleeping bag. We'd been looking forward to this moment all afternoon and we were not disappointed.

JUNE 11: DAY 26

We got up at 5:30 and set off as soon as possible. It was cold and cloudy and already the wind and waves seemed to be picking up for the day. The children went back to sleep and we paddled on as long as we could before being forced ashore at 7:00 on a rocky beach. We quickly built a warm fire and heated up some cocoa, then we had bacon and cereal for breakfast. Afterwards we baked a bannock, something we hadn't been able to do last night. By 9:00 the wind had shifted and it was safe to set out again.

We had our morning snack on a nice sandy point and later stopped for lunch on another sand beach. The sun came out for 10 minutes and we lay snuggling on the sand out of the wind, soaking up the glorious rays. It felt so warm! The kids had fun digging in the sand.

Gradually the day was improving. We paddled through some more showers in the afternoon, but there were also several periods of sun. About 4:30 we came to a nicely mowed area by a wilderness cottage. There were two latrines, a fireplace and no one around. The country is a little swampy here and it was too good a site to pass up. We stopped for the night.

Well, we have certainly been getting enough practice with cold wind, rain and waves this week. We hope it clears up tomorrow and gets warmer. Margie and I both have leaky boots and we are tired of cold wet feet and numb fingers. We went 16 miles today.

JUNE 12: YOU'RE NOT FRENCH?

Today the weather was beautiful -- calm and blue. Early it was in the 30's and we paddled through a cold mist to the town of Quyon. There

39

we stopped to phone relatives and report that we were still alive. On the little beach by the water's edge, we built a fire and cooked the rest of the bacon to go with our porridge. The sunshine was streaming down now and we sat there deciphering a French newspaper we had picked up. There was a large article devoted to the fabulous exploits of the celebrated Shepardson Family and their hazardous passage through Ottawa. We lapped it up. We also learned that we have just survived the coldest temperatures ever recorded anytime in the month of June for the Ottawa area, both lowest nighttime temperatures and lowest daily highs. Thank goodness that stretch is behind us.

About 10:00 we reached the dam above town and spent 3 hours getting around it. It was a miserable obstruction. Oh, to be back with the voyageurs and have only rapids to contend with! The dam was miles wide and we tried to begin by landing at the power house in the center. Just to get there we had to lift over a log boom and outmaneuver an eddying flotilla of pulp logs, but it was to no avail. No one there had ever heard of a boat passing by their dam. Incredibly enough, this massive structure has been created with no apparent thought as to how to get around it. We were sent to try the south shore. The natives there were dumbfounded. We talked to several and they would have us believe that no one has ever gone up their river. Typical was the final conversation we had with the old retired gentleman living in the house by the corner.

Me: That's quite a dam.

Him: Going downstream?

Me: No, going up. Where is the best place to portage around?

Him: You can't.

Me: (Reluctantly) Well maybe on the other side of the river?

Him: Nope. I've lived here 40 years and there's no way around over there. You can't go any farther.

Me: Is there a road around?

Him: No. You have a car?

Me: No.

Him: Well, you couldn't drive around anyway. The next landing is ten miles up at "Querx" (?)

Me: (Shouldering canoe) Well, thanks.

Him: Where you going?

Me: (Striding off) Querx.

As usual, luck was with us. We had not gone far before a telephone truck kindly offered to carry Margie, the kids, and all our gear around.

Better yet, he knew the way and it was only a few miles. I continued down the dusty road, alone now with my canoe. They a hydro pickup truck came along and he stopped also. He too knew the way and I sat in back holding the canoe as he drove through little side roads and ditches to arrive at the far side of the dam. The telephone man arrived about the same time and everybody helped unload. Everything had happened so fast that it was only now, after the carry, that anyone finally thought to check if we were French. We have noticed for days now that the first thing Ontario residents do is ask if we are from Quebec. They don't mean to insult us, but they want to know. At first I used to hesitate before even admitting that I was brought up near Montreal, but gradually I've learned that this confession elicits only sympathy.

By now it was 1:00 and very warm and we stayed right there at the top of the bank to eat lunch. Miles off we could see a massive red mountain of iron ore tailings. We were told it was two miles around and a quarter mile high, and it certainly looked it. The Japanese are purported to have bought the rights to it. They are coming over soon to mine it and then fill the original hole back up and landscape it! We were also told that the river current was so bad it would take a 15 horsepower motor to ascend the rapids in the next few miles.

We left right after lunch and it turned out that the rumors about the river were nearly right. The current was indeed strong and progress very slow, but foot by foot we managed to advance. Three times in the next few hours we stopped to rest and swim and we all spent the afternoon half naked working on our sunburns.

After supper we paddled an hour and a half till 8:00 and then set up camp during a beautiful sunset. A hard day, but a good one.

JUNE 13: PULP DODGING

It was Friday the 13th today. We generously gave lady luck several opportunities to strike us down, but she passed them up and tonight we are camped on a lovely beach just outside Bryson.

We left camp at 6:00 this morning and sped down Lac des Chats with the wind at our backs. Breakfast was on a nice rocky outcropping. The country has been growing more scenic as we continue along and our breakfast spot felt like real canoe country. The day was warm and sunny and about noon we came to Portage du Fort. That was the end of the easy part.

41

The carry itself was not bad, perhaps a quarter mile, but we spent a slow, difficult afternoon working our way up from there against the current. There were numerous log booms to negotiate and floating logs to avoid. In places we were forced to line up rapids, crawling over cliffs and around trees to do it. It's really quite surprising how well a canoe can go upstream. By using the little eddies behind rocks, darting in and out of little coves, etc., we managed to ascend some fairly good rapids. We would creep right up to the eddy edge until just our nose peeped out and then yelling "Hit it!" we'd surge forward, paddles flashing. Once the river narrowed right down and we were forced to paddle up between two log booms, dodging the logs which came fluming toward us. They had tremendous momentum and would seem to suddenly leap sideways at us. We glanced one and the jar was appreciable. Still luck was with us and we inched forward weaving our way through. That's something the voyageurs never had to face.

By late afternoon we reached a second portage -- the dam before Bryson. We'd been advised to portage on the right but the access looked formidable. Floating pulp logs simply made it impossible to reach shore anywhere near the dam and we would have had a long difficult carry around. Still we should have tried it. Instead we carried up a trail through the woods on the left and portaged to where we could slide down a twenty-foot rocky bank to the water above the dam. What a mistake. Once in the canoe we had to paddle out around a rocky point, which put us dangerously close to the dam. Immediately we were caught in a strong current sweeping by the point and were forced slowly backwards. For long minutes we battled hard and were clearly losing. We have big paddles, mine is over 6 feet long with a huge blade, and we wielded them vigorously. We tried desperately to pull ourselves sideways out of the main current. Nevertheless, ever so slowly, we were being swept back towards the powerhouse openings. The noise of the turbines was tremendous. Whirlpools and eddies were sucking at the boat. Then suddenly, we broke free of the main current and began to creep ahead. The fight was not over but once out of the main current the outcome was certain. It sure pays never to give up, but it also helps to have the necessary endurance. Only a few weeks ago we would not have had the strength to last those furious minutes. The weeks of upstream work have strengthened our paddling as no trip has ever done before. We continued on playing the eddies against the strong currents until about 6:00.

The kids did really well on this long day, although Randy seems to be going through a stage of being as obnoxious and obstreperous as possible. Of course, he is at his worst when tired.

Today we passed the 500 mile mark. Upstream progress is slow, less than two miles an hour lately, but fortunately we enjoy the hard work on a beautiful day like this. There is a fierce pleasure in knowing that you can travel relentlessly all day long and never get tired.

We met two canoes today and told them we were going to Alaska. They gave us three cheers. Hooray for us.

JUNE 14: FORT COULONGE

Shades of Swanzey. The local youths had their Friday night blowout on our beach last night. Things were pretty noisy at times, particularly between 4:00 and 4:30 in the morning. That's when they decided to race their cars at the tent and slam on the brakes. The bright car lights and flying sand made it hard to sleep but we got the last laugh when one of them got stuck just outside. They were there quite a while cursing and shoveling and whirling their wheels in deeper and deeper. We lay there chuckling just inside until eventually they broke free. That seemed to pretty much end the night's activities. When we got up at 6:30 there were only 2 carfulls left and they were pretty done in. I started the breakfast fire and soon they staggered off.

Yesterday we were forced to make one of the two major decisions facing us on the Ottawa. Grand Calumet Island lies just a few miles north of Porage du Fort; it is 15 miles around the west side and 22 on the east. The question was whether to go the long way or to take the shorter route with its presumably stronger currents. We had studied the maps and weighed the alternatives as best we could. After a careful analysis and prolonged discussion we had gotten out a penny to flip. Dissatisfied with the outcome of the first toss, we decided that such a major decision should really be best out of three. The Coin Gods were adamant, however, so we set out to go the long way around. After experiencing the strong rapids and currents around the lower end of the island, though, we don't regret our decision. Assuming the other side is even worse, it is probably time saved to paddle the extra seven miles. We have all the difficulty we can handle right here.

Today was warm and muggy with very little wind and we continued to face a strong, steady current. It was too mosquitoey to get near shore

43

so we paddled pretty steadily throughout the day. About three we came out from behind the island to rejoin the main river. Another hour brought us to Fort Coulonge where we stopped to do a week's shopping. The sky drizzled a little but was mostly just threatening. The menacing clouds were enough motivation however to speed us on our way, and we hustled out of town in less than an hour. We were in a hurry to find a campsite and we ended up with a beautiful one - a huge sandspit island at the mouth of the Coulonge River. We had a delicious supper: hamburgers with rolls, fresh milk, corn, tortilla chips, and vanilla pudding for dessert.

To tell the truth, I am starting to get tired of the Ottawa River. Every day is slow and hard when you go upstream -- you can't rest a second without the canoe's slipping back. Tomorrow we face our second major decision when we reach Allumette Island. The north shore is 14 miles long and the south 25. The difference (11 miles) is too much to contemplate. We shall forget the coins and simply strike out along the north side, portaging where necessary.

JUNE 15: FATHER'S DAY

What a "yecky" day. It was cool (in the 50's) with heavy rain showers off and on all day long. This morning we left at 6:15 and paddled until about 8:00 when we stopped for breakfast on a sand point. At least there have been a lot of nice beaches along this stretch. Breakfast was all the french toast we could eat -- a whole loaf of bread and a bottle of syrup.

The kids didn't have much to do as we paddled along in the rain so we sang songs, "oldies but goodies", and played guessing games all morning. Just before lunch Margie got a nice rest in the middle of the canoe when Tina moved up front to paddle for 40 minutes.

For long stretches the current and riffles were essentially as strong as we could progress against. Finally at 3:30 we reached an island just before the Culbute Rapids near the head of Allumette Island. We paddled all the way around it (about 2 miles) before deciding that the best place to camp was exactly where we had started from. What a discouraging waste of paddling effort. We stopped early, partly on account of the poor weather and partly because we had not the will to face the next 2 to 3-mile stretch of rapids. We are expecting some challenging portages there as there is no evidence that anyone ever comes this way.

44

At least the strong currents we have been facing are good training for the big lakes to come. Maybe we shall be able to whip off 30 miles a day when we finally reach level water. It is after supper now and the sun is starting to come out. It looks as if tomorrow will be clear. We have been watching a family of foxes romping across the way.

For the first time in my life I broke a paddle today. Actually it only split, from the tip nearly up into the shaft. It happened when I clunked a rock while paddling furiously up a little rapids. It was a favorite paddle and a demoralizing experience but I soon learned that it made a pleasant hissing noise as the water passed through the crack.

It is too bad to keep harping on our difficulties all the time, but there really are days that seem to be dominated by hardships. As one of the early French explorers, Pierre Radisson, wrote after his trip up the Ottawa River, "It is a strange thing when victuals are wanting, work whole days and nights, lie down on the bare ground. ... (one feels) the weariness in the bones and the drowsiness of the body by the bad weather that you are to suffer". After a month of uphill paddling I empathize with the state of mind which produced such a sentence.

JUNE 16: NO PICTURES

Today was a beautiful day. We had breakfast at camp before starting out. The plan was to face the Culbute Rapids on a full stomach. Fully prepared for the worst, we set out and immediately encountered a tremendous streak of good fortune. We began by trying to force our way up the Quebec side and right away we found the rotted remains of an old wooden lock hidden at the back of a big eddy. Many of the old floor beams and a few of the side boards were still in place and we simply waded and carried up the floor-boarded channel. The top was blocked off by a huge logjam of debris, but we struggled over it and that was it. The first of the Culbute Rapids was behind us and we had neatly bypassed it. Just before the second set we paddled into a little side cove, and there in the back, by sheer chance, we found a half-mile trail. Amazing luck. A half mile is a long carry of course but this one was made more pleasant by the hundreds of pink lady slippers dotting the trail and the knowledge that we were avoiding a severe rapids. By 10:00 all the rapids were behind us and we were coming out on beautiful Allumette Lake.

The lake was very windy and we struggled hard. A logging tugboat was going upstream also and we managed to overtake, then pass it (admittedly it was dragging a bunch of logs). It was a part of the crew sent out each summer to clean up the strays. This should mean no more logs floating our way or littering the beaches for the rest of our trip.

The lake was beautiful in the crisp blue weather and had loads of sandy beaches. We took a lengthy lunch -- swim -- rest stop on a gorgeous crescent beach hidden in a little cove. There were tall whispering pines in back and a little rock island out front that the kids waded out to.

By supper we were off the lake and once more heading up river. Dinner was on another beach (Pointe au Bapteme, a long sandy point among pines which was the site of the traditional baptism of novice voyageurs). Soon after that we came to a secret government installation. For several hours we had been passing "Government Property, Protected Area, No Trespassing" signs, but until then we had seen no sign of life. Our topographic maps showed nothing -- but here in the middle of nowhere on the Ontario side was a huge installation. Soon we came to a gigantic sign "NO PICTURE TAKING". We took out the camera and snapped photos left and right but nothing happened. At 9:00 just before sunset, we gave up for the night and set up camp under one of their signs. We tried hard to get by their private streak of property but it was just too long. Tomorrow we shall leave early.

The river is very calm and beautiful tonight; truly picturesque. The right (Quebec) side slopes steeply down from a range of miniature mountains flanking the north shore while the Ontario side is far more level. Both sides are heavily forested and uninhabited except for the mystery installation a few miles back. At the last moment the sunset kind of fizzled.

The children slept from 7:30 on in the canoe this evening and tonight we are all in the same tent. Randy had nightmares last night and ended up coming in to join us sometime after midnight. He dreamed a bear was sitting on his sleeping bag and was afraid to stick his head out and check. It turned out to be Tina's feet. Anyway, Margie had to go get him -- I was busy pretending to be asleep.

JUNE 17: ONE MONTH

We have been out a full month now and in some ways it is starting to tell. The children are sunburned and Margie has sore arms. With me,

46

it is my fingers. My fingers are certainly adequate under normal use but each summer after about a month of paddling the same couple of finger joints start to give out. Part of the reason is undoubtedly that I always paddle on the right side -- never on the left. Anyways the progression is all too familiar. In a few more weeks I shall not be able to clench my right hand in the morning and will begin each day by building a breakfast fire. Gradually toasting the fingers over a slow fire gently curls them into paddle-gripping shape for the day.

Today we were both feeling unenergetic, probably due to several hard days in a row. We got up around 6:00. We could hear a dull chug-thugging noise and soon a logging tugboat, trailing its load of logs, loomed out of the fog. The day's first rays piercing the early mist, and the slow thudding of the heavy motor as the boat passed between us and the mountains across the way, made a memorable scene. We were off and paddling by then and the mist had thinned to the point where we could clearly distinguish the stately wading birds riding the tail end of the boom. They stood there gazing intently into the water's depths, and passed us by in silent majesty.

In about an hour we reached the end of government property and stopped to build a morning breakfast fire between some rocks. The day warmed up quickly but never got hot, remaining in the low 70's. By noon it had clouded up some but the kids went wading and swimming anyway. A wind was springing up and we were anxious to be off, so we held the lunch stop to less than an hour.

Eventually we reached a dam and a one-mile carry. As far as we can determine it is the last serious obstacle we face on the river. We were barely starting to unload when a couple who were fishing on the gravel beach offered to drive us around. We learned from them that we had paddled right by two of Canada's nuclear power plant facilities. The first, a research site, was what we had passed yesterday evening, and the second was only a mile or so back. The second we had recognized for what it was but had not stopped to investigate. The river had been very fast there and we were intent upon our business. We accepted their offer of a ride and piled into the back of their old pickup. The canoe was perched on top and we held on tightly as they lurched and sped over bumps and potholes and around corners. The truck stalled a few times but before long we were at the top of a 50-foot dam.

Launching was a problem. The river was a backed-up lake, and the waves were coming directly onshore. There still wouldn't have been much trouble if it hadn't been for all the logs in the water. Nevertheless we managed to jostle them aside and paddle out a hundred yards to a boom.

We have crossed many booms in the last two weeks but I have never described the technique. It is a precarious exercise requiring extreme agility and balance. The idea is for each of us to stand on the log -- one on each side of the canoe. The force generated by lifting on the gunwales, coupled with our weight, is enough to submerge the log and allow the canoe to float over. Sounds simple. The problems are:

1) the logs are slippery and unsteady

2) the incoming waves are distracting

3) the log generally sinks slowly but steadily and you can't be sure just how far down it will go before twisting out from underneath you.

When the procedure is performed in the middle of a wavy lake as we were doing today it becomes truly exciting. The waves were jouncing the logs so much that we found it nearly impossible to even land and get out on one. After a few attempts and a wetting though the mission was finally accomplished. The hardest parts were:

a) getting out

b) getting the canoe across

c) getting back in

(Some days nothing is easy.)

The wind continued strong for the rest of the afternoon. The lake was gradually widening and the waves were getting bigger. About 4:30 we gave up and landed at a tiny grassy clearing that turned out to be a widening in an old logging road. It seems to be the only spot for miles around that is flat and clear enough for a tent.

It is very buggy here with mosquitoes, blackflies and no-see-ums. It is rarely that we have all three at once. We had supper down on the rock beach where the wind kept the worst of the bugs away. It is nice to spend an evening where we have a chance to get the accumulated sand out of everything. The canoe should be 50 pounds lighter tomorrow!

JUNE 18: FISHING SECRET NUMBER ONE

I started off by entitling tonight's report "The Big Pike", but after thinking it over I've decided to reveal one of my most cherished fishing secrets. We do a lot of trolling on our trips using a handline. So do most trippers and all of us are accustomed to regularly pulling in the 2 and 3 pounders that so infest northern waters. But have you ever wondered why a chosen few, using your identical outfit, seem to consistently pull in the lunkers? The secret is in the feet. In order to catch a fish, a really big fish, the experienced troller will invariably remove his boots and stow them out of reach. This not only insures a strike on the trailing lure, but almost guarantees a fish of munificent size. Inevitably, once the boots are away and your toes out wriggling in the sun, you will snare a prize. There is no chance he'll get away either. No, he'll head right for the canoe and with minimal assistance from you vault right into the back of the boat. No need to reach for the pliers, he'll spit the hooks right out, and there'll you'll be: snapping teeth, loops of line, disgorged triple gang hooks, flopping tail, sliming blood and razored fins all scrabbling at your bare feet. Naturally, you will not wish to try this technique too often. Anyway the method produced a huge pike for supper today. We ate all we could but finally ended up throwing some chunks away.

Last night it rained and stayed muggily warm, right through till morning. Margie and I got very little sleep; we had let too many mosquitoes and no-see-ums get into the tent with us. The kids slept well in theirs, though.

We got up about 6:30 and left immediately to paddle the few miles to Driftwood Provincial Park for breakfast. There were so many bugs there, however, that we decided to have a cold breakfast and eat it sheltered inside the two little houses (one each for men and women) that had been erected there. The kids amused themselves by running from shed to shed (safety zones).

Travelling conditions were good today. It was clear and cool with only a weak wind and the children spent much of the time sleeping. We hooked our huge fish early, and when we came to a nice spot at three, we stopped for the day. We are camping on a big rock ledge under some pines on the Quebec side and are about 30 feet above the water. It is a beautiful place with everything so blue and green and crisp. It is such a nice spot we shall stay for breakfast. We have only put up the one tent as the ground is too rocky to hold the children's tent pegs. We took pictures today of a mink, some loons and another logging boat. We are starting to get a little bit excited. It is only 30 miles to Mattawa where we shall leave the Ottawa River. There are quite a few mosquitoes and black flies around now.

FISHIN'

SANDERS, '84

50

JUNE 19: MATTAWA

This morning was overcast and cool but the bugs were up early and waiting for us. We used to put dried apple slices in our morning oatmeal for flavoring. Then we went to raisins and next to the slightly smaller currants. Today, however, we just set the oatmeal out a few minutes uncovered. Just like Brer Rabbit and the tar baby, the mosquito hordes got first one leg, then another, and finally both wings and their foreheads stuck. They wiggled a moment and then gave up.

We had a snack about 10:30 but couldn't stay on shore very long because it was so buggy. The black flies followed us out onto the water in a cloud and only gradually dispersed as we managed to leave them behind. At lunch we decided not to risk the bugs by landing and, instead, spent the time offshore in a cove slowly drifting backwards. Soon after, the day began to deteriorate. A cold rain settled in about 1:00. After a couple of hours everyone was getting wet, cold and miserable despite our warm jackets and rainsuits. The current was picking up and the shoreline was impossible to camp on: steep brush-covered cliffs and hills marching right down to the water's edge. We had mistakenly passed up a scruffy swampy beach spot on the Quebec shore around 3:00 and it turned out to be the only level spot in 30 miles. We flexed our shoulders and paddled on determinedly through the rain. The kids sat bailing in the middle, chanting "I want supper in Mattawa!" Finally, about 5:00, we reached a last corner and there, two miles away, was the town! With whoops and cheers we paddled on, though not exactly speeding because of the current and tired muscles. We debated briefly the possibility of setting up camp in the pouring rain and building a fire on the muddy bank outside town, but it was not much of a discussion. Margie would not discuss it. She jumped out of the canoe and ran up the bank to a motel. We finally ended up at the Mattawa Hotel with a double room and bath with a special rate for poor, half drowned canoers. We had hot dogs and french fries for supper, a warm bath and a dry bed. Heaven! It put a big dent in our budget but nobody is complaining. We all had fun seeing ourselves in the mirror tonight. Margie has visibly bulging muscles in her back and arms now, and I have grown a bushy beard. Today we went 30 stupendous uphill miles for a total of 635.

51

JUNE 20: EXPLORER'S POINT

Mattawa is an historic village which grew up around an old fur trading post, and the incoming Mattawa River marks a major turning point in our journey. Running through an ancient geologic fault from Trout Lake near Lake Nipissing, the river has been travelled by men since prehistoric times. This ancient route was visited by Champlain in 1615 on his way to Lake Huron, then followed and improved upon by the voyageurs. The 14 major carries and other difficulties were consistently described in the journals of the fur traders and explorers over the next two centuries. The route was an integral part of the Northwest Company's "highway" west from their Montreal headquarters to their annual rendez-vous at Grand Portage. The river is short, running no more than 40 miles, but here more than anywhere one appreciates the backbreaking jobs of the early voyageurs. Struggling, 8 to 10 men per canoe, they lined and portaged their heavy cargoes past the numerous rapids and falls. Each of their 36-foot canoes could carry up to 8000 pounds and the individual voyageurs were each responsible for 6 ninety pound packs (pieces) as well as their own personal gear on each of the carries. A normal load was 2 such packs (180 pounds), but it was not uncommon to see men carrying 3 or even 4 at a time across the portages.

It was still raining hard when we woke up this morning so we loitered around the hotel and then went out to do a little shopping. I bought a new pen and am no longer engraving my reports on the paper with a faint stubby pencil. We had both breakfast and lunch in our room and then finally, reluctantly, we pushed off in the rain about 2:00. The current was very strong there and a townsman offered to tow us around Explorer's Point to the mouth of the Mattawa with his motorboat, but we declined with thanks. It was still raining, windy and bleak but at least we were starting out warm and dry from the hotel.

We soon discovered that the portages on the river are all marked and measured and there is an interesting historic placque at each one. We got by the first three, namely

a) Portage du Plain Chant (falls where the singing spirits live?)

b) Portage de la Rose (Thorn Rapids -- mentioned in all the journals from the 1600's on)

c) Portage Campion (named for an early traveler).

We stopped for the evening about 6:00 and, glory be, the rain let up and the sun came out in another half hour. We are camped beside the

52

river in Champlain Provincial Park and nearby is an exhibit including a huge 40-foot birchbark canoe. It is 6 feet wide and is, of course, huge. The plaques say the voyageurs commonly worked their craft 18 hours a day at rates of 4 to 5 miles per hour, and covered the distance to Grand Portage from Montreal in 6 to 8 weeks. These figures are somewhat inconsistent but they made us feel good. If the trip really took them 8 weeks then their progress was not substantially better than ours. Of course, we have left our 3 tons of cargo at home.

JUNE 21: PARESSEUX FALLS

Now that we are well away from town my new pen has stopped working and I am again engraving the journal with a faint pencil. Today was a great day. It was foggy early, so we slept in and ate breakfast right in camp. We left about 8:00, just as the sun was starting to burn through the mist -- everything was really pretty and quiet. The water rose several more inches in the night due to all the rain runoff and is now very high. The lily pads are anchored a foot or so beneath the surface and all day long we could see them down below, straining at their stems.

Before long we began the day's portages. It certainly saves searching time to have them all marked with signs. The children run right over, then Tina reads the historic plaque to Randy. The plaques are all on the upstream side and give us something to look forward to as we struggle across. Each contains an interesting historic tidbit. We started with Portage des Roches (150 paces) which was an incredibly bad trail -- all rocks. We managed to paddle and line up the next rapid and avoid a portage. Unfortunately, later in the day we made up the lost portage by doing one twice, or in two parts, or perhaps we found a new one somehow.

After a pleasant paddle through cliffy country the river closed in till we were paddling up through a black granite canyon leading to La Porte de l'Enfer ("The Gates of Hell"). The Indians were reputed to have obtained their red war paints from the ochre in the shallow cave there. Naturally the kids wanted to climb up and explore the cave despite the poison ivy covering the bank between us and it. We carefully picked our way along until we could see the back wall of the cave, about 6 feet in. That was enough to satisfy everyone's curiosity and we returned to the canoe.

Next came 4 portages in quick succession.

a) Portage des Paresseux. This carry of 402 paces around scenic 30-foot Paresseux Falls was named for a pair of lazy trappers. Legend has it that a brigade from Montreal lost one of their craft here. The brigade then went down the nearly 350 miles to Montreal to fetch another canoe and trusted the trappers to portage their loads around while they were gone. They made the 700-mile roundtrip in such short order (two weeks) that the trappers had not yet finished portaging when they returned.

b) Portage de la Prairie - 287 paces.

c) Portage de la Cave - 100 paces. A 19th century traveller, John Bigsby, described this section of the river as rarely maintaining ''an equable and moderate rate for a mile together; some descent or obstruction is continually occurring.'' It was here we did at least one extra carry.

d) Decharge des Perches - 200 paces. It is at this point that the voyageurs could finally throw away their poles (perches), as paddles were sufficient for the rest of the trip.

We made it to a small lake (Pimisi Bay) and a nice picnic spot for lunch. We rested and Margie soaked her hand, which she injured this morning on a portage when she slipped on a wet root. The trails in general were fairly poor today. There were nice docks at every landing but because the water is so high they were all at least a foot under water.

After lunch we did only one more carry, the famous Portage de Talon, making 7 for the day. This short steep portage was only 275 paces but was considered by the voyageurs to be the worst between Montreal and Grand Portage. It was all way up and way down between big rocks and deep puddles. It reminded me of portages in Labrador where I crawled over huge rocks on hands and knees with the canoe balanced on my shoulders. The difficulty here was partially compensated for by the beauty of the 40-foot cascade dropping in two falls between 100-foot rock walls. George Simpson, ''the little governor'' of the Hudson Bay Company, described the carry as ''...truly picturesque; the river from being a considerable width, here branches into a variety of channels,...on either side are stupendous rocks of the most fantastic form; some bear the appearance of Gothic castles, other exhibit rows of the most regular and beautifully carved Corinthian pillars: deep caverns are formed in some; while others present a smooth level surface...''. The day was quite warm by then and we were all tired by the time we finished.

Tonight we are camped on a grassy point on Lake Talon where we have a table and outhouses -- all the luxuries. The kids went swimming today. We also met a few canoes taking weekend trips downstream to Champlain Park. It was a good day even though we only covered 11 miles.

JUNE 22: VASE RIVER

Today was probably as hard a day as we'll put in all summer. Thankfully the weather cooperated by not raining, however, and tonight we are camped on the shore of Lake Nipissing at the mouth of the Vase River. After yesterday, I thought we'd never do 7 portages in a day again and yet, today, we accomplished at least that.

We started off at 6:30 planning to breakfast at Portage Pin de Musique (456 paces). It was so buggy there though that we just carried across and ate on a big rock in the middle of Robichaud Lake. The next carry, Portage de la Mauvais Musique (undoubtedly named for the infernal humming of the millions of mosquitoes there) we did like lightning, literally running across with our heavy loads -- the mosquitoes were so thick. Although that swampy carry has now been terraced by the labor of hundreds of voyageurs, it was here, in Mackenzie's day, that many men fell and were crushed to death by weight of their huge canoes.

We thought that there would be only one more carry after that, into Lake Nipissing, and we settled down to steady paddling trying to get there before the wind rose. We paddled without stopping till 1:00, then took ten minutes to eat in the canoe while the kids paddled. Continuing on we reached the end about 2:00 and then the fun began. Following in the footsteps of Champlain etc., we set out over the height of land through swamps and beaver ponds to the narrow, shallow La Vase River. This miserable, abominable, marshy swamp took us 5 hours of hot continuous work to cover 5 miles. Small wonder the voyageurs, emerging from this area, shouted with relief. There was no evidence that anyone had ever come this way. There was a lot of carrying through dismal swamp, smashing through beaver dams, and pushing through weed and lily-pad-choked ponds and sloughs, with us half lost much of the time. The heat and bugs were terribly oppressive. The old beaver dams were so overgrown that we could not even push the canoe through the brush and trees growing out of them. There was no current to give us a hint which way to go and the water was so clogged with growth we could barely budge the canoe forwards. Finally after the first three hours (and two miles) we stumbled into the winding Vase River and, comparatively speaking, things picked up. We finally reached Champlain Park on beautiful Lake Nipissing at 7:00, after 12 hours of hard work, and set up camp. Tomorrow we get hot showers, a laundromat and food shopping.

Interestingly enough, it snowed here Monday. In Timmins there was enough to cover the ground.

I am using Margie's hand cream this summer and it helps a lot. My hands used to get cracked and bleeding on long trips but now they just get cracked.

JUNE 23: THE HOLY PIZZA

Margie and I slept in until 6:30 this morning and the children didn't wake up till 7:00. We had pancakes for breakfast, and then the kids ran off to play at the beach and playground. We showered and washed clothes and Margie took the bus to go food shopping -- very convenient. When she returned there were a reporter and a photographer from the local newspaper waiting to take some pictures of our family. We all tried to look busy while the photographer took some "candid" shots. The reporter confided that he was always sent out to interview the kooks. I am not sure that we made it to the top of his list though as he already has several good cross-country specimens to his credit. His favorite was the Vancouver pizza maker who one day discovered the image of the Lamb of God in his pie. Realizing that he had a divine mission to reveal this miracle to the world, he had set out on foot for the east coast carrying the pizza strapped to his back. Apparently he got at least as far as North Bay.

After lunch we had an ice cream and repacked the food. Repacking Margie's supermarket purchases is always good for an hour's entertainment. It mainly involves debulking and lightening wherever possible. Boxes and jars are thrown away and the contents placed in plastic tubes and baggies. The remaining unpackables are placed in a cardboard box which rides along on top of our gear until it either disintegrates or space for the contents materializes in the packs. This year we are using only three of our four large Duluth packs. We used to use pack frames but found them an unwieldy abomination in a canoe. The crushable Duluth packs each carry about 75 pounds without any trouble and we can easily

56

accommodate 10 days store-type food along with our gear in the three packs. Next year we shall bring our fourth pack because with it and judicious shopping we seem to be able to carry approximately one month's supplies. The big advantage of three packs over four, though, is that the portages may be made in two trips. There are four regular sized loads for the two of us -- the three packs and the canoe. With four packs I must suffer on one of my trips by either taking two packs or a pack and the 100 lb. canoe.

Finally we were ready to leave at 2:30. Of course, the predictable happened. Lake Nipissing is big but surprisingly it had been like glass all morning long. It was still calm when we pushed off and the air was nearly still. Half an hour later though it started to get breezy and by the time we had crossed the first big bay we had to stop for the wind and waves. After a rest it seemed calmer so we rounded the point but were soon forced ashore again, this time on a sandy beach where we ate supper and may end up spending the night. We had planned on a long evening paddle when the lake would be calm. Very frustrating!

JUNE 24: LAKE NIPISSING

About 9:00 last night I found a big old turtle hiding in the rocks by the shore and I brought him into camp for the children to see. Randy got out his toy stuffed turtle that he sleeps with and we had scenes of turtle meeting Turtle. Later I had to help the old turtle back down to the shore. He was such a slow walker.

Shortly thereafter we gave up waiting for the wind to die down and spread out the tarp and sleeping bags to sleep. Immediately the wind let up and the mosquitoes swarmed out. Somewhat disgruntled, we got up in the dark and erected the tent. We all crowded in to spend what turned out to be a miserable night. Margie was restless and stayed up most of the time with the flashlight killing bugs all around us while the rest of us tried to sleep. It was hard to rest though with the light flashing in our eyes and the sounds of triumph as she caught another "bloody one". Finally we got up at 4:00 and set out by 4:30 in the dark. The wind was down and the lake had calmed to big smooth swells which gradually flattened out as a big red hazy sun came up. We paddled by a huge rocky "seagull island" just as the sun was rising and the hundreds of gulls

the ENCOUNTER

SANDERS, '85

wheeling and mewling in the air over our heads sounded like the opening scenes of an old Tarzan movie. The gulls were terrified that we would molest their ugly little offspring which paddled pitifully around in the water crying feebly, unable to fly or even flutter.

We spend a lot of time singing in the canoe, particularly on rainy days, and today Margie took the opportunity to teach the children another oldie:

"Birdie birdie in the sky."

This year's favorites, however, seem to be "You can't get to heaven" and

"You can't ride in my red wagon.

Axle's broken, back seat's draggin'.

Same song, second verse.

Little bit louder,

Little bit worse

YOU CAN'T RIDE IN MY RED WAGON.

AXLE'S BROKEN, BACK SEAT'S DRAGGIN'.

Same song, third etc.''

A few stanzas of this last is bound to quickly drive any parent batty.

We paddled right along through the morning with only a very quick stop for a cold breakfast, and by 12:00 we were entering the French River. Lunch was a long rest and swim period, and afterwards we did only a few miles before stopping for the day. Today was very hot, 84 degrees in the shade, and in the afternoon the wind was strong in our faces. We are camped on a nice rock; we really don't have much choice since there is nothing but rock around here. This evening the kids spent some time feeding the seagulls. The birds are quite friendly and will come in very close for a taste of our delicious bannock. Now as dusk settles in, the wind is beginning to die down.

There is no discernible current yet in the French River. Everybody is tired, the sky is clear, and we did 25 miles today.

JUNE 25: THE UPPER FRENCH

I understand the voyageurs could, on occasion, do the entire French in a single day. We, on the other hand, accomplished only 12 more miles today, and a frustrating effort it was.

We started off early and got in an hour or so of paddling before breakfast. The upper French is full of islands and after eating we wasted over an hour casting about for the best route. We had decided to take the Little French River around a big island when we met some Indians who suggested that the other side was really better, so back we went. There was a good portage there, about half a mile, and the day was getting awfully warm. Once over, we threw down our loads, stripped, and plunged in for a swim before continuing. There was still no discernible current and by lunchtime it was getting quite windy so we took a long break. Afterwards we tried to continue, but progressed no more than a mile before giving up on account of the wind. We made ourselves comfortable on another rocky spot and waited until after supper, when the wind was dying down a bit. We then paddled on for an hour, stopping at a tiny sloping sand beach for the night. Really it is the first non-rock spot we have seen since joining the river and it is barely big enough for both tents.

We have had excellent bannocks lately. Also the pine trees really smell sweet and refreshing. Too bad we can't bottle the scent for this winter at home.

JUNE 26: THE MIDDLE FRENCH

There were terrible thunderstorms starting about 12:30 last night. We had an awful lot of close crashing thunder and lightning and we were later kept awake by a small river coursing through the tent until about 3:00. I had ditched the tent in anticipation before retiring but there is not much you can do when camping in a leaky tent at the base of a rocky slope. On nights like this I used to sit up in the tent clutching my down sleeping bag in my arms to keep it dry. This time though, with my Polar Guard bag, I just wallowed soggily, drowsily regarding the storm as just another good test for the new materials. We could hear the kids talking in their own tent during the lulls, but they never complained.

Today was surprisingly difficult even though we didn't get up until after 6:00 and stopped for the evening by 4:00. The wind harassed us mildly all day long. We stopped to eat breakfast with a large party of 7 canoes (the first canoe group we have seen). They were just getting up after a wet night on a rocky island. They were a "camp" group and couldn't seem to get a fire going. It seemed inappropriate to build one for them so we ate a cold breakfast and then gave them our empty cereal boxes to start their fire. They are really lazing along. Their schedule calls for them to reach the point where we are camped tonight, some 5 to 6 days from now.

There were 7 marked rapids on our maps today. For maps we always use the 1:250,000 scale (4 miles to the inch) topographic maps. Almost all major falls and rapids are marked on them and with rare exception these are adequate for northern travel. They lack a lot of detail of course but one soon gets used to them.

After scouting out the rapids on today's stretch we chose to portage one, line one and shoot the rest. Learning to scout out rapids is as important as learning to run them. It is something that needs to be practiced. Be sure to do a thorough job for if a rapid is worth scouting, it is worth scouting well. Check every inch all the way to the end because lives may depend on it. If necessary throw in sticks to get an accurate reading of the current. Also a pole may be used to probe barely submerged rocks and ledges. Memorize the best route through and, just as importantly, plan out alternatives. Besides all this, scouting is an excellent chance to relieve yourself unobserved.

Occasionally after scouting out a stretch of rapids you will decide to try lining. Lining (letting a canoe downstream with ropes) may well be the most deceptively difficult and most seldomly mastered canoeing technique there is. Everybody loves to practice shooting rapids but no one wants to go out and practice lining for an afternoon. Linable rapids lie in that narrow fringe between the almost runnable and the must portage. As such they are often powerful, difficult obstructions with the potential for truly serious accidents. Never underestimate a rapid you have decided to line. Using a piece of string to shepherd a canoe through a rapid you wouldn't dare run is always a dicey proposition.

The country around here has not really been to our liking. The scenery is fine, but not spectacular. Of course, we are not the first to notice all the rock and the absence of dirt. Radisson, who travelled the same route in the middle 1600's, remarked, "The most parts there abouts is so sterill that there is nothing to be seene but rocks and sand, and on the high wayes but deale trees that grow most miraculously, for that earth is not to be seene that can nourish the root and most of them trees are very bigg and high." Further the river is a navigational nightmare -- all islands and bays, and our maps are not too accurate. Lastly, there are crowds of people. We were both looking forward to this river as one of the summer's highlights, but there is none of the solitude we had hoped for. The overwhelming impression is one of motorboats everywhere. They are almost never out of sight. The shores and islands boast numerous summer camps and fishing lodges and there are simply scores of fishermen puttering around with their native guides. Two nights ago a float-plane landed just out beyond our campsite. The pilot threw out his anchor and stepped out on the pontoon to try a few casts, then jumped back inside to fly down the river to the next "hotspot". Of course the kids find it all very exciting.

JUNE 27: CAPSIZE

This morning we got up early and paddled the 7 or 8 miles down to Recollet Falls for a late breakfast. It was a great day for travelling: cool and partly cloudy, with an occasional light wind at our backs. After portaging the falls we just sped along, eating lunch in the canoe and not stopping till 2:30 for a snack break on a rock island. As we began to get down toward Georgian Bay though the river turned into a real maze of islands and channels and we passed literally hundreds if not thousands of islands of varying sizes. Our map was worse than useless and we failed to discover Voyageur Channel, the most direct route for us to take. The river empties into Lake Huron in a mazed mess many miles wide that defies description. The area is a huge delta comprised of rock islands and several main channels, and the Voyageur Channel we wished to find was not even on our map. Still it was all downstream and after our snack we continued on, not particularly concerned. As we progressed the current began to pick up and the islands closed in. We started shooting little riffles and rapids and then suddenly we were at an effective dead end. We had come down to a pool whose narrow outlet between two rock islands was a little falls nearly choked with debris. Still we were not worried for there we met another party of canoe travellers.

There were 4 men with two canoes and they were pondering the chute there as we arrived. Being more knowledgeable than ourselves (they had been down the river before), they knew that they were lost. They had excellent large-scale topographic maps and delighted in showing us just how badly lost we were. At the end, all the channels leading to the bay drop, some precipitously, others less so. Apparently we had chosen one of the worst. Looking over the falls though I allowed as I could probably run it and so win through, but would rather not. This casual remark so encouraged one of their number that they determined to try it. I yelled out for them to hold on while I ran for my camera, eager to film what must be a certain debacle in their smaller, heavily loaded boats. Sensing my undisguised excitement at their impending misfortune, they decided to reconsider their prospects. After some discussion we all agreed to retreat upstream and seek a better channel. We went first and by cleverly using an eddy and cross stream ferry managed to ascend the first riffle back. The next canoe tried and failed but made it on the second attempt. The last canoe made it also, but shipped considerable water and almost swamped in the process. They had been down the river before and had the good maps, so we waited for them while they bailed.

They then led us meandering amongst the islands and dead ends until finally they "recognized" what they assured us was the best channel. It was a heavy rapid running down between rock walls and then branching left and right as in a capital Y around a rock island, and then continuing tumultuously out of sight on either side. I am generally not bashful about running rapids but I was dubious this time. I don't like to commit my canoe to a course I cannot see and I had little faith in my companions. They were certain that they knew what they were doing, however, and only warned us to be sure to take the right fork. It was late afternoon now with no place to camp and no obvious alternative so I reluctantly agreed to accept their judgment. They were anxious to go first and I politely acquiesced. Stressing that the right fork was the only passable one, the first canoe took off. It shot forward and immediately bounced into the left wall, swamped and caromed into the left fork, followed by two flailing swimmers. The second canoe now seemed reluctant to proceed and hung back, so it was up to us to plunge after their friends. Sending the kids to the floor (they already had on their life-jackets) we braced ourselves and hurtled towards the fork, the shout "Stay to the right!" ringing out behind us. We reached the fork just as the swimmers were swept over a falls on the left with a loud yell. Spotting an eddy just before the lip of the falls, I decided to take a slight chance. Standing and bracing, I managed to pull the canoe left after them at the last moment. I figured to pause in the eddy at the brink and decide where to go next, but luck was with us. I was still standing and as we swept down to the edge I could see a small chute in the falls ahead, so we twisted into it to slide down into the pool beneath. We crossed the pool slowly, rescuing packs, floating swimmers, and broken dimestore paddles. On the far side we parted company, they wet and shivering to go east, we to go west. In another hour or so we came to where the real Voyageur Channel emptied out and we stopped on a rock to cook supper.

It was a still evening and so after supper we put the kids to sleep in their sleeping bags in the middle of the canoe and paddled out to see Lake Huron. Coming out onto a big lake or ocean is quite an experience. It is a little scary as the secure banks of the river are left behind and there is only the vast open space ahead. It took us an hour or so to thread our way out among the islands but by 8:00 we were in open water. It was beautiful. The water was a bright turquoise green and the ever-present rocks were variegated hues of pink-peach. There was only a long smooth gentle swell and we continued on through the evening. It was a beautiful sunset and soon a full moon rose in an otherwise clear and darkening sky. We finally stopped for the night on the far side of Point Grondine. The water is very shallow hereabouts with big rocks everywhere, both above and below the surface. It would be hard to conceive of a more challenging piece of water if the surf was up. There is the everpresent danger of having a big swell just deposit you with a crunch on one of the barely submerged boulders. Lake Huron is beautiful though and we are both deeply impressed. Today, particularly this evening, was one of those times that we live for. All we could do was smile and smile as we saw that beautiful lake opening up around us. We did about 37 miles today, really a pretty long day.

JUNE 28: GEORGIAN BAY

Last night we slept perched on the top of a smooth rock just off Point Grondine and a very poor night it was. We had landed after dark and had immediately set up the tent on account of the mosquitoes. Unfortunately a breeze soon came up. Because we were unable to use pegs in the sheer rock, the wind kept flapping and blowing the tent around. Also there was such a bright moon that it felt like dawn inside the tent and every hour or so we checked the watch to see if we could leave yet. Still the rock was extremely smooth and we managed to get some rest. Finally, at 4:30, I could stand it no longer and got up.

The wind came up swiftly with the dawn and so did rain. We spent the morning weaving around rock islands trying to stay hidden from the big surf which was forming out in the open water. It was very cold at breakfast and it was still cold and raining by lunchtime. We did not cook a bannock last night so we had a good excuse to build a lunch fire. We landed on another of the thousands of rock islands and built a roaring blaze. The fresh warm bannock tasted delicious and it was fun huddling around the fire in the rain. In less than an hour though we were off again, but we only went a mile or so before giving up for the day. We landed on the lee side of an island, the last one before Killarney that's big enough to hold a tent. As usual it was all rock and scrub pines, no sand or dirt, but we have all been having a good time. There is a family of mink here and the kids stalk them through the rocks. We have also found the year's first blueberries, five of them, which we are saving to split up for dessert tonight. There is really no way we could have gone farther today as the next few miles are totally exposed. The surf is bursting ten feet into the air over the rocks on the windward side of our island and the kids in their raincoats are playing in the resulting showers. The water is beautiful, really turquoise, and we are all enjoying the sight of the big waves on the rocks. We landed at 1:30. Today we went 16 miles for 794. No one minds an occasional rainy day (too much).

JUNE 29: INJURY

We left early under cloudy skies, but not without trouble. Our usual practice is to gently deposit the children, still sleeping in their bags, into the canoe last thing before taking off in the morning. This way they can get an hour or two of extra sleep before breakfast while we paddle along. Today, however, Margie fell on the slick rock while carrying Randy down to the boat. In an effort to protect him she fell full on her knees on the rock and has been hurting since. She can't walk very well and it is also hard for her to bend her knees or paddle.

It was only a few miles to Killarney but by the time we reached the point there the waves had already grown to big swells and we were in some difficulty. A dark cloud was racing over the water toward us and we were barely into the safety of the channel before a steady rain and obscuring fog bank enveloped us. We immediately stopped at a deserted cottage on the outskirts of town and quickly roused the kids and packed their sleeping bags away. Then we settled down to cold breakfast in the shelter of the cottage porch and listened to the blaring of the channel's lighthouse foghorn. It was startling how fast the fog, rain and big waves had rolled in. We'd been only moments ahead of real trouble. There would have been no way to land on the cliff-bound coast in the mile before Killarney. We'd had some difficulty with the backwash from the cliffs as it was in rounding the point.

Eventually the rain and fog abated and we crossed the channel to the town. Margie limped hobblingly off to do a little food shopping (fresh bread and brownies) while the children and I hung around the marina getting weather reports and general information about the coast ahead. It was still foggy when we left, but our route now lay across the relatively sheltered Killarney Bay to Badgely Point, and we set out by compass. The bay was fairly calm although we did take shelter on an island in the middle when another short violent storm swept by. Rather than paddle some 15 miles out of our way around Badgely Point we decided to carry over the peninsula. There was a small pond in the middle of the carry so it really turned out to be two fairly short portages. Margie had a lot of difficulty but made it across okay while I portaged the gear. Lunch was on the shore of Frazer Bay. There was a pretty pebble beach there with rocks of all colors, many spotted or striped. I played rock throwing games with the children and Margie was able to lie down resting her knees. After lunch, fog and rain came in again, and we went only a couple of miles before stopping for the day at a coarse sand beach. Well, this was another day no one really worried about sunburn. Hope that tomorrow is a little better weather and that Margie recovers. It was in the 50's today.

JUNE 30: DREAMER'S PENINSULA

On a warm morning such as we had today the mosquitoes can be a real nuisance. They are particularly annoying when you are taking the tent down and first setting out.

We were up by 5:30 and as often happens millions of mosquitoes had decided to sleep on the roof beneath the fly. Naturally, I woke them up. You can't defend yourself properly when you are pulling out the stakes, disassembling the poles, and stuffing the tent away and the hordes settle all over the backs of your fingers and hands and face. It takes determination to ignore them and continue with the camp chores. Fortunately it takes us no more than 10 minutes or so to be up and off.

On a still morning such as today, however, they follow you right out onto the water and it can take as much as half an hour or more to outpace them. The kids snuggle deep in their sleeping bags but the parents simply endure. You can move your legs around to protect them and the paddling movements of your arms protect your face and upper body. The one place you can't protect, however, is your fanny. We have cane seats in the canoe and the mosquitoes gather in the bottom of the boat away from any wind and take turns piercing us through the cane holes from underneath. It is amazing how many bites you can acquire this way and your seat remains itchy for hours. Fortunately the solution is simple. We start out every morning, rain or shine, wearing our rain pants and this effectively thwarts the mosquitoes as they can't bite through the coated cloth.

We had breakfast on Dreamer's Peninsula, a point that looks like an island (dreamer) and isn't. Rather than paddle around we chose to simply carry across the narrow isthmus. This is the second time in as many days that I have chosen to portage rather than paddle. I must be getting old. Margie's knees are still too sore to portage anything, but she seems to be getting better; thank goodness. Afterwards we continued on out into the North Channel of Lake Huron and had a leisurely lunch and clothes washing break at Flat Point. The country is very rugged and the rock hills come right down to the shoreline. We tried twice to continue in the afternoon but the wind had picked up from the west and we made very little progress. After supper the lake was still rolling, but the white caps had mostly gone and we were able to do another 7 miles. About dusk we stopped at a beautiful campsite. I was very tired today but I think a lot of it was due to the small meals we have been having lately. A voyageur needs 5000-7000 calories a day.

JULY 1: NORTH CHANNEL

I forgot to take the flashlight to bed last night so I had to wait until

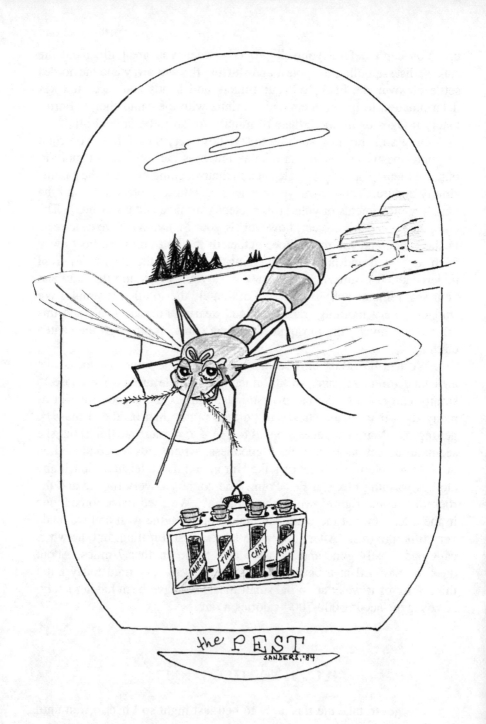

the PEST

SANDERS '84

it was light enough to read the watch (5:15) before getting up today. Again the bugs were terrible, but at least they made for a quick getaway. It is hard too know what to do about bugs on a canoe trip. Basically, the three most irritating species are mosquitoes, blackflies and no-see-ums. Repellents work on them all of course, some better than others. There are many commercial preparations on the market and each year we try a couple of new ones, hoping for a miracle substance. We also bring along our own concoction. The exact mixture was passed on to us by an old hand in northern Ontario and we were sworn to secrecy as regards its proportions. I can reveal though that it contains pine tar, citronella, mineral oil and whiskey and is really no better than anything else. Everyone is familiar with mosquitoes but in the north black flies can be at least as obnoxious. They are silent, last all summer, draw blood and crawl under clothes at neck, wrists, ankles and beltlines looking for a warm place to bite. If you find blood trickling down behind your ears you have been visited by a black fly. No-see-ums are most pesky on warm nights. Even during the day though they are almost invisible. They attack in hordes, are small enough to pass through almost any material, and their bites burn like fire. Their only redeeming feature is that after 20 minutes all traces of the bite are gone, whereas a black fly bite can linger on for days.

Well, it was overcast with showers all day long and the channel remained calm although it didn't hurt any that we were protected behind islands most of the time. In the afternoon Tina took over for Margie and paddled a full hour -- good for her. About supper time the rain finally stopped and we found a good rock campsite. We paddled 29 miles today and now we are all in our damp (but not wet) sleeping bags for a good night's rest.

JULY 2: BLIND RIVER

Good weather at last. A nice blue day with lots of sun and still refreshingly cool. We paddled the 19 miles to Blind River by 2:00 and then spent three hours shopping and doing other errands. We would have gotten there much earlier but the wind had risen in our faces and made the last three miles extremely tough. The waves were big enough that we should have stopped sooner, but it is hard to quit when you can see

69

the town right there a mile or two away. It looked calmer when we left the harbor at 5:00, but it really wasn't. Two miles, one nerve-wracking hour and many waves later we finally found a sandy cove, a scarce commodity in this rocky country.

The supper following a food shopping day is always a big event and we did a lot of fancy cooking. I suppose some campers would be horrified by our utensils. Boy Scouts in particular like to keep their pots clean inside and out. To this end they soap the outside before every meal and scrub them clean afterwards. I guess this works alright for groups who must share their pots and who are usually out for only a week or two. At the other extreme, however, there are those who have their own pots and feel a rinsing in cold water is sufficient, augmented by scrubbing with sand when available. Often these are the same people who like to travel with a minimum of dishes -- maybe 2 pots and a mixing spoon, with one cup and spoon per person. We fall somewhere in between. We travel with a set of 4 nesting pots, plus a bowl, cup, spoon, and fork per person. When we are done cooking we put a pot of dishwater on to warm up while we eat. We don't try to clean the outside of the pots though. If they get sandy or dirty when they are put together again, it is no trouble to rinse out a pot before using it next time. We used to use soap to wash our dishes but that leaves a soapy taste if they are not rinsed well enough. Usually a steel scrubby and hot water take care of everything.

This year we have experimented with another easier method -- just set your bowls and cups out after eating and let the rain wash them. We have had plenty of occcasions to try this.

The wind didn't die down after supper so we went straight to bed. I had to get up in about an hour though to construct a driftwood dike around our camp. Gradually the waves are eroding our little beach away and now the tent is right on the water's edge (at least for the biggest waves).

JULY 3: THESSALON POINT

Another beautiful day, but a little hotter than yesterday. The children went swimming at breakfast, lunch, afternoon and supper and they are sunburned tonight.

We pretty much paddled from 5:15 till 2:00 and then, since the lake was roughening up, we stopped until after supper. Later we travelled from 7:00 till 9:00 with the kids asleep in the canoe. The north shore here has been pretty deserted. Tonight though we are on a rock island right near Thessalon and we can see the point a couple of miles off stretching way out to sea. We really should be paddling around it tonight while the waves are down, but we are pretty certain that tomorrow morning will be calm also. Besides we are a little tired.

It was fun paddling along in the early morning and again this evening. A lot has been written on paddling and there are several schools of thought as to what constitutes the best technique. My advice is not to worry about it, but then we are a little unorthodox. First we never change sides. I paddle on the right and Margie on the left, day in and day out. Further we make no effort to stroke at the same time. In fact, our natural rhythm is for me to take 2 strokes for every 3 of hers. Finally, I use a paddle that is somewhat larger than average. Although I am 5 feet 8 inches I am very uncomfortable with anything less than a 6 foot paddle (perhaps a little shorter in a smaller canoe), and the bigger the blade the better. There are at least two advantages to a big paddle:

1) you can easily paddle while standing; that is, you don't need to lean over, cricking your back. I may only stand for a half hour or so a day on lakes but on shallow rivers I will stand almost continuously, particularly on rapidy sections. This is the best way to puzzle out the obstacles ahead and be able to react smoothly. There is a casual euphoria to standing relaxed in the stern while a maze of rapids and streams unwinds beneath your keel.

2) a large paddle is essential for rough water, be it severe rapids or windy lakes. Strength and experience will avail you little if you haven't a large enough blade to really reach out and grab some water when conditions are threatening. It takes a big paddle to "manhandle" a canoe in an emergency.

As far as learning to paddle goes, my advice is to learn by going solo. It will take a little longer but you will be more confident of your skills. A few hundred miles of solo paddling teaches you more about your craft and how to handle it than any number of instructional manuals. So wear a life preserver and experiment. Try standing, kneeling and sitting. Paddle from the bow (facing the stern), from the stern and also from just aft of center. Practice until the canoe is just an extension of yourself, until you feel total pinpoint control in any situation. Establish a smooth and easy rhythm. Employ the muscles of your legs, back and stomach. A sternman leans and twists with every stroke. Master a natural

71

stroke and you will discover an easy enduring strength that will allow you to paddle hard for hours on end.

We certainly have big appetites now. We just ate a whole apple pie for a snack and we could easily have eaten a couple of more.

JULY 4: MICHIGAN

We had a comfy rock to sleep on last night. This morning we got up and paddled around Thessalon Point before sunup. It was another good travelling day, adequately warm, no rain, and the weak wind behind us. Tonight we really are starting to tire and we have resolved to sleep in tomorrow till 5:30 or maybe even 6:00. We have put in 5 solid days of big lake travel and covered 130 miles (32 of them today), and the pace is beginning to tell. Generally, 20 miles of lake travel per day is enough for us but we have been averaging 26. Still in all, we are very pleased with ourselves. Tonight we are in Michigan and the North Channel is essentially behind us. It is only 18 more miles to Sault Ste. Marie and we hope to pass through the locks tomorrow. Bring on Lake Superior! Who knows, we might even reach Grand Portage by the end of the month.

We are camped on someone's beach tonight on a Michigan Island and they are not quite sure what to make of us. We were given a bag of orange gum drops and some cookies. The big event of the day (besides reaching Michigan) was the passage of a huge 800-foot freighter by our campsite. It was not more than 100 feet off shore and the kids were very excited. Tina has her own camera and took several pictures. So did we. Oh yes, I finally counted my 100th plane today. I started counting back on the Ottawa, the day before the Culbute Rapids.

JULY 5: SAULT SAINT MARIE

Well, we had great hopes of sailing up to the Soo locks by early afternoon, but things didn't turn out that way. Difficulties kept cropping up. First, it was raining when we woke up. We were planning to sleep in anyway, so it didn't upset us much. We got up at 6:30 during a lull and ate breakfast, pushing off about an hour later. Right away we noticed quite a strong current running against us in the narrow channel and it took an hour just to go the first mile or so. I don't know why it never occurred to us that there might be a current in the narrow waters between lakes Huron and Superior. There is a 20-odd-foot difference in water levels between the lakes and the going is very difficult. Also, while crossing the wide area above Neebish Island, we started to run into a strong headwind which continued the rest of the day. We also had a bit of excitement there in crossing the main shipping channel. The wind and current had essentially stalled us in the middle when a freighter started to bear down on us. It was hard to judge speeds and distances but we took a chance and continued to cross and made it safely over in front of his bow. There were scattered showers all day long but the real nuisance continued to be the wind. We were soon reduced to pushing our way through the bullrushes in order to progress at all. It was simply too stormy out in the open water. It gave us a lift, however, to pass a motorboat, anchored, sitting out the gale in the reeds.

We had a wonderful respite at lunchtime. When we nosed our canoe into the shore to eat, people came out of a nearby cabin for a chat. They invited us in where it was warm (and not raining), then they filled us up with popcorn and milk. As we were leaving they stuffed the kid's pockets with candies -- enough snacks to keep them supplied for a week!

I'm not sure what there is about children that brings out the best in people, but the kids are always receiving little gifts. Usually it is candy but sometimes toys or pennies. Occasionally people give the parents things also. The most appreciated gifts are fresh fruit and milk. We'll all be quite spoiled by the time we get home.

About 4:00 the sun started to come out and we reached a picnic ground some two miles before the locks on the U.S. side. There was a coast guard station there and they radioed ahead for us and then reported that we would not be allowed to pass through the American Locks. They reported further that the wind was gusting at 25 knots which, combined with the strong currents, made it clear to everybody that we could not safely cross the river to try the Canadian side. Tonight we are camping at the picnic ground and plan to try crossing early tomorrow. There appears to be some chance that we shall be allowed to use the Canadian Lock. We are very excited about actually getting out on Lake Superior, our last big obstacle for the summer. Lots of huge freighters have been passing by all evening. In the dark they are all lit up like little cities. Some of them are 1000 feet long and less than 100 feet offshore. They

73

tower over us. We have now been 954 miles.

The first lock here was built on the Canadian side in the late 1700's by the North West Company in order to avoid the substantial rapids which drop some 20 feet here. The lock was less than 9 feet wide and was intended only for canoes and batteaux. The huge canots de maître would reach the locks about 35 to 40 days after leaving Lachine. The company had constructed a larger vessel for Lake Superior and the voyageurs would leave about a third of their cargo at the docks for the ship to carry on to Grand Portage. By lightening the freighter canoes here the voyageurs were able to travel with more speed and safety across the lake. The ship was also used to carry all the provisions for the return trips of the nor'westers (the voyageurs wintering west of Grand Portage). In the course of a season the ship could make 4 or 5 round trips.

The original lock was destroyed in 1814 when the Americans attacked the company trading post. Today, two of the world's three largest locks are here and the system has the greatest tonnage-moving capability of any locks system on earth. Needless to say I have been reading the local literature.

JULY 6: LOCKING THROUGH

It was tough, even without the wind, going up the river early this morning, but we made it to the locks by breakfast time. They get very few canoes through here, less than one a year, but they were glad to service us. They swung open the big metal doors so we could paddle into the lock. We waited for a sailboat to join us, then the doors slowly came back together. We passed up to the lock officials a 70-foot rope which they made secure and the sailboat did likewise. Once that was done, they started letting water in from underneath. Gradually our boat rose until we were 20 feet higher and now on a level with Lake Superior. The upstream doors opened, and out we paddled. Afterwards we toured the museum there and learned that the present Canadian Lock is only 69 feet wide and so can't handle the big freighters we have been seeing.

After the strong current in the river, it was a real pleasure to get out on Lake Superior. Today was very hot and clear and the kids swam a lot. On one sand beach they could walk out half a mile and still be only thigh deep. The lake stayed breezy most of the day with small one- to two-foot sized white caps and this, combined with the shallow water, made the paddling difficult. Later, after supper, the waves subsided to good sized swells and we moved out around rocky (but impressive) Gros Cap. A mile or so beyond we made camp on the golfball-sized rocks forming a little beach between two jutting rock points. The sleeping will be a little slanted tonight because the beach has no flat place wide enough for our tent. Well, we took our first 20-mile bite out of Lake Superior today and it felt good.

JULY 7: WHITEFISH BAY

We had pretty good travelling weather today, cloudy with the wind mostly behind us. We paddled steadily with about two hours off for meals, snacks and a swim. We had to try twice to cross Goulais Bay. The first time we were turned back by big waves but further down the bay was narrower and there was less wind. The waves were still about 3 feet high but there were no white caps and we made the two and a half mile crossing without incident.

At breakfast I found a hand carved wooden decoy which must have gotten away from somebody. It had been washed high up on the rocks with other debris by the spring storms. Anyway, we rescued "Willie" the duck and the kids have adopted him. Tonight they have built a little rock pool out in the water for him to play in. We are camped in the opening to Batchawana Bay (an offshoot of Whitefish Bay). The surf must really be running farther out on Whitefish. Every couple of minutes the water level rises 6 to 8 inches, liberating Willie from his pool. The children are just now bringing Willie in and putting him to bed before he gets away. Whitefish Bay is where the Fitzgerald went down a few years ago. She was one of those huge freighters and had set out for the Soo Locks from Thunder Bay despite gale warnings. She'd made it this far before the storm struck. The ship went down so fast (with all hands) that no one had time to even radio for help. Pretty sobering to think that there can be storms like that. Sitting on shore tonight, looking out to sea its hard to believe that they get 50-foot waves here occasionally.

We went 26 miles today for a grand total of 1000 -- a real milestone. Our hands are getting pretty sore from paddling though. Margie has been keeping a list and reports that so far this summer we have lost:

a) one bailing sponge
b) a cooking mitt
c) Tina's hat
d) Tina's windbreaker
e) Tina's jersey
f) Randy's matchbox tank.
Not bad for so many stops and portages I suppose.

JULY 8: WINDBOUND

"I have clinched and closed with the naked north,
  I have learned to defy and defend;
  Shoulder to shoulder we have fought it out -
  Yet the wild must win in the end." (Robert Service)

"We must stay often in a place 2 or 3 days for the contrary winds; for (if) the winds weare anything high, we durst not venter the boats against the impetuosity of the waves, which is the reason that our voyages are so long and tedious." (Radisson)

Lots of violent thunderstorms in the night whipped the lake to a froth. I peered out of the tent at 5:30 but it was obviously no go so we rolled back to sleep. The day was clear, sunny and cool (60 degrees) with a steady 15 mph wind and we spent the time sleeping, eating and lying around. Today was one of those times when we are glad that we brought two tents. We used ours for sleeping while the kids made a playhouse out of theirs. Although it was a little too cool with the stiff breeze to relax outside, it was an almost perfect drying day for our clothes washing. The lake remained a mass of whitecaps all day long, but by 8:30 p.m. the wind was beginning to die down. We've gone to bed hoping for better conditions in the morning. A day's rest was good for everybody.

JULY 9: FIFTY MILES

"We neither desire to be idle in any place, having learned by experience that idleness is the mother of all evil..." (Radisson)

Well, we made up for yesterday's rest with a vengeance today. Determined not to be windbound in the same place again, we rose early and left at 5:30, as soon as it was light enough to see. Well, almost light enough; Margie's wet socks got left behind on the beach.

It was a calm cloudy morning and the kids were tired so they slept late till 9:00. Anyway we were really surging with energy. We made 15 miles in 4 hours before even stopping for breakfast, a tremendous pace for us. (Margie was beginning to grumble though about all those miles on an empty stomach.)

Later the sun came out and the breeze gradually changed direction, flattening the swells completely. We passed several rock cliffs and huge rock points today. It was really spectacular. In places the rock comes straight down into the water. The water itself is green and so clear it is frightening to look over the side of the boat. You can look down and clearly see the rock cliffs dropping off another 20 to 30 feet below the surface and you get the feeling you are actually falling as you pass over these underwater drops. The rock has been mostly pink with streaks of black, green and white through it. We saw several small caves. Between the rest day and the calm water we were able to travel almost continuously.

We had already covered 40 miles by supper and yet afterwards we were still going strong. The canoe was literally hissing through the water as we raced into the sunset. It was one of those days when you feel you can paddle forever and it was with some reluctance that we finally stopped at 10:00. The setting sun found us far from any sand beach so we just put up the big tent on rocky gravel and deposited the sleeping children gently inside. It was really an incredible day; fifty miles of lake travel, an unheard of distance for us. We were glad though to get by the miles of dangerous rocky points and bays while the weather was so calm. It's not hard to understand why the voyageurs put in 15 to 18 hour days. It is hard to stop yourself on days like this. There is an exhilaration to the travelling life that is hard to express. Listen to the words of an old voyageur which were recorded on the shore of lake Winnipeg in 1825 when he was over 70 years old:

"I have now been 42 years in this country. No portage was too long for me; I could carry, paddle, walk and sing with any man I ever saw. No water, no weather, ever stopped the paddle or the song. I spent all my earnings in the enjoyment of pleasure ... now I have not a spare shirt to my back. Yet, were I young again, I should glory in commencing the same career again. There is no life so happy as a voyageur's life; none so independent; no place where a man enjoys so much variety and freedom.''

JULY 10: DEVIL'S WAREHOUSE

Today was a little slower. We started later than yesterday and took longer snack and meal breaks. I had diarrhea today and felt very tired this afternoon, probably the aftereffects of yesterday's stupendous effort. We finished passing Montreal Island, the Lizard Islands and Leach Island and were just reaching the Devil's Warehouse about 3:00 when the wind came up from the southwest and it began to look stormy. We had already done over 20 miles in less than ideal conditions so we simply set up the tent and called it a day.

Devil's Warehouse is a spectacular cliff-sided island a mile or so off-shore. The whole lake has been picturesque lately but the rocky promontories and long headlands are nervewracking to pass. Many of them are miles long, very high, and solid rock dropping steeply into the sea. We steadily inched our way by them hour after hour, praying that the water would remain calm. The fearsome shoreline would simply gobble up and crush the unwary canoeist in any kind of wind or swell.

JULY 11: CAPE GARGANTUA

We left just after 6:00 this morning and started out around Cape Gargantua. Wind and waves have carved the rocky islets and shoreline hereabouts into grotesque shapes. By sunrise there were already big swells and the wind was making it choppy. Rounding the point itself was rather tricky as the waves bouncing off the rock walls set up a turbulent backwash and we found it difficult to control the canoe or to progress. The huge black and red rocks, the blue water and white foam were certainly beautiful though. There was no way to land and so we just ate breakfast in the canoe as we jounced along. It is quite like the ocean here, except of course you can drink the water. Breakfast was an unusual affair even for us. There we sat bouncing up and down on the waves, passing the Cheerios. Next we reached over the side and scooped up some of the clear green water to mix our Instant Breakfasts. We had to take turns eating so one person could remain on duty to keep the canoe from washing onto the rocks. It was with real relief that we reached the big bay before Cap Chaillon and stopped on the beach there to wait out the weather. About 2:00 we were able to set out again and continued another 10 miles to a nice campsite in Old Woman Bay.

We travelled behind reefs and islands whenever possible today to lessen the waves and did 21 more miles.

JULY 12: MICHIPICOTEN

In the morning we got down to Michipicoten Bay without too much trouble and we sat a mile or two offshore at Perkwakina Point debating what to do next. The next 100 miles of shoreline will be totally deserted. There will be no roads, communities, houses, or summer camps, just rock with occasional sand or pebble beaches. We had 4, possibly 5, days of food left and the weather was perfect. We thought that we could easily cover another 20-25 miles today leaving only 75 or so to reach the next town (Marathon) and resupply. The alternative was to shoot the day by:

a) going over to the point to check in at a Coast Guard Station we could see there, and then

b) paddling a mile or two further out of our way into the bay to look for a food store.

"A prudent man foreseeth the evil, and hideth himself: but the simple pass on and are punished." (Proverbs 22:3) Really there was no choice and we started over to the Coast Guard Station.

The coast guard man on duty was asleep but we banged around the premises until we woke him up. He acted glad to see us and we spent over an hour chatting. We learned quite a bit including:

1) There are special radios for marine forecasts. The weather prediction is concisely encoded in a 15 digit number which details the conditions for the next 24 hours and the numbers are read out continuously over the

radio. One of the main topics on any canoe trip is the weather (the other is food), and a little marine radio should be an irresistible attraction to anyone planning a Great Lakes canoe trip. Indeed it would be only good sense to carry one considering the dangers and difficulties of such travel. At any rate today's forecast is for scattered thundershowers later on.

2) There are manned lighthouses every 50-60 miles or so from here to Minnesota. Many of them are on islands too far offshore for us to visit but the next, at Otter Head, is only a mile or so out. The keeper there has now been radioed to expect us in a few days. This way, if anything should happen to us there will be someone to send out a search party. I said that we would probably arrive at Otter Head by the morning of the third day but was told not to count on it. (We were also regaled with exciting tales of helicopter rescues of shipwrecked travellers who had been plucked from various rock and cliff faces after storms.) Really though I think that my estimate was conservative and I actually expect to hit Otter Head in two more days without much trouble.

3) There is a food store in Michipicoten Bay. It was Saturday noon by now and the coast guard radioed ahead to make sure that it would stay open for us. No one seemed to think we could possibly reach Marathon within the next four days and all applauded our decision to stock up.

We finally said goodbye and paddled the mile or so across the bay to town. Really it was only a village -- 4 houses and a general store. There was a huge dock though as Great Lakes freighters stop in here twice a week. They drop off limestone and coal dust which is carried out of town by train. We did some shopping, bought some "Kool Pops", and left.

The next 15 miles of lake were beautiful, lots of clean rock separated by sandy beaches. In the afternoon we only went about five miles before stopping to take a long swim, rest, wash break. After supper though the wind died down, and the lake became glassy smooth. We got out the kids' sleeping bags, tucked them in, and paddled on another 10 miles. By sunset we were within a mile or so of False Dog Harbour when we came to a little beach and decided to call it quits. We covered 28 miles -- a very full day. Without the stops we would have surely broken 40. Still it is good to have 10 days' food with us once more. The predicted thunderstorms never materialized.

JULY 13: DIARRHEA

Today was a little slower. We had some diarrhea and made frequent stops throughout the day. Perhaps yesterday's water back in Michipicoten Harbour was not so pure. Still, the nice weather continued and we persevered. "Weatherman Randy" played with the thermometer and reported hourly temperature readings, mostly in the 70's.

This afternoon lots of fog patches rolled by. It was a breezy sunny day and all of a sudden a fog bank would envelop us, completely obliterating the shore. It was kind of exciting. Just as suddenly though the fog would be gone, drifting farther down the lake.

In spite of our problems we managed to cover over 20 miles again today. In fact, we have done 143 miles in the last 5 days for an average of 28 and one-half. We are within easy striking distance of Otter Head now and should reach the lighthouse tomorrow afternoon, a day ahead of schedule.

Today's health problem focused our thoughts on that important commodity, toilet paper. There are two commonly accepted theories as regards toilet paper. Of course, most people agree you should bring it, but how do you keep it dry? Some authorities advise not putting all your eggs in the same basket. They advocate safely tucking a roll (carefully waterproofed) deep into every pack. This way there is always bound to be some dry paper somewhere. Others suggest that you do put all your eggs in the same basket and then guard the basket. When afflicted as we were today, however, there is certainly something to be said for the former approach. It was reassuring to realize that no matter which of our identical packs we delved into we would be quickly rewarded.

JULY 14: MOOSE HUNTING

We covered a total of five miles today and we had to set out 3 separate times to accomplish even that. We were just preparing to leave camp after a leisurely breakfast this morning when we started hearing thunder. We peered around but couldn't see any storms headed our way so we set out. We knew that both Redsucker Cove and Ganley Harbour were coming up in the next two miles and figured there was no real danger of getting caught out in the open. We were badly fooled. Once out of our sheltered cove it was obvious that conditions had deteriorated in the night. The lake was all lumpy with 6-foot choppy seas that had us bobbing every which way. We inched along the mile or so to Redsucker Cove and with great relief went ashore on a little beach. It had been a hair-raising mile and we were glad to be safe. We sat out a rainy morning in a broken down log shelter there and then tried to travel again after lunch. The rain and wind were gone but the lake was still a mess. Another mile and we were safely ashore in Ganley Harbour. We stretched out on a little shelf of a beach and slept through a few hours of light drizzle. Eventually the cool dampness started to bother us and we got up to leave. We hoped that with the light drizzle and fog the lake would have settled down. Unfortunately it was worse than ever. We have a big canoe but when it sits on the pinnicular top of a steep wave you just brace and wait to see whether you'll slide forward or backward or maybe down one of the sides.

We always keep a close eye on the approaching waves but here we were just plain scared to look at them. They would come towering up on our left hindquarter and it just took our breath away to see them hanging there one after another so high above us. On the downdrops you wondered what would stop you at the bottom. It was just plain awful. Since the wind was down they were not surfing and breaking and that is what saved us, as a wall of breaking wave would have been pretty hard to deal with. I thought about throwing out our cooking pot sea anchor and decided not to. What I mostly thought about though was how did I ever get there? This lake is so treacherous. You come out of a calm cove sheltered by an island, turn a corner past a rocky point as we did, and suddenly there you are with no way back. At that point you are only 100 feet from safety but it is too late as there is no way to safely turn around. You must try to continue past the cliffs until the next safety spot. In travelling like this you age hours every minute. Your paddling is mostly ineffectual and the greater percentage of your effort goes into preserving the canoe's orientation to the coming waves. The worst moments come when you must ply out to sea to avoid a backwash or even worse, a shallow spot. Let the water get less than 20 feet deep and suddenly the waves appear to race forward and lurch upwards. Actually of course friction with the bottom is slowing the underside of the wave while the wave's continued momentum forces the top to pile up and leap ahead.

Fortunately relief came quickly. We plunged around a little island and there before us was the opening to a rocky cove. It was about 100 yards wide and 500 yards deep and with the drifting fog we could not really distinguish the far end. There was no continuing, however, and we surfed in welcoming the comparative shelter. Both sides of the cove were lined by steep cliffs but we could not return to the lake. Fortunately at the end we found a gorgeous beach. We surfed ashore, completely harrowed, to spend the night.

The place here is beautiful. There is a series of three sand dunes covered with beach grass marching back to a forest of conical pine trees. We have set up the tents out of the wind behind the second row of sand dunes. It should be good sleeping tonight. The fog is really rolling in now. The surf pounds out front and the tops of the scraggly northern pines are waggling in the wind, but it is cozy nestled in the tents.

With the lake the way it was today we couldn't help wondering at supper when it would be safe to travel again. This is always the way when travelling; when conditions are good you wish to travel hard for fear they will deteriorate, but when the weather turns ornery you quickly begin to fear it will always remain so. Anyways it appears we may not reach Otter Head tomorrow morning. At supper we began to take stock of our food situation. There is still no problem as we have 8 days worth left and it is no more than 70 miles to Marathon. Still the kids decided it was time to start foraging. There are many edible wild foods and it is always fun, even exciting to take the wild foods book and discover new ones. We are real amateurs, however, and usually settle for fish, berries, rock tripe and occasional tubers. These were all well known and relished by the early explorers. Their journals are filled with glowing testimonies to the natural foods. Typical was that recorded by Radisson with regards to the nutritious northern lichen, ''Tripe des roche, a species of lichen, which being boiled resolves itself into a black glue, nauseous but not without nourishment.'' Anyway the children decided to catch a moose. There are tracks everywhere on the beach where the animals have been trampling up and down. The kids dug ''prairie dog'' holes in the sand. The plan is for the moose to step in a hole and break his leg in the dark -- then we shall rush out of the tent and scoop him up for breakfast. Even on three legs a feisty moose could probably still elude us so we ended up digging pairs of holes strategically placed. The improved plan is for each moose to break two legs, thus completely incapacitating himself. The children have conveniently placed the holes near the cooking fire and the entire plan appears to be a sound one. Already they have tripped up two mommies and a daddy and it is not even dark yet.

JULY 15: REVERBERATING COVE

Last night thunderstorms started about 12:00 and continued until 3:00. It was really wild. One after another they would come rolling into our little cove thundering and bouncing off the walls until it felt as though the ground was shaking and our innards were all aquivering. It rained tremendously hard and when I peeked out to take a look the lake was white with froth. By 2:00 we had puddles even inside our sleeping bags. When dawn finally came I went to pry the kids out of their tent into the canoe and there they lay, like melting popsicles in their soggy baggies. We dressed them in dry clothes and then set out. They spent the whole day fluffing and blowing on their sleeping bags trying to dry them.

Well today was less than mediocre. We had only gone about 100 yards when a thick fog bank rolled in and stayed for the day. What discouraging travelling, especially after yesterday. Whenever fog appears it is a problem for canoeists. Even morning mists, though beautiful, can be dangerous and disorienting. I still vividly remember a misty morning on the Missinabie River a few hundred miles north of here. We were paddling on what we took to be a completely calm stretch. The river was fairly wide and we couldn't see either shore for the fog when the current slowly started to pick up and we began to hear a dull roaring. Suddenly a sign reading "WARNING, DANGEROUS RAPIDS" appeared out of the mist ahead of us. Visions of rushing rapids and swirling eddies leading directly over a falls danced through our heads. Fortunately, however, nothing more substantial than light class II rapids materialized and we passed safely through. For sheer frustration, however, the kind of foggy travelling we had today has got to rank pretty high.

The waves were still disconcertingly large and the fog was so thick we couldn't even see them approaching until they were already looming up beside us. Visibility was less than fifty feet, and yet we didn't dare to stay that close to the rock cliffs lining our route on account of the heavy backwash. Fortunately on foggy days one can travel out of sight of land by the sound of the waves crashing against the rocks. At least that is the theory. In practice it is a little tricky. I know for a fact that we completely circled one good-sized island one and a half times. Our difficulties were compounded by the fact that we don't have a map for the 10 mile section of the lake that we are on now. As a result we are hopelessly confused. Because of the fog we have had to bob into all the little bays and around islands etc. with no real idea of what the shoreline even ought to be. We passed the place where we are camped tonight four times before deciding that we had better just give up for the day. We don't know where we are or how far we went but it's certain that we paddled miles and miles! Useful miles are different however, and these we have estimated at 13. We don't believe we can be more than 2 hours from Otter Head now.

We passed some tremendous (apparently topless) cliffs today. Also two yellow grosbeaks are socked in here on the beach with us tonight. You know the fog is pretty bad when the birds have to walk to get around!

JULY 16: OTTER HEAD

I had a hard time sleeping last night. I kept waking up thinking that I heard people walking around outside, but everytime I unzipped the tent and looked out, nothing was there. Margie was dead to the world and I couldn't wake her. Finally I could stand it no longer and got up in the predawn grey. This time I was luckier. There running down the beach away from me was a caribou family. We have seen caribou before, but never this far south. They are very scarce here and it was really an incredible piece of good fortune to see them. A good omen for a good day!

We got off to a very early start. The lake was clear and calm and we reached the lighthouse at 8:00. It was just starting to rain as we arrived and we grabbed up our breakfast fixings and dashed up to the house. The keeper, Elwin Richardson, was expecting us and made us feel very welcome. It was so pleasant to feel warm and dry while we listened to the rain outside. Elwin had of course been monitoring the weather lately, and would not have been particularly concerned even if we had taken another day or so to arrive. Lighthouse keeping is a pretty lonely job. He is out here 8 to 10 months a year with mail every couple of weeks and occasionally a visitor. He has a radio of course (we got the new weather forecast) and sometimes his wife is there. We used his stove to cook breakfast and later Margie was able to wash her hair in his bathroom sink. Actually we were some inconvenience to him as he had to go down in the basement to turn on the stove. It is a gas stove and he is very careful with it. He lights it maybe once a week, does all his baking, and then shuts it off, preferring not to trust the pilot light. You can't be too careful when you are way out and alone.

It was fun talking. He confirmed my caribou sighting by showing us some pictures he had taken of them in the winter. He also described some of the storms he had seen here over the years. Frightening! Fifty-foot waves hurling drift logs up against the side of the building. He was also the last person to see the doomed freighter Fitzgerald on that fateful day when it passed by here on its way to disaster in Whitefish Bay.

About 10:00 the rain seemed to be letting up some and we forced ourselves to continue on. Unfortunately the respite was only temporary, and we had more showers during the morning after we left. In fact huge black clouds and thunderstorms out on the lake kept pace with us throughout the day. We are determined to travel when we can, however. Again today there were big fog banks out on the lake but they never drifted in to shore. Elwin told us of one summer when he was continuously socked in by fog for 33 straight days. Brother!

As the afternoon progressed the wind rose and we finally took refuge in a small cove just past Simon's Harbour. Tonight we feel safe. It is only about 40 miles to town and there is a rough trail along the coast from here to there.

JULY 17: PIC RIVER

It was an excellent day today; warm, clear, and almost no wind. We travelled from 6:00 till 6:00 stopping only for breakfast and lunch. We are just a little past Pic River tonight and shall get in to the town of Marathon tomorrow without much trouble. We need to visit a bank (cash traveller's checks), post office, laundromat and food store.

We met a canoe today, the first one since the French River. They had just started out this morning and were on a trip down to Otter Head and back. I hope they know what they are doing. Today was a beautiful deceptively calm day, but after being on the lake for a couple of weeks I was tempted to ask, "Do you really understand what a chance you are taking?" They were a retired couple in a small canoe with their two pet dogs resting on a rug in the middle. I wanted to alert them to the perils of the lake but didn't know how to go about it. Any such advice would probably have sounded a little strange coming from a couple with two small children in their boat anyway. As it was we really didn't communicate too well. The conversation started roughly like this:

86

Them: (Putting on clothes) Gee, look another canoe. Where did you come from?

Us: New Hampshire.

Them: Ha, ha, New, hoo, hee, hee, ha, Hampshire. When did you ha, ha start?

Us: Middle of May.

Them: Ha, ha, hee, hee, haw

Us: We came through the Soo about ten days ago.

Them: Soo, hoo, hoo, hee,hee, -- where are you ho, ho, going?

Us: Alaska.

Them: Ha, ha, ho, haw, hee, har.

It was obvious that our credibility was a little low and so we passed on without any warnings or advice. There really are techniques that need to be mastered in order to travel safely here though. For instance, just landing the canoe. The problem is most days it is like the ocean with the waves rolling in, looking for an opportunity to smash a canoe. Our solution is to have everybody leap out before the breaker line to prevent an accident on the rocks. We stand there in the surf as the waves crest up and down from ankles to knees. We face seawards, watching the waves and holding the canoe offshore while we toss our duffel over our shoulders, hoping it will land far enough up on the slanted shore so that the kids can grab it before it rolls down to the water. Then we pick up the almost empty canoe and leap nimbly over the cresting surf line to deposit it gently up on the beach. This goes on virtually every time we land.

A peculiar thing happened about 3:00. We were paddling on a clear flat calm sea when suddenly from offshore came a smooth swell but no wind. In a few minutes more wind did come and then the waves grew and roughened quickly. We travelled in waves for the rest of the afternoon. It was a strange experience going from calm to waves so quickly with no hint of a storm or even clouds.

Most travellers have their own set routine once they land for the night and we are no exception. We generally feel like:

    a) going swimming

    b) flopping down for a rest on a rock in the sun

    c) getting out some snacks

    d) going berry picking

    e) doing anything but "work."

Instead however, we immediately:

    a) clear a campsite

b) set up the tent

c) gather firewood, and

d) make up the beds.

Then, if there is any time left we will rest or play before starting supper and picking up for the day.

Well, this was a good day and we are looking forward to getting into Marathon tomorrow for breakfast.

JULY 18: MARATHON

Marathon is a company town. In 1946 it was carved out of the wilderness by the paper company which even today dominates the community. The people and the company treated us wonderfully well but I must still report that they are very guilty of polluting the lake. Approaching the town this morning we had to pass through an extensive "pond" of floating foamy white suds which extended out perhaps half a mile from where the pollutants were being pumped into the water. It was like paddling through pack ice. The canoe broke apart great blocks of foam and a long trail of separated floes was strung out behind us.

We got into the harbor well before breakfast and sat out there in the middle, slightly puzzled. I got out the monocular and stood up to get an even better view. Peer as I could, however, I could see no place anywhere to beach a canoe. The entire shoreline was blocked off by pulp log debris and floating log booms. It turns out that the townspeople have no need of a shoreline as they don't have any boats. The lake is considered too treacherous for boating and too cold for swimming. How reassuring! Anyways we looked around and finally chose a spot right near the paper company where we could get in pretty close. What a reception we got! By the time we beached, a company official was down there to greet us. He put a company truck at our disposal and had us escorted around town to do our shopping, laundering and to visit the town newspaper. Later we received a quick tour of the paper company itself. No one had had any idea that we were coming but they certainly treated us well. I guess it was a unique sight for them to see a family come paddling off the lake into their harbor.

We left Marathon shortly before noon, heavily loaded with new supplies, and quickly ran into difficulty. The weather had turned rapidly worse during the few hours we had visited in town. Not only had the sky darkened, but also a strong whistling wind had arisen, and we paddled out of the snug harbor to find a sea we could not deal with. We scudded along a mile or two before the wind, digging ourselves deeply into a bay we knew we wouldn't be able to paddle out of. Finally we found a safe sandy nook in which to land. It started to sprinkle, so we put our stuff under cover and settled down to lunch. It rained and blew all afternoon and we made plans to spend the night. We delayed setting up camp though, hoping that the wind at least would let up. Supper was a soggy affair -- hamburgers and potato chips in a pounding rain. Finally about 7:30, as it was starting to get dark, the rain paused. We quickly erected the tents and tried to build a log/brush shelter around them to ward off the wind. It was a pretty hopeless situation though. Violent thunderstorms continued to blow through and knocked the big tent flying. We tied stuff down to huge logs and hoped for the best. We put the kids to bed together in Margie's sleeping bag and the two of us sat up late around a roaring campfire waiting for things to settle down. Eventually of course they did -- thunderstorms never last forever. We retired to our soggy beds using my sleeping bag as a pad and the kids' wet bags as our covers.

Our tent is four years old now and somewhat overworn. In any good storm it is almost as bad as sleeping on a screen porch. Next year, somehow, we absolutely must manage to come up with a new one. For extended trips we have always found that a 3 to 4-man tent is about right for two adults. Ideally a canoeist wants a spacious, light, waterproof, bugproof tent that can be quickly assembled by one person. It should also be highly wind resistant. We are currently using the 4-man Timberline which, while an excellent tent, does have drawbacks:

a) The zippers give out after a year or so and have to be replaced. (This may be partly due to the children's tendency to try and walk through tent screen doors without unzipping them.)

b) The floor leaks around the corners after a couple of years.

c) On wildly windy nights like tonight the aluminum poles may warp and twist. We had three bend badly this evening, but fortunately I happen to carry a few spares tucked away for just such an eventuality. I bring them along every year but haven't needed them until now. Still, one accident makes all the precautions worthwhile. It is the same with our first aid kit. Every year we replace old pills and expand our kit even though we hardly ever use it. On a wilderness trip you have to depend upon yourself for every emergency. If you don't have what you need,

the DREAMS

SANDERS, '84

you improvise or do without; so it gives us a feeling of security to be as prepared as possible. One ruined pole, to return to our present "emergency," is worth four years of carrying a spare.

JULY 19: ROUGH TRAVELLING

We got up to a thick crushing fog this morning and ate breakfast slowly on the beach hoping that the visibility would soon get better. There was no improvement however, and we pushed off at 9:30 to try and paddle around every nook and cranny. We quickly discovered that the waves were still dangerously large from last night though, and after searching for some three miles we finally found a place where we could safely land again. We ate lunch there and sat around a fire until 1:00 when the fog started to lift. What a surprise! We were right next to a long 2-mile cliff which had train tracks etched into them about 100 feet up. In places where the cliff was too sheer the tracks just tunneled through the rock. The improved visibility somehow made the waves look smaller and we started out once more, but conditions were still borderline and after the cliff we landed again. In another hour the sun came out and we couldn't resist trying one last time. The lake was still too rough however and in another mile we stopped for the day. Hopefully by tomorrow the waves will have calmed down some from last night's storms.

JULY 20: THE LAKE SUPERIOR 500

We paddled 29 miles today and progressed steadily all day long, stopping only for a half hour breakfast and a 45-minute lunch. We had planned to continue on after supper but the sky looked so threatening that we set up camp instead on the forested edge of a crescent-shaped beach.

On days like this travelling reminds us of the Daytona 500. We dash into the pits, so to speak, for a quick refueling at meals, and then we are off and paddling. Actually at breakfast it was still pretty wavy and we didn't even try to beach the canoe. First we found a fairly sheltered cove. Then, to avoid landing and having to get wet by unloading the canoe, we emulated the drift logs by resting our bow on the edge of the surf line with the stern pointing out. When this is properly done the canoe simply bobs up and down a few feet from shore without drifting or blowing away. We discovered the method by watching the pulp logs which can maintain this position for hours.

We have been over 300 miles on Lake Superior now (for a total of 1260) and really things seem to be going pretty well. Last night we camped in a narrow, shallow sandy cove where the wind and waves caused the water to ebb and flow. At times the level would rise as much as a foot in only 5 minutes. We had paddled behind a big island to get shelter from the waves when we found the attractive, sheltered beach to camp on. A little investigation showed that we had happened upon more than just a quiet beach. There was a trail through the brush leading to a large cleared campsite complete with homemade latrine, tables and benches. It was a restful change of pace to eat our supper at a table and sleep on level forest ground. We were entertained by a flock of cedar waxwings. Margie couldn't remember ever having seen them before and she waded along the shore following them as they flitted from tree to tree. The kids were wading too, playing with the "tide" as it rose and fell every few minutes.

We all have spots of bad sunburn but the cloudy weather lately has been a help. Still we are starting to look forward to the end of the lake. It is less than 200 miles now to Grand Portage. Today's song:

WHITECAPS
(to the tune of "Raindrops Keep Falling....")

Whitecaps keep falling in my lap
Breakers keep combing through my hair
But I don't see / That they bother me
'Cause I just keep on paddlin'
Though the sea gods are surfin'
We'll soon be there...
200 miles and we'll be there.

JULY 21: NIPIGON BAY

It rained some in the night and continued until we got up. We built

92

a fire at camp and cooked birdseed porridge (Red River cereal) for break-fast. It was rainy and cloudy all day. Also the wind was offshore, out of the north, and gave us considerable trouble crossing the bays. Although we are both experienced travellers, we find the canoeing here very tiring emotionally. Much of the shoreline is rock and cliff, impossible to safely land on. After a few hours of travel a nervous tension builds inside you as you eye the rock walls, the waves, the clouds and the wind, trying to gauge what is safe and what isn't. Wind and waves can come out of nowhere so that a traverse of only a mile across a bay or between islands can tatter your nerves, even in good travelling conditions. With the wind strongly offshore as it was today, there is the additional worry of getting blown out too far and being unable to return. It became pretty clear today, though, that our nerve is slowly being sapped. Rather than risk the three-mile crossing of Schreiber Channel to Copper Island we decided to hug the much longer north shore and head into Nipigon Bay. It would be a lot shorter to travel along the outer islands though, and tomorrow we shall have a second chance. We are camped tonight right near Crow Point and in the morning we may try the three-mile crossing to Simpson Island.

Margie was feeling poorly today and by late afternoon both she and the kids were seasick again. The constant big waves have been bothering them for several days now.

By this time we are all used to the routine for travelling on rough water. When wind and waves first come up we have the children put on their lifejackets. The next step is for us to put on ours and have the children lie down. When the canoe starts surfing then Margie and I kneel down on the floor. By this time, of course, we are looking for a landing spot. Well, we did another 26 miles today despite the rain and generally poor weather.

THE LAKE SUPERIOR BLUES
(to the tune of "Old Smoky")

Canoeing the lakeshore, I've paddled so long;
Oh, where is a campsite? I don't feel too strong.
I've paddled and portaged, all the long way
And now I'm so weary, with no place to stay.
First wind was against us, then it rained and it poured
But I didn't wear raingear, because it was stored.
Now it's too wet for a fire, and my fish got away
And it's a whole month yet, till I get away.

JULY 22: MOOSE NUMBER ONE

We set out at 6:15 this morning and crossed to Simpson Island before breakfast. Despite the early hour the bay was already choppy, and rather than risk a landing we ate breakfast just offshore in the canoe. Later we started through Moffat Strait, intending to pass around the south side of St. Ignace Island. We had barely started through, though, when we spotted a big moose in a grassy cove. We were able to paddle and drift in quite close and ended up taking half a dozen pictures of him. We seem to run into moose pretty much every year but it's still aways a thrill. They are so big when you get up close. Later on, continuing down the Strait, we paddled right through the biggest flock of loons we've ever seen. Twenty-three were visible at one time.

All in all it was a partly cloudy but scenic day. We passed a few cliffs, some heavily wooded islands, and many red gravel beaches. We continued paddling after supper and finally set up camp on a marshy beach on Fluor Island just as it was getting dark. It was another long day and we covered 34 miles.

Randy is sick now. His temperature hovered around 102 degrees today. Hopefully, rest and a few aspirin will cure him.

JULY 23: MOOSE TWO THROUGH EIGHT

It was hard to sleep last night; it sounded as though the moose were going to step right on our tent. They were sloshing and stumbling around on the beach all night and one was still there when we got up in the morning. Actually it was hardly morning as it was still pretty dark. Anyway while we stood there watching, another moose swam the channel from St. Ignace Island to join the first at our site. We left soon after and spent the next couple of hours dipping into little coves along Black Bay Peninsula. By being careful we managed to sneak up on five more moose, including a mother with two calves, in the early dawn stillness. We finally managed to get what we thought would be the "definitive" moose pictures, then we landed for breakfast.

Today was bright and clear, but unfortunately breezy out of the south/southwest and we were forced to sit out the hours from noon till 7:00. After supper we paddled a couple of fitful hours, but the going was

94

very rough and we ended up with a lousy rocky campsite. Margie has taken to wearing her gloves again while paddling. She doesn't like to do this as she feels it is effete, but sunburn has been wrecking her hands. She gets blisters on the backs and the knuckles swell up; then I have to do all the paddling.

This afternoon two kayakers joined us for a couple of hours. They were sailing a la catamaran, using a single sail and running with the wind. It was exciting to meet fellow travellers. We exchanged addresses and snapped pictures of each other. They are eight days out of Grand Portage heading for the Soo. It's hard to imagine that we may finally be off the lake in another week. Travelling with the wind as they were, they were able to leave a few hours before us.

Randy is still quite sick. His temperature is now over 103 degrees. There is not much we can do as we are still quite a way from a town or doctor. We try to carry a fairly complete first aid kit but for now we are sticking with aspirin.

Each year before setting out we make an appointment with our family doctor to get advice and medicines. We also carry a wilderness medicine book. Generally we need only bandaids, but occasionally the kit comes in handy for bee stings, etc. A couple of years ago we had a more serious accident when a companion broke a finger while lining a canoe through some rapids. The line was wound around her hand and when the canoe tipped and filled with water it yanked a little too hard on the rope, ruining a few fingers. Fortunately we met a real doctor a few days later. Other years our kit has simply been outmatched. I am thinking in particular of the summer Margie was suffering from hypoglycemia and the trip I came down with appendicitis.

JULY 24: WIND

Well, as always, we started out with high hopes for travelling today but, as often happens, our hopes were dashed by wind. By 7:00 there was a strong south/southwest wind (in our faces) and white caps were forming. When we stopped for breakfast after 3 miles we chose the best place we could because we knew we would be there quite a while.

We were really quite fortunate. The kayakers had told us of a sheltered cove behind an island where there was a padlocked, deserted fishing

95

shack and we landed there. There was a grassy clearing and we spent the day lying in the sun. The children picked berries and from time to time we measured the wind velocity. It was incredible. By 2:30 in the afternoon the wind was gusting from 35 to 40 mph. A big 100-foot commercial fishing vessel came sneaking in between the islands but when it got out into the next channel we could see the waves spraying right over the top of the boat.

The wind was still strong after supper and we set the tents up back in the woods where there is some shelter. Randy still has a fever (102 degrees) but seems to be a little better today. There is an old grindstone here and I took the opportunity earlier to sharpen my axe. An axe of course is an almost indispensable tool for wilderness travellers. It is also the one thing that can guarantee a fire during a streak of miserable weather.

On days like today it is nice to have a watch along. It keeps us from eating meals and going to bed too soon. We have tried camping without a timepiece but with our temperaments we are pretty uncomfortable without it. A watch:

a) adds structure to our day. The few times we have tried to "get away from it all" and obey "nature's natural rhythms" have not been all that successful. Nature's rhythms seem to dictate that I have my third meal for the day sometime before noon. This leads to an uncomfortably long evening. Occasionally the watch stops as it did a few weeks ago and we arbitrarily reset it in the morning. The actual time is not important. We just need to know roughly when meals are due and how long we have paddled. Fatigue has a way of coming upon me very suddenly and I find the only way to avoid it is to snack or eat fairly regularly.

b) helps us defend against the children. Without a watch it is hard to convince them that every time is not snacktime and that now is really nap or bedtime.

c) is a useful navigational tool. Eventually you learn to judge pretty accurately how far you have paddled in an hour even under different conditions. This can be a big help when you are travelling on foggy days or in island studded country or through featureless terrain. Of course I suppose that if you don't care about time then you are probably not concerned with location either.

d) can artificially add a whole new topic of conversation if you leave it at home. The few travellers we have met who travel without a watch seem to spend a good deal of their time wondering about the time.

e) helps Margie keep me in line. Without it I would be hard to restrain. Frequently I awake between midnight and 3:00, and if it weren't for the watch I would surely pop out and start to take the tent down. As it is, however, I am not supposed to start the day before 4:00. Also, I'm not supposed to paddle past midnight, even when conditions are excellent.

JULY 25 THE PAPS

There was just a spot of rain in the night and we awoke this morning to find the wind had shifted 180 degrees and was now whistling out of the northeast. It was nearly as strong as yesterday but the direction was more favorable. We left early and started sneaking behind islands and around points. The day was clear, blue and windy and we struggled on. The scenic highlight for me came when we made our closest approach (3 miles) to The Paps. These two lofty (1200 foot) lifelike mounds rise suggestively out of the otherwise flat Black Bay Peninsula and were a famous landmark christened by the Voyageurs. We have been able to see them for a couple of days now (they are an unmistakable sight) and today we finally reached them. Margie is just as glad to have them behind us.

We reached Magnetic Point late in the afternoon and stayed for supper. The point and adjoining Magnet Island are named for their pronounced effects on compass needles. We noticed some distortion but have actually seen worse deflections from magnetic rocks and islands in previous years on trips father north.

The wind has been gradually weakening all day long and we have decided to try crossing the neck of Black Bay later this evening. It is a wide risky crossing and will take us two hours or so but the alternative is unthinkable, a 2-3 day paddle in along the shoreline of the bay which is about 50 miles deep.

Right now we are going through all our gear and repacking it. We have a 9-mile carry coming up in a few days at Grand Portage and we have decided to mail as much of our equipment home as possible beforehand to lighten the load. It looks as though we shall be able to part with at least 40 pounds. Included in the unnecessary pile are:

a) the children's toys and books, including rock and bottle top collections

b) tacklebox, spare fishrod, and canoe repair kit.

c) children's tent and Willie the duck.

d) changes of clothes, footgear, and big tarp.

e) some cooking utensils, extra bug repellent, towel, and dozens of little odds and ends.

There is only another month left in the summer and we figure we can pretty well last with what we are wearing, a pot, a tent, an axe and sleeping bags. We shall also leave one spare paddle behind. All in all we have completely filled one Duluth pack with things to mail home. Let us hope the weather is good in August because we will be ill-prepared for long periods of rain and cold.

We started out to cross the neck of Black Bay about 8:00 last night and it took quite a bit longer than we had estimated. In general things went smoothly although we did encounter a surprising amount of wind and turbulence. The waves would shift directions unpredictably. They would come rushing into the bay for about half an hour and then, suddenly, switch and come rushing out. It was very strange, but we just kept paddling. About 10:00 the sun set and the full moon came out bright and cold. We were paddling right towards the Sleeping Giant on Thunder Cape and he was beautifully outlined. About 11:00 the northern lights started, bright white and green dipping curtains. Finally at 12:00 we stepped ashore, some 18 hours after starting the day, and discovered that we had managed in the dark to land on a sand beach, the first one we had seen in 3 days! We pulled the canoe above the breaker line and left the kids in it to sleep out the night. Then we spread out a ground cloth and sleeping bags to catch five and one-half hours of sleep before starting out the next morning. We had worked awfully long and hard (from 6:00 until midnight) for only 26 miles, but we both felt good about it. It is a pleasure to travel when you can and Black Bay is one big obstacle now behind us. The next problem will be Thunder Bay. We have heard that the voyageurs in their 36 foot canoes could take as little as 12 days to do this entire lake, rafting up in sheltered coves during storms but generally not ever stopping. Good for them, but we are only human.

JULY 26: THUNDER CAPE

When we woke up there were three foxes cavorting on our beach. It wasn't really light enough to take a picture so we just pushed the canoe back into the water and paddled off. We continued pretty steadily until about 10:30 and covered another 35 miles. We are getting hungry now to be off the lake.

Thunder Bay presented us with a real question in strategy. The choices are either to island hop across the mouth of the bay or to lose two days by following the shoreline. The trouble with island hopping is the first hop. It is a six and a half mile leap to Turtle Head on Pie Island, the nearest point to the outjutting finger of Thunder Cape. With the right weather conditions I might make such a leap except for the geography of the situation. The narrow point of the cape is just too small a target and once we pushed off it would be effectively impossible to return if a wind came up making it unsafe to continue across. Anyways we have decided to go into and around the bay in order to

1) get more food at Thunder Bay. It seems unlikely there will be many stores at Grand Portage and we plan to stock up for the next 2 to 3 weeks with fairly light food for portaging though Minnesota.

2) visit Old Fort William. The village is an historic recreation of the old fur trading post and we are anxious to visit it. The kayakers of a few days ago told us about the fort and even the children are excited about seeing it now. Time is no problem when you have the whole summer free.

3) mail off our pack of nonnecessities.

The lake was pretty calm this morning and we rounded Thunder Cape right at noon. After eating lunch in the canoe and paddling a little more, we stopped on a rock beach for a rest. The kids played (Randy is much better today) while the adults flopped down on the rocks and slept for half an hour. When we set out again the wind and waves were behind us and we breezed along another 7 miles before stopping for supper. By 7:45 it was calming down and we pushed off to cross the bay just in front of Caribou Island. We were aiming for a light on the north shore and just as it was getting really dark we finally pulled up at a little 9-acre island with a house on it. We paddled around the island to a dock and Margie went up to ask permission to sleep on the shore for a few hours. Our hosts, Eunice and Bev Porter, were as gracious as could be. They had a beautiful campsite on the island but insisted that instead we spend the night in their guest house. What a marvelous evening! After settling the children into real beds we followed our hosts back to their living room for an hour of chatting over tea and cake. Later, back at the guest house, we were able to shower, pat dry with ''Bill Blass'' towels, and then drop into a luxurious bed. Looking in the full length mirror tonight, me bearded and both of us tanned and weatherbeaten, we were struck by what a "rugged" looking couple we've become. Really, the Porters could not have found a scruffier bunch to sleep in their guest house.

Well, we have paddled almost clear around the impressive Sleeping Giant now. It is a huge rock cliff mountain formation and is clearly the outstanding terrain feature for many miles. As such it is the basis of many local Indian legends and superstitions.

JULY 27: SASK POOL 4

We knew that we would get off to a slow start this morning and we did. We got up a little late, had breakfast and spent some time with our hosts. They insisted on giving the children new toys and us a bag of fresh fruit. There was no way to adequately thank them and it was about 10:00 before we pushed off for the town of Thunder Bay some 12 miles in the distance. The sea was calm and the temperature warm as we paddled steadily, trying to reach the city breakwater which would shield us the remaining miles to the Kaministikwia River. We planned to get as far up the river as we could today and visit Old Fort William (11 miles upriver) tomorrow. We had no way of knowing that we were about to experience an unforgettable lesson.

Being naturally wary and quite alert, we had nearly 15 minutes warning, but squandered the first few moments not recognizing or quite believing what we were seeing. It began just about noon when we were within two miles of the breakwater (and safety) and less than a mile offshore. Our first inkling that all was not normal came when I spotted a blue line on the horizon, no more than 8 miles out to sea on our left, and remarked on its oddness. We should have acted then. Three or four minutes later I observed aloud that it must be the wake line of some giant ship because we could now see that it was only about five miles off and that it appeared to be advancing line of breakers. This was foolish speculation on my part of course as we have seen a lot of freighters and none have left a wake of breakers. We still had about a mile or so to reach safety and paddled steadily on. We should have turned to shore and fled. About this time a small plane began to circle directly overhead and this engaged our attention (I guess the pilot could see better than we could what was about to happen). Anyway, things began to move quickly and it was no more than another couple of minutes before we realized that we were in trouble. We could now see that we were being approached by an ocean of whitecaps rather than a single breaking wave. Still, every-thing was dead flat calm around us. Nevertheless, we began to race for the breakwater. We didn't make it. Too late we decided to turn and head directly for shore. In less than five minutes the lake around us went from flat to small smooth swells, big swells, and steep swells; then came the wind, whitecaps and finally combers five feet tall. We have shot a lot of rapids over the years and suffered our share of misfortunes, but never have I seen things go to hell so quickly. To move unexpectedly from dead flat calm to giant seas in only a few minutes was a new one on us. We weren't far from shore by now but all our attention was focused on the steep breaking waves around us. The plane which kindly stayed with us thoughout the ordeal was totally ignored. We were too busy fighting to maintain our balance and keep off the dangerous rocky shoreline. It seemed like forever but was probably no more than 15 minutes till we finally found a place to lift out, nearly breaking our poor canoe.

What we found was an artificial harbor formed by a paper company dock. By timing it so the waves were bouncing up instead of down we could stand up to reach the level of the dock. Margie managed to pull herself out and then I threw up the kids and the packs. The hardest part was getting the canoe out, but by timing our efforts to coincide with the crest of a big wave we managed to lever the boat over the edge of the dock to safety.

It was late lunchtime so we sat on shore and ate. We have been here all afternoon now and it is very frustrating. We are less than a mile from the breakwater and safety, but there is nothing we can do. We still can't believe how quickly things can sour on this lake.

Supper will be a problem. We are on paper company property and two security men have been by to tell us we can't build a fire as it is too dangerous. It was clear that they don't want us here but they didn't dare suggest we launch into the ocean. We don't carry a cookstove but tonight it would be nice to have one. We also can't hike to town without crossing a picketline; the workers are on strike. We settled for a cold supper of Spam, corn and pudding. As miscellany I observe that:

1) Randy is now well.

2) Tina has just been stung by a bee. Someone gets stung every year but usually it is me while I am gathering firewood.

3) The next time I cross the Great Lakes it won't be in a open canoe; maybe I'll use an unsinkable, indestructible, ocean going kayak and a sail.

Finally, about 9:00, the wind was gone and most of the white was

101

off the lake. We started off in the gathering twilight to paddle the last precarious mile through steep swells to the breakwater. Once inside the entrance we were safe and looked around for a place to land. We were in a city now and finally chose to set up directly beneath Sask Pool 4, one of the world's largest grain elevators. It was dark when we landed and we set up quickly and put the kids to bed. Although it was Sunday there was a lot of activity around and the workmen invited us inside to snack in the employee lunch room. We had exciting tales to tell of course but, due to our thinness, we must also have looked pitifully hungry. Everybody took turns feeding us homemade bits of supper from their lunch pails. When they heard we planned to visit the old Fort, they told us to expect a big welcome. They'd seen the annual reenactment of Rendezvous where a brigade of canoes comes paddling up to the Fort amidst cheers and a cannon salute. Of course, no one knows we are coming, but we are looking forward to talking with the people there and maybe spending the night nearby.

It was getting late again (third night in a row) and we declined hot showers to toddle off to bed. Actually, the sleeping was not too good. Grain cars were shunting all around throughout the night, and the rumbling and bright lights made it hard to sleep.

JULY 28: OLD FORT WILLIAM

Today we finally visited Old Fort William, but the day was not without its frustrations and disappointments. We were able to get an early start and reached the Kaministikwia River for breakfast. The original fort was built near the river mouth but the reconstruction is eleven polluted miles upstream, so we started up the river. We hadn't gone far before we stopped at a boatclub dock for information and errands. We were pretty well into the city and Margie left to go food shopping while I went off to see about shipping our nonnecessity pack home. Disappointment number one; the cheapest method I could find was still $36. As a result we have decided to save our money and portage our Great Lakes rock collection etc. through Minnesota. I also learned that we have a problem brewing. Our current plan is to try and reach Kenora on the north shore of Lake of the Woods this year. The trans-Canadian railway passes through there and we want to take it home. I stopped in at the railroad station

102

today, though, and learned that you have to have a reservation to get on a train in this country. Alas. Next I checked in with the bus station. It turns out that they don't take credit cards. Great; we don't have enough money to get home. Oh well, that is a problem which is still a month away.

We ate lunch under a bridge while it showered and then we continued upriver. It is true that I am not in a very good mood tonight but I really think that the Great Lakes Paper Company is the worst polluter that I have ever seen. They have singlehandedly destroyed the Kam. R. and the noise their giant operation makes is deafening. As we paddled slowly upstream past their plant the stench of the dirty water was overpowering. We feared that the canoe would corrode away beneath us. Dead fish floated everywhere while others struggled and flopped on the surface for breath. Upstream of GLP Company property, conditions quickly improved however, and soon the water was relatively clear.

When the American imposition of customs duties forced the Northwest Company to abandon Grand Portage in Minnesota, the company reorganized and established their inland headquarters at Fort William in 1803. For nearly 20 years the Fort was the major depot and trans-shipment point for furs and trade goods. Each summer it would spring to life as over 1,000 voyageurs converged here for the annual Rendezvous.

We paddled on till nearly 3:00 growing more excited as we neared the Fort. Before rounding the last bend in the river, we cleaned up the canoe a bit and let the kids paddle in the middle (their usual spot). Then, 4 paddles flashing in the sunlight, we triumphantly approached the Fort. We passed the parking lot and paddled around the point to a big dock at the front entrance of the palisade. And now a word of caution if you are travelling by canoe and wish to visit the Fort. First, the river is polluted; but second, when you reach the Fort you are emphatically not welcome. This was made very clear to us. They have an efficient tourist processing center here and real voyageurs are out of place. We were ordered to shove off as our canoe was not authentic and would spoil the atmosphere. We offered to hide it in the bushes but nothing doing. We were sent a half mile back downstream to the parking lot where there was a small private landing. We tied up to the NO TRESPASSING sign there and went ashore.

The Fort is really quite elaborate and is based on excavations and early drawings of the original. We enjoyed touring the buildings and grounds and talking to the residents but the visit had been marred by our reception. Typical was our first conversation with a resident "voyageur"

103

in period dress:

Me: Hi.

Him: Hi, where did you come from?

Me: New Hampshire. We just paddled here coming through Montreal.

Him: Oh, yeah. Heh, heh. Sure.

Me: Yes. We came through the Soo Locks about 3 weeks ago.

Him: Sure. (Pause) You're not serious are you?

Me: Yes.

Him: (to Margie and the kids) You're not serious?

Margie: Yes.

Him: Well, you can't land a canoe here.

Well, you get the drift. Eventually we talked to the man in charge who thought our trip was great, but no, there was no place to set up a tent for the night unless we wished to sleep on a gravel bar another half mile upstream. We thanked him and later left to go downstream. The only voyageurs they can handle there are the ceremonial ones. We ate supper at the refreshment stand. Then, as we were walking back to our canoe we were accosted by a security guard. It turns out that it is illegal to tie a canoe up to the dock at the parking lot also. After paddling over 1400 miles we're not even allowed to get out of the boat! Slightly miffed, we left.

The evening was dark and stormy with thundershowers as we raced downstream looking for a tolerable place to spend the night. Violent storms were breaking out all around us but somehow they mostly missed. We were about three miles from the lake and it was getting dark when we finally found a place to pull over for the night. This makes four late nights in a row and I am feeling a little irrritable. There were two barking German Shepherds (dogs) here when we arrived. I was hoping that they would attack so I could have the questionable pleasure of tearing them limb from limb, but no such luck. They trotted off leaving us to set up quickly and go to bed, our aggressions unreleased.

JULY 29: MINK BAY

We got up early and started off in time to get down to the lake for a nice sunrise and breakfast. The Sleeping Giant was clear in the distance and we took a couple of last pictures before heading south. The weather was fine today -- in fact, too hot. We found ourselves stopping to rest in the shade every hour or so. We are just plain worn out after the last several days. At least the children had plenty of chances to swim. We gave up for the day about 5:00 in Mink Bay.

The fire is a little smoky tonight but it does keep the bugs away. We are long past being concerned about smoky smelling clothes and hair. Tonight we are doing a little steam cooking. This is really the best way to do gingerbreads, cobblers, blueberry/cranberry loaves, etc. You take two close fitting pots and place a couple of pebbles and some water in the outer one. The inner pot is filled with the dough and then nested inside the larger with a lid over the whole works. This is very effective and makes delicious breads. It is an error however to let all the water boil completely away.

We saw an otter today. We have about 25 miles to go now to reach Grand Portage and we hope to do it tomorrow. What a relief it will be to get off the lake and into Minnesota!

JULY 30 & 31: GRAND PORTAGE

We started out early this morning under cloudy semi-foggy skies. It rained all through our breakfast stop but then gradually the day started to improve. We had lunch at Pigeon Point in Minnesota and then the excitement started to build. After 25 days and 525 miles of travel on the lake we were finally coming to the end. We rounded Hat Point about 3:00 and there it was. We gave out 3 cheers and paddled in to the reconstructed fort. At last! We were awfully glad to arrive but still it is sad to be leaving the lake. It has come to be an old friend.

Grand Portage Fort is much smaller and more low key than Fort William and they gave us the warm reception we'd been looking for. Ranger Gordon Lindemann was quite impressed with our trip and told everyone he saw all about us. We had a lot of fun being celebrities. Later we paddled across the bay to spend the night at a nearby campsite.

Grand Portage of course was the original rendezvous site for the western fur trade. The old Indian route west was via the Pigeon River which empties into the Lake a few miles north of here. The problem was that the last 20 miles of the river are simply not navigable. The solution

105

was a nine-mile "grand portage" carry south and east from the river to where we are now. The trail lies in Minnesota and therein laid a problem. When the U.S.-Canadian border was eventually drawn, the Americans discovered that they owned the carry. They promptly imposed a tax on everything passing through their territory. It was no longer practical to use that route and in 1803 the rendezvous shifted north to Fort William on the Kaministikwia River.

During the heyday at Grand Portage however, hundreds of voyageurs would arrive from Montreal in their huge canots du maître during the first week of July. In the meantime the elite "hommes du nord" or "Norwesters" would be coming in from their wintering grounds in the far northwest. The Norwesters were the cream of the Voyageur crop, or so they thought, and they referred to the Montreal group (somewhat derogatorily) as the "mangeurs de lard" or "porkeaters". The porkeaters, living at home with their families in Montreal through the winter, and having bacon to eat on trips, were considered to be somewhat inferior. At any rate the Norwesters would disembark at Fort Charlotte, 9 miles from Grand Portage, on the Pigeon and carry the furs across. There were 16 "poses" or rest stops along the trail. Later they would be returning with the new trade goods to hurry north to the Athabasca region before the onset of winter. Their "canots du nord" or "north canoes" were somewhat smaller (26 feet) than those of the Montrealers and would carry 4 or 5 men and a load of approximately 3 to 4000 pounds. Like their bigger brothers they were made of birch bark. A flotilla of 4 to 8 north canoes constituted a brigade.

Ranger Lindemann told us he would arrange a lift for us across the carry if we cared to wait and we quickly accepted. We have been dreading the nine-mile portage with all our heavy stuff and canoe. As it is the records show that there are more than 90 carries from Montreal to Lake of the Woods and starting as we did from southern New Hampshire we will have carried well over a hundred times before the summer is done. At any rate we were more than happy to spend a day visiting at the Fort. We spent the time taking a little hike on the portage trail (without packs) and viewing the many movies they have available at the visitor's center. The fort had several hundred visitors today and we also had fun playing king of the castle sitting there conspicuously on the shoreline with all our gear and canoe.

In one room of the main building they keep old voyageur clothes which they let the visitors try on, so we all got our pictures taken in period dress. Randy wore a capote, the heavy essentially waterproof felt-like coat used by the voyageurs. The rest of us dressed in calico shirts, tuques and sashes. The heavy sashes (ceintures flechees) were worn by the voyageurs to prevent hernias caused by the strain of carrying heavy loads across the portages. Of course, I use Margie instead of a sash and have found it equally effective. Putting the heavy stuff in her packs seems to eliminate any need I might have for a sash. By using a tumpline to help support the weight the old time voyageurs could carry 200 or so pounds balanced on their backs. Unfortunately, Margie has never mastered this technique and seems to be effectively limited to about 80 pounds or so. As far as hats go, though, I believe that we may bring tuques ourselves next year. A hat is essential gear on a canoe trip. It keeps out rain, sun, bugs and cold. We have always used felt crushers but as the years go by and I grow progressively more bald I have been thinking that the added warmth of a tuque would be nice. Felt hats have their place; they are good for saving special feathers and flowers, and we place them over the kids faces during sunny naptimes in the canoe, but they are a nuisance in the wind when they must be fastened on with a chin strap. Also a good crusher takes a couple of years to acquire the proper woodsy character.

Finally, right at closing time we got our ride. We put the canoe and gear in the back of an old pickup and jounced across old logging roads to the far side of the carry. We wound up and up, leaving the lake far behind in the distance, and now here we are on the Pigeon at last. How exciting! Right here it is a narrow, reedy little stream and we can hardly wait to set out tomorrow. After a month on the open lake everything seems so small and confined. Because of the ride, of course, we were able to bring everything along without trouble, but we did leave two things behind. The first was the laminated paddle I made Margie for Christmas last year. It had just seen too much hard use and we decided that the shore of Lake Superior would be a fitting place to retire it. The second is a little more serious and we did not discover it until after the children were in bed. Somewhere today Margie lost her wallet. This is too bad. It had $90 in cash, some traveler's checks and our only credit card in it. I still have enough money for food for the rest of the summer though. We just can't get home again. Oh well.

107

AUGUST 1: PIGEON RIVER

What a day! The morning started early for Margie who got up before dawn to start walking down the old logging road towards Grand Portage. She was still concerned about her wallet and hoped at the very least to phone a bank and deactivate her lost credit card. In about an hour however she was back at camp and woke us all up. A mile and a half back she'd found her wallet where it had bounced out of her hip pocket and out of the truck onto the road. She was ecstatic! I was happy too.

After breakfast we started up the Pigeon. It was grassy on both sides, but not dead water; in fact there was a pretty good current -- against us of course. Also a breeze came up in our faces. Before too long it got so shallow that we had to wade. It was a warm sunny day and the water was a lot warmer then the mountain streams we were wading back in May. Still, after an hour or so the fun was going out of it. We had a brief paddling stretch, then lunch in the canoe and finally more wading. The wading was really not too bad and we bypassed two portages in this way. Admittedly, we never saw a trail but still we probably would have dragged rather than carried anyway. Thus, when we came to a one-mile portage trail bypassing the final set of rapids we decided to simply continue wading. We were already wet -- so why not! This was very dumb. Portages exist for reasons and travellers should think long and hard before passing one up. For a one-mile carry we were about to pay a terrible price. We were to spend the next five hours ascending the last mile or so to South Fowl Lake. We spent the first hour pulling the canoe up an ever steeper stream bed. Towards the end we were carving out our own channel, pulling rocks out of the river bed with our hands. Eventually we reached what appeared to be an old log dam where we got out and portaged a quarter mile or so. Since we assumed that the dam marked the outlet to the lake we were surprised to discover that we were still on the river. There was nothing for it but to continue wading. Unfortunately we were gradually working our way into a ravine and soon the mountain brook became just plain impassable. It was time to start scouting out an alternative. Margie and the kids spent the time splashing around in a little pool while I hunted and searched through the woods for the portage trail. I never found it. Our rule of thumb is that bushwhacking is not necessary. There is always a better way. We have had this lesson reinforced time and time again. If you have to bushwhack the chances are that you have done or are doing something wrong. We have seen it happen to others,

108

still it was galling and frustrating to have it happen to us. It will be a long time before I pass up another well-marked carry. Suffice it to say that after a half mile of forcing our way through the dense brush we managed to bull our way out to the lake. There was a tortuous vertical descent to the water at the end of our ravine but everything has ended well. The trail is a lot clearer now than before we came through. I felled several old trees with my canoe as I came crashing through, and Margie broke off a lot of branches with her pack. We lay on the shore of South Fowl Lake and lapped up an instant chocolate pudding, then we paddled off to find the nearest campsite. We found one with lots of raspberries, a grill and a latrine. It is a nice grassy clearing beneath some pines. We only went 11 miles or so today but everyone is exhausted. At least tomorrow should be easier. So much for the Pigeon River.

Margie is putting the kids to bed now but after that she has an essay she wants to write. If you are travelling with children it is important to have an inexhaustible collection of stories. The same old favorites will be told repeatedly of course but there are always times when they want a new one. They come in handy at bedtime, naptime and during those boring rainy days when you are just paddling along. Usually we bring books to read for bedtime stories and that is what Margie is doing now. Most evenings she spends a half hour in their tent reading while I pick up around the camp.

QUE SERA, SERA

Early in the trip I decided my theme song for the summer would be "Que sera, sera"; what will be, will be. At home I tend to be a structured person who gets upset with unexpected changes of routine. But outdoors you just can't be that way. You don't really "conquer the wilderness"; you are merely passing through. You have to learn to live with whatever comes. Of course it's wise to make plans, often several plans, to allow for different circumstances. Just be ready to change them if conditions aren't right.

There were many days we planned on travelling but there was too much wind or rain or lightning, so we stayed put a while. Other times we travelled more slowly than we expected to and ran quite low on food. (Fortunately we always carry enough to get by for a couple of extra days.)

It is really important but difficult to remember this philosophy when dealing with kids. Try not to yell when they spill water in the new bag of gorp. Try to stay calm when they go wading in their last dry clothes or sliding down a muddy bank in their only clean ones. When they accidentally kick sand in their supper or drop their spoon in the dirt just look the other way. After all, it could happen to anyone. . . Besides if you can manage to ignore it, the child -- even a 5 year old -- can often take care of things well enough on his own. He is the one who is wet (sandy, etc.) and if he doesn't mind why should you? If he does mind he may learn not to do it next time.

There are enough times the kids have to do things our way, such as wearing life jackets or getting up early. If you can let the little things go by the trip goes much more smoothly. I must admit though, it's awfully hard for me to remember sometimes.

AUGUST 2: MOUNTAIN LAKE

Today we worked the canoe for a little less than 8 hours. Progress was slow but steady and we covered 14 miles. It was overcast all day with minor showers and the mosquitoes were pretty thick in the woods. We ended up portaging 4 times (132, 140, 40 and 90 rods), making 2 trips on each carry. Tonight we are camped three-fourths of the way down Mountain Lake and tomorrow we expect to make a run that will position us to arrive at Gunflint Lodge the next day.

Now that we are in Minnesota we have to start watching the maps a little more closely. There are lots of little lakes, streams and carries here and you have to always be aware of your position. Actually there is less to map-reading than meets the eye. I like to spend hours poring over maps in the winter and around the evening campfires on the trail but not infrequently all this careful planning is obviated by a single on-the-scene inspection.

We are hoping that tomorrow will be our last full day of uphill travel for the summer. Once we cross the height of land portage into North Lake we shall be in the Hudson Bay watershed. The water will be flowing west to Lake Winnipeg and then northeast from there to Hudson Bay via the Nelson. It will be an exciting moment. Each year the best of the porkeaters were given the opportunity to become Norwesters. If they accepted there was a little initiation ceremony performed at the height of land. It involved both a baptism and an oath. The fledgling Norwester was sprinkled with the dew from a wet cedar bough and then asked to

110

swear that he would never:

a) permit another voyageur to pass the spot without similar initiation, and

(b) kiss another voyageur's wife (without her permission).

AUGUST 3: STAIRCASE FALL

Today we followed Margie's old Girl Scout song, "The Far Northland." The shortest route west is to take the "Long Portage" (2 miles) from Rove Lake to Rose Lake. Instead, we took a long cut, the three far shorter carries from:

"Lake Duncan to Clearwater
To the Bearskin I will go
Where you see the loon
And hear its plaintive wail.
If you're thinking in your inner heart
There's swagger in my step
You've never been along the Border Trail."

Actually, the voyageurs were known to use this alternate route also.

Today we continued our new routine of getting up around 6:00 and eating breakfast at the campsite. There is really no point in dashing off early to avoid the wind in such peaceful country. We travelled from 7:30 to 4:30 and only went 14 miles. The combination of portaging and inland heat, however, leaves us just as tired as the longer lake days did. We carried four portages (3/4, 1/4, 1/4 and 1/4 miles) to end up at the far end of Rose Lake. The last carry, Stairway Portage, lived up to its name. There are two sets of stairs there consisting of 28 and 99 steps, respectively. The kids loved them. There is a pretty falls there also, but it was quite dry this time of year.

Coming out of Rose Lake toward Rat Lake, we traversed a shallow swampy area of water where the bottom was all soft mud. We'd heard that the voyageurs used to imagine that the mud was sucking down their canoes and I can understand their feeling. Even with Tina paddling, the canoe slowed way down as we passed over this stretch. It was a weird helpless feeling.

111

Camping in this country is sort of like musical chairs. Everybody picks up in the morning and dashes off. The trick, however, is to find an unoccupied site late in the afternoon. The local ground rules are no more than 2 parties or 10 persons (whichiever is smaller) allowed at a camp. Thus, the last ones to stop for the evening are somewhat like "Charlie on the MTA" (who couldn't get off that train). Theoretically, they may have to paddle all night and try again the next day. We finally ended up tonight at a noncampsite on the Canadian shore. I supposed technically we are "cheating" by not staying at a regulation site.

Lately the children have been helping out a lot. Tonight Randy put up their tent while Tina made the fire. It certainly makes setting up camp a lot easier for us, especially on days like today when we're lethargic from weariness and heat.

Well, we are in real canoe country now, and I saw over 20 canoes today: everything from snooty experts in their own hand crafted stripper canoes to bumbling duffers in their sportspal sponsons. The most amusing occurrence happened at noon. There were people everywhere today and at lunch we drifted in to eat at an occupied campsite (and use their latrine). The couple there was just out for a couple of days and were very friendly. We were barely ashore before they asked whether we knew anything about tents. They had a regular pup-style tent, distinguished only by its glorious color scheme: red ends, one red side, red floor, and one blue side. They remarked that they had borrwed it from friends and that it seemed to have extra poles. I allowed as how that was not unusual; I carry extra poles myself. Slightly incredulous, however, I went over to examine it and wiggled it with some disbelief before calling Margie over to have a look. It is not ever day that you see a tent deliberately pitched on its side. Still, it seemed sturdy and it was certainly clever the way they had suspended it.

AUGUST 4: GUNFLINT LODGE

It rained gently in the night with some thunder and lightning. It let up for a few minutes in the morning though, long enough for us to break camp and set out. The wind was very strong out of the east, gradually switching to the south, and we hurtled right along.

It is easy to keep gear dry when you are paddling on a rainy day.

112

First place a few branches and sticks under the packs; this keeps them off the wet floor. Then just throw a tarp over everything to keep stuff dry. The water will run freely to the back of the canoe where it can be easily bailed, rather than soaking into the packs. The situation is far more difficult during portages though, when everything is uncovered and you are most vulnerable, but today we were amazingly fortunate. We had to make four portages and the rain cooperated by stopping briefly for each one.

We have been looking forward to reaching Gunflint Lake. Last winter Ernie Schmidt, a complete stranger who had heard of our plans, wrote and asked us to stop in for a visit if we made it as far as Gunflint Lodge this summer. Gunflint Lake is several miles long and it was about 3:00 before we finally pulled in to the Lodge at the west end. It had been a cool rainy day and we were anxious for a visit. Ernie lives on nearby Loon Lake and was not at home, but it worked out very well for us. The lodge people bent over backwards to make us feel welcome. They chauffeured us to a food store, let us use their washing machines and dryers, and introduced us to a sauna.

We had never used a sauna before and were somewhat taken aback, but they couldn't wait to show us how to use it. It was a little room with wooden benches and a huge stove. They built a roaring fire in the stove, tossed a little water on some heating rocks and closed the door. The first minute was not too bad and we even threw on some more water. Those Minnesotans must be tougher than we are though. It seemed like only a few seconds before we began to get dizzy and hunkered down. The steam was so thick you couldn't see anything if you were more than six inches off the floor. Soon I was down there crawling around like a snake trying to find the door. It was so hot they darn near cooked me before I could escape! Still it was a lot of fun.

About suppertime Ernie returned and we were driven over to his 5-acre property, where we were invited to spend the night. Actually we had to sleep in our tent there as they are still in the process of clearing a space for their cabin. In the meantime they also are living in a tent. It is really a pretty elegant setup though. We have never seen a tent before that has an oriental rug on the floor.

Ernie is a canoeing expert and we spent a very enjoyable evening with him and his wife. Ernie is an "old-timer" and knows everybody in canoeing. He was on the "Today Show" with Hubert Humphrey and is a good friend of Sigurd Olson and Eric Morse. Ernie asked how long

113

Lake Superior took us. I told him and I guess it was a few less than it took Eric (whew -- we hadn't realized what pressure we were under!). Ernie quickly pointed out, though, that Eric had been windbound eight of his days.

AUGUST 5: DEVIL'S ELBOW

This morning we were treated to a sumptuous breakfast, then driven back to the lodge and our waiting canoe. We faced a windy, whitecap-covered lake, and it was a pretty tough crossing to the start of the Granite River. It was tougher though for another group with smaller canoes. They left considerably ahead of us and elected to paddle around the end of the lake to avoid the full force of the wind, and we ended up arriving well ahead of them. We all stopped for lunch on Blueberry Portage. The children picked nearly a quart of berries besides what we all ate. Tomorrow we shall have blueberries in our cereal and blueberry bannock for lunch.

The water is very low hereabouts so we were able to run a few of the lesser portages and avoid some carries. Minnesota must be the only place in the world where the portages are almost fun though. First, they have such well-groomed trails. It is like strolling along a wooded path in a city park. Secondly, there are canoe racks every 40 rods or so on most carries. These are extremely convenient. You can set the canoe down with a minimum of fuss and go back for your second load. Thirdly, there are lots of sweating co-participants. Minnesota is fairly crowded and some of the portages remind me of the opening half mile of a marathon. Everybody comes bursting along the trail and with such high spirits. There is a certain amount of gamesmanship involved as we all try to make portaging appear delightfully easy. You must stagger along with all you can carry and act as if you are having a wonderful time. If you can do all this with both a pack and a 20-foot canoe you garner extra "prestige" points of course.

Actually the participants generally fall into several well-defined classes. The largest is made up of neophytes. They bungle across with an improbable collection of paraphernalia requiring at least 3 trips. They are always friendly, bubbling with enthusiasm, and usually have one member on crutches. Then there are the select and somewhat snooty experts. They dash by jauntily wearing light packs and a canoe. They make only one

114

trip and have little to say to the rest of us. The teenage camp groups are in a class by themselves. The first week out they are miserable but effusively outgoing and full of inquiries about conditions ahead (how is the next portage?). By their second week out however these groups have "toughened up" and are best ignored. If questioned they will reveal with unbearable condescension that they have paddled miles and miles and seen it all. They are full of themselves and their new found prowess. Then of course there is us. We are as obnoxious as anybody. After a summer of travelling we have an iron strength and an efficiency to match. Although we are a heavily loaded family canoe, we pass over the carries and across the lakes with a deceptive casualness that leaves all but the most determined travellers behind. Naturally, we are insufferably pleasant to all we pass. Randy is particularly loathsome as he passes out advice to struggling neophytes on how to pick up their canoe, or how to paddle, or comments on what small fish they're keeping.

We tried to stop today at 4:30 but the musical chairs aspect of Minnesota was already in full swing. Every site seemed to have four or even five canoes pulled up at it and we reluctantly continued. Then, miraculously, on the main canoe route though Devils Elbow we came to a vacant site! It is a beautiful spot. We set up camp and settled in for the night.

A couple of other canoes have passed by and we invited them to stay but they all declined.

Well it turned out that we didn't have the site to ourselves after all last night. To make a long story short let me note only that Minnesotans have a strange sense of humor or perhaps it is only that they are just true sports. Whereas an Indian or northern traveller would quickly take his rifle to any bear which dared invade his camp, the Minnesotan prefers to entice, yes even tease the local bruins. The lonely evenings are made more entertaining by lodging a pole high between two trees and then, just before retiring, one's food and gear is tied to the pole to dangle just out of any bear's reach. The bears, of course, are true sports also and come woofling around the tent sites each night to play the game. Imagine the bear's pleasure then at finding our outfit stacked tidily beneath our overturned canoe. It was a dark night and our flashlight burned out weeks ago. Also I am a tolerable sport myself. Thus I was loath to take my camp axe and interrupt his fun. Fortunately, the bear was a young one and relatively inexperienced. He did not even think to eat our traveller's checks. This was a very pleasant surprise. Like all Americans I am well aware of the extreme hazards one runs in carrying American Express. Last winter it seemed that scarcely an evening would go by without the TV's showing some poor newlyweds dashing back to their hotel in tears after losing all their checks in some foreign city. This is the second time in only a week that we have nearly lost ours.

AUGUST 6: LITTLE KNIFE FALLS

It was a beautiful day today. We travelled against the wind but it was never too strong. We had lunch on a little gravel shelf about three fourths of the way down Saganaga Lake. Explorer Alexander Mackenzie claimed the lake took its name from the many numerous islands. The name of the lake has been translated to mean "lake with many islands," "lake of bays," and "lake that bewilders," but with our modern maps we had little trouble navigating. In 1775 this lake held the country's most northwesterly post, established by the French.

We shared our lunch with 2 guides and mentioned how crowded the campsites had been last night until we miraculously found a deserted place on Devil's Elbow. When closely questioned, we described the place more fully and they laughed and said the outfitters were warning people away from the site as there had recently been numerous reports of marauding bears there. We confirmed these rumors.

The afternoon was stiflingly hot and we did some warm portaging. The best carry was Monument Portage which, as the name suggests, is marked by international "monument" markers defining the border. The water is very low this year and all the carries are somewhat longer than normal. Monument carry proved a little too long for at least one unlucky camper. She had just brought a canoe over the carry and was attempting to set it in the water off the end of a small unsteady pier. With one misstep she fell into the muck along with her canoe to the surprise and amusement of her friends. Their laughs changed to helping hands however when they realized she was shrieking in near panic. She was floundering in the deep, soft, almost quicksand-like mud and could hardly get back onto the dock.

After observing this incident we were doubly careful to walk on all available branches and boards unloading the canoe but Randy managed to fall in anyway. He was immediately up to his thighs in mud, which

116

is a pretty scary feeling. Margie was only a step behind however, and soon had him out. We swam and rested for a while afterwards, but otherwise continued steadily till just before supper.

We were able to create a campsite just a mile or so above Little Knife Falls. It is a fairly good spot and we were soon joined by 2 Outward Bound leaders who sent their troops a little farther on (but not out of sight). In this way the six of us were able to spend a pleasant and fairly quiet evening. We pooled suppers and then sat around the fire roasting popcorn and sharing routine campfire talk. Later they showed us how to "bearproof" our food. Their rule of thumb is to get the packs ten feet up and three feet out from the nearest tree. With 80-pound packs this a considerable feat. They were shinnying up and down trees and swinging from the branches stringing crossropes and other guys. They were soon successful though and no one was hurt. Still I was somewhat disconcerted to find the packs now swung directly over the peak of our tent.

Well, it was a good day. We covered 20 miles, did 4 portages and met a lot of people. Early tomorrow we should reach Knife Lake, named for the felsite rock formation there. This is a hard, finegrained, blue black rock with conchoidal fracture and sharp (knife-sharp) edges. The local Indians at one time shaped both tools and weapons from it. (I have acquired a little informational pamphlet on the area.)

AUGUST 7: POLAR BEARS

We saw an awful lot of people today. It was not uncommon to have 10 to 20 canoes at a portage and men would be queued up in lines at the end of a carry, each with a canoe on his shoulders, waiting for room to launch. It was very hot (84 degrees by 10:00) and the kids went swimming more than once. Everybody was kind of tired so we made it an easy day starting out about 8:00 and continuing on until 3:30. Even so we portaged 4 times and bypassed 3 others with a little judicious wading of rapids. It was wet work but easier than carrying on a hot day.

By stopping at 3:30 we were able to choose a nice big private campsite in a cedar grove. We had it to ourselves for over an hour before being joined by another party. There is a high sturdy "bear pole" here and we were able to get our stuff well into the air.

While young folks may like to sing (and drink) around a fire at night

117

in the WILD

SANDERS, '85 ©

118

I find as I grow older that it is enough to simply stare into the embers enjoying the present and remembering times past. Travellers are natural story tellers and it was not surprising that after putting the kids to bed we adults soon settled into a round of bear stories around the fire.

Over the years we have had a number of experiences with bears (including the most recent at Devil's Elbow). Someday I expect to be an "oldtimer". As such I will need an inexhaustible supply of well-rehearsed stories and so I am always glad to get a chance to practice. Anyway, we traded yarn for yarn, each striving to top the other. I told them about the night with the wounded bear in the campsite, about the cub we once caught in a laundry bag, about the bear who jumped into our canoe to get a fish and so on. I have lots of material but even so the competition was fierce. These fellows seemed to have a never ending supply. Finally though, as the fire began to die down, I brought out my ace in the hole. Black bear stories are fine in their place but a good polar bear tale is something else. The big white bears are the one creature that hunts down man as prey.

It was late one summer (early fall) a few years back. After a month or so of travel we'd come down to Hudson Bay and were making plans to go out around Marsh Point and on up the Nelson. We were heavily loaded and travelling slowly as we'd been carrying a fellow traveller and his gear for the past couple of weeks (he'd lost his canoe in a bad rapid). Anyway there were five of us, counting the children, in one overloaded canoe and we had stopped in at the defunct York Factory Hudson Bay Post. The caretaker gave us some stiff warnings. The polar bears had been pesky lately and just the past week a young archaeologist had been chased up the bank from his morning washing. A couple of Indians working nearby that day had a third standing guard with a rifle. Such an atmosphere makes one wary. At any rate we were warned not to land or camp on either Marsh Point itself or the first 20 miles of the Nelson. The bears patrol these waters to catch any seals or whales which wash ashore.

We set out about 3:00 to catch the tide which would enable us to paddle across the foreshore mud flats that extend out into the bay for some miles. We were just approaching the point when we saw the bear. Big and white, he ambled off the tundra ahead of us and into the water. He was way ahead and after the obligatory picture taking we lost track of him. It wasn't long though till we rounded a point and saw him swimming a 1/4 mile offshore. The bay with its tides and the swift tricky waters induced by the 2 outpouring rivers is no place to fool around, so

119

we determined to keep close to shore and go inside the bear. Our error soon became apparent. The tide was going out and the bear wasn't swimming, he was lying on the mud bottom. Soon the canoe was scraping. Arming ourselves with the camp axe and a couple of emergency signal flares, we stepped gingerly out and started to drag by. I was determined to use the flare to paint him a bright orange if he decided to make a pass at us, but he was content to let us go, this time. With hearts in our mouths we waded by. Once we were past he got up and went ashore. But then began a game of cat and mouse. Night was coming and we were tired but every time we approached shore the bear would step out from behind the underbrush and off we'd go. By 10:00 it was dark but we were too scared to land now. It soon became pitch black and midnight found us tired but still wading, now against the current up the Nelson. The river is miles wide there and we were some hundreds of yards off shore but it was still shallow. It was then I received the jolt of my life.

Me: (Loud whisper over the THUD THUD of my heart) What's THAT?

Margie: Where?

Me: (terrified now) Up ahead.

Margie: (Flicks on flashlight and shines it on large white object up ahead)

Me: (I rarely swear) Damn!

I wish I had a picture of how fast we jumped in the canoe and paddled backwards out of there. That polar bear was waiting out there in the dark in the water not 75 feet up ahead.

The Nelson is miles wide there with wind and current and ebbing and flowing tides, and ordinarily I wouldn't think of crossing it. We crossed it in the dark that night though, built a bonfire on the beach on the other side and slept so close to it that I still have the ember ash holes in our sleeping bags as souvenirs.

Two days later we met a trapper who said the fire was a big mistake; fires attract polar bears.

AUGUST 8: FOREST FIRE

We tried to get off quickly today but the heat (68 degrees) and high humidity made every movement a chore. Nevertheless by 7:30 we were off and paddling and soon reached Prairie portage into Basswood Lake. At one time this area was rich in fish and game, and when the French were in possession they had several trading posts on the lake. The lake's Indian name translates literally as "lake of dried berries", but we found only scattered blueberry bushes. We had a lot of time to look for them though as the wind was very strong and we were grounded from 9:00 to 10:00 on Bayley Bay and later from 11:30 till 2:00. Otherwise we paddled into the wind, which fortunately took care of the humidity.

Our lunch stop was on the Canadian Ranger Island where we stopped to talk. Unfortunately we had just missed two men in a canoe coming east from Rocky Mountain House. They plan to reach Montreal in September and it would have been fun to talk with them and share experiences. (We later learned from Ernie that they made it.)

Soon afterwards we came upon a forest fire burning on an island but a plane was already there taking care of it so we went on. We landed at United States Point at 4:15 to bake a bannock and eat supper. There was a group of five brash young men there already. It was their first time out and they had rented their equipment and rudely rejected all our advice, in effect telling us to mind our own business. The problem was they had built a bonfire in the pine woods on dried and decaying pine needle duff and the ground around it was smoking. We are extremely careful about fires anyway but after being sensitized by the burning island this afternoon we were particularly concerned by their recklessness. There was little we could do though, so we built a small cooking fire on the rocks by the shore. There we heated up one of our freeze-dried concoctions; dried bits of beef, dried peas, and flavored noodles. It was too salty but, worse that that, there wasn't enough to fill us up. Normally we would bake an extra bannock to fill out a skimpy supper, but we are running low on flour and decided not to this time. For dessert there was instant pudding followed by water and lots of tea.

Some freeze dried meals are more filling than others but even on short trips we find that there is not enough bulk or fat in any of them. We prefer lots of oatmeal (and fish) for breakfast, and bannock plus cheese or nuts (and fish) at lunch. Supper is more varied; usually fish or a one pot meal based on noodles, rice or lentils. For snacks we find both gorp and leftover bits of bannock are good for staving off starvation. They are both excellent for children as there is nothing to clean up and they're nourishing. If they fill up on that instead of supper (which rarely happens) at least they have had something that will stay with them, and there will just be that much more supper for everyone else.

After dinner was over and the dishes packed away, we settled down on the shore to wait for evening when we hope the wind will finally die down. We would like to reach Basswood Falls at the west end of the lake later tonight. We certainly aren't going to stay here with these maniacs.

I forgot to mention one of yesterday's amusing incidents. (We are such heartless cads.) We met a large party on a portage, one of whose members was all crippled up. He was hunched over and limping badly. In fact, even with his staff it was all he could do to hobble along and his girl friend was staggering along trying to help support him. Being naturally nosy we had to find out what had happened. It turns out that he had fallen out of a tree while trying to bear proof his food for the night. We restrained ourselves and neither of us started laughing until we were well out of earshot.

Well, the wind eventually died down and we set out at dusk to cover the miles to Basswood Falls. Since it was dark when we arrived we quickly set up camp on the Canadian side and lifted the sleeping children into bed.

AUGUST 9: CROOKED LAKE

The world is changing and I don't like it. It used to be that when you met someone on the trail you just naturally stopped to chat or "boil the kettle". After being out a while you welcomed the chance to talk. I always invite travellers to eat a meal or spend the night with us, but I find now that I am the exception rather than the rule. Of course I am talking about Americans and Minnesota now, not the north. I believe the changes in travel etiquette here have been inspired at least in part by

(1) the overcrowding. There are an awful lot of canoes in Minnesota. It would be ludicrous to suppose that you could stop to talk with everyone you met.

(2) a change in people's attitudes. A high percentage of today's travellers are relatively inexperienced. Quite naturally then they are very "into" their own personal trip and wish to be left alone. Also many of them are following a pretty strict schedule and are in a hurry -- we should talk!

(3) the regulations and their enforcers. The overcrowding here has inevitably led to a degradation of the environment and the rangers are zealously pursuing a course designed to minimize the impact of so many people. In doing so, however, they are changing the whole outdoor experience. For example, consider the following selected rules (and they are rigidly enforced):

a) no one can bring cans into the wilderness
b) no one can camp at an unauthorized site
c) no more than 10 people may be present at a site at a time
d) fires must be built in designated fireplaces
e) no live growth may be cut

and there are others.

I understand the reason for all of these. Thoughtless travellers were strewing their refuse through the wilderness. Anyone who has seen the unsightly dumps the northern Indians make of their camps would be tempted to applaud rule (a), but think again. One result has been that travellers either purchase the exhorbitantly priced freeze dried foods or try to get along on a rather poor diet. Admittedly this last is avoidable but the truth seems to be that people have a hard time constructing balanced meals without cans. Travel in Minnesota and see what people are eating before you scoff too much. We could not quite eliminate every can from our packs so we have had to bring a few with us. Naturally we burn them afterwards and then carry out the remains (this is the ideal solution). The zealousness of the rangers is staggering however. We met a group who claim to have been pulled over and searched by an airplane. They were then fined $25 for having a grape jelly jar.

Rule (b) makes sense too. Allow people to camp anywhere and that is just what they will do, wreaking havoc where they stay. But (b) coupled with (c) leads to real problems. Some areas have more than 10 travellers per available site it seems. What do you do when every site is full? Crash with people who vehemently don't want you or create your own site. Until today we had made our own when necessary but tonight we camped with others and it was decidedly unpleasant. There were 13 of us at the site and the others were in a lather that the rangers would come and confiscate all the gear and canoes. I pointed out that this would be pretty difficult as there would be 13 of us against, most likely, 2 of them but they assured us that such confiscations occurred. Clearly, rigidly mindless enforcement is deteriorating the camping experience. When travellers can no longer act decently or even humanely toward one another for fear of the authorities something is wrong. The musical chairs aspect of campsite finding would be more amusing if it were not for the deadly seriousness with which it is played. A tragedy is brewing in Minnesota and it will happen the night some poor group is forced out onto one of the big lakes with a storm and darkness coming. Many people don't have the survival skills necessary to realize when some of the rules must be broken and someday someone will pay the full price.

The reasons for (d) are clear also. There are a lot of inexperienced people out here who are inadvertently capable of starting a forest fire. Then too a fireplace with its blackened logs and rocks can scar a spot for years. Still it is annoying to have to sneak a quick guilty little fire in secret seclusion when I am travelling hard and wish to eat a warm meal.

As for the last rule, (e), I am often guilty here. Margie and I both sympathized with the boys' trip leader who had his camp inspected and was then fined for having cut a live tent peg. This was not a good thing for the boys to have done I suppose, but the incident only hardened my heart toward those ubiquitous (and so far invisible) rangers. I'm sure I would have had them spinning a month ago when I cut a particularly well branched and leafy healthy young tree down without a qualm. We wanted it to use in the bow of the canoe as a sail one windy day and I'm sure this act took the prize for something.

Anyway, I was so worked up about the rangers earlier today that if someone had declared open season I'm not sure which I'd have gone after first, the bears or the rangers. The former takes the unprotected food and then the latter takes away any remaining cans and jars.

Well, today started off very nicely. We had breakfast and then rather than take the mile long portage around Basswood Falls we paddled bits and pieces and managed to break the obstacle into 3 short carries. By lunchtime we had completed two more carries for a total of 5. We picked a lot of blueberries and then everyone went swimming. The water is a lot warmer than Superior of course and it was very pleasant.

By 4:30 it was clouding up and we were getting tired and we started to look for a place to spend the night. We passed half a dozen sites in the next hour and a half but the occupants were decidedly not interested in having company. On the contrary they were quick to point out that there was no room for another tent or that with our 4 we would be over 10 people. We were on Crooked Lake now and already past both Thursday and Friday Bays. Finally about 6:30 on Saturday Bay we found a site with 2 tents and no people. We landed quickly, set up camp and were eating supper in less than a half hour when 4 canoes (9 people) returned. They had been out on a day trip and were they furious at our presence. It probably didn't help any that I had invited them to stay for the night before I realized that they were the owners. They were a camp group led by a 20-year old camp guide and we were plainly told to leave. We were direfully told of the consequences that would occur should the rangers come but by then I wasn't listening. It was clear that they would not be able to muster the wherewithall to physically eject us so I had gone back to my log seat to finish supper. Today is my birthday and we celebrated by breaking out the canned peaches and having them with blueberries and raspberries for dessert. The entire site was clearly despoiled by our presence though so the other group took their sleeping bags down to the beach to sleep out under the stars. Helpful as always I wandered down to tell them that it was going to rain soon, but the guide told me this was a typical Minnesotan evening and there was no chance of precipitation. Perhaps, but we are back in our tent in the woods now and it is pouring pretty hard here.

I believe we shall leave pretty early tomorrow as we don't wish to spend another meal with these people. Besides being unwelcome we are getting a little anxious about our food supply. We are travelling a little slower than we expected and International Falls is still a good ways off.

We saw four bald eagles today. I'm officially 35 now.

AUGUST 10: PICTOGRAPHS

It is hard to put in a good day's travel this late in the season. There just aren't enough hours of daylight. You can't see anything till 5:30 in the morning and then by 9:00 it is almost black night. Our neighbors retreated to their tents sometime in the night so we had the beach to ourselves this morning. We set off before 6:00 and reached the end of Crooked Lake in time for breakfast. We built a teensy weensy invisible fire on the rocks there and had some porridge. Sufficiently fortified, we picked up and portaged the half-mile of rapids following Curtain Falls but soon wished we hadn't. Except for the 23-foot falls most everything appeared pretty runnable. The trail makers must of course be pretty conservative with so many people around. Still we were surprised. We are more accustomed to paddling up to the lip of a falls and then setting out again directly below. It was such a nice portage trail though we never thought to resist it. There was one more quarter-mile carry and then that was it for the portaging today.

Shortly before noon we reached the Indian pictographs on Lac La Croix and were very impressed. Although not large they are colorful, striking and surprisingly realistic depictions. Lac La Croix is very large and there is some dispute as to the origin of its name. It:

a) is shaped like a cross

b) is the site of an old cross that stood at one time on one of the islands

c) is the lake on which Sieur de la Croix drowned in 1668. So take your choice.

About noon we found a deserted campsite with an undrowned fire so we stopped and baked a bannock. The lake remained calm all day and we paddled till 5:00 to reach a lovely campsite on Island 41 (they are nicely numbered) for a total of 23 miles today. We have now been 1648 miles in 86 days -- not a terribly good average.

It was cloudy all day with scattered showers but nothing is really wet. We have been studying our maps and believe that there are only 3 more portages to International Falls -- whoopee! We plan to make it in 4 more days when our food runs out.

It is almost dark now and a forlorn group of Boy Scouts just went by. They declined our invitation to stay, pointing out that our two parties would total more than 10. Some of the little scoutlets looked pretty woebegone but they had just been harassed yesterday. They caught hell for having fresh marshmallow sticks. Those rangers don't miss a trick!

AUGUST 11: VERMILLION LAKE

There was a little rain last night but not enough to really bother us. We ate breakfast in camp this morning then pushed off at 7:30. It was cloudy and rainy all day but so warm that we didn't bother with rain gear, just stripped down and enjoyed it. There were more pictographs down the lake but they really weren't of as high quality as yesterday's. We took a couple of pictures anyway though. We were able to stop on a nice sand beach and run around for a while this morning and now tonight we are camped on a second beach, this one on Vermillion Lake. I believe we have safely passed out of the boundary water's Superior

Park and are in the more lenient Voyageur Park. Whew!

Late this afternoon it cleared off and we went swimming. Now, after supper, the lake has completely calmed down and apparently the 20 miles and portages we did today were not enough for the children. First Tina took the canoe out solo to practice her skills and now the 2 of them are out paddling around. Really they look kind of cute paddling about in that big empty canoe. Randy's feet don't touch the floor and he bobs all around the seat as he paddles along trying not to offbalance himself. They can't wait for a canoe of their own. Margie and I can't wait either. We long for the day we can stop paddling and portaging an overloaded 100-pound barge through the wilderness and go back to a normal sized craft. We are wondering now if by the third (final) summer of our trip we can switch to 2 smaller canoes. It should be a fairly easy summer -- pop down the Mackenzie from Great Slave Lake, pass over the Rockies and then 1500 miles down the Yukon. Except for the carry over the Richardson Mountains it should be a breeze.

The rodents have been a nuisance this summer. They got into our packs again last night. They don't eat as much as bears but they seem to chew holes in every last baggie. I am thinking next year of bringing 6 of the biggest mousetraps I can buy. I think if I just set them out with a little dab of peanut butter each night I should be able to augment our food supply. There are certainly lots of squirrels and mice around. This fall when we get back home we shall have to go to the library and find some good recipes. I suppose there are some risks involved -- like what if we catch a skunk poking around?

We are only 70 miles from International Falls now.

AUGUST 12: NAMAKAN LAKE

There was some rain in the night and more in the morning but we got up and left anyway. Generally we like to save a cold breakfast for emergencies. We are so close to International Falls now though that we decided to go ahead and eat our last one and so save the bother of a fire. Cooking in the rain is always a problem. Many modern travellers solve the difficulty by bringing a stove. We tried a stove when we were first married but have not carried one since. The disadvantages to stoves are:

1) they are hard to warm up by

127

2) you can't cook bannock, fish etc. over them

3) they require fuel

4) they are just one more thing to carry.

Actually, if you are going to be travelling in the north you need to be better than good when it comes to fire building anyway. A canoeist should be able to create a blaze anytime, even on the third day of a hard three day rain. Of course, there are lots of tricks. I always have dry birch bark or tinder in my pack as well as a dry stick or two. In the evening I also throw a few dry logs under the canoe, in case of rain, before I retire for the night. The main thing to remember, however, is to take your firebuilding seriously and prepare carefully before you light the match. In a real downpour I will spend as much as 15 minutes or more locating exactly the right tree before I saw it down and split it up. Everybody has his own firebuilding quirks, of course, and I am no exception. I enjoy starting a fire with a match or even my well-used metal match but you will never catch me using a firebow or magnifying glass. In particular I disdain the liquid "Indian Birchbark" used by the Indians. Their potent method of firebuilding consists of draining a cup of this fluid from their motorboat gas tanks, splashing it on the logs, then standing well back and throwing lighted matches. Admittedly the technique is very effective and I have never seen it fail.

Well, it was cloudy all day with some rain. About 10:00 we met a huge turtle, and shortly thereafter a mother bear with 2 big cubs came down to drink in the water beside us. Unfortunately they left while we were still rummaging around looking for the camera and we only got a shot of their behinds.

At lunch we stopped and napped at a really beautiful island campsite. Voyageur Park is lenient in their rules and has gorgeous spots to camp.

Next stop was a set of Indian pictographs (only fair this time) and then out to Namakan ("place where there are many sturgeon") Lake. It was so windy we could go only a mile before being forced ashore on a little islet. We waited all afternoon and evening but the wind never let up (it did rain more) so we finally just set up the tent for the night -- planning to leave early in the morning. It is too rocky for the kids' tent (needs pegs) so we are all crowded together in ours on a slanted shelf on the lee side of the island. The lake is fairly large and appears to be a navigational challenge with all its islands, bays and channels.

AUGUST 13: HOUSEBOATS

It rained last night but there were no thunderstorms to really clear the air. It was muggy, warm and showery again today. We got up before dawn and left about 5:30. The children slept in the canoe and we travelled about two hours before stopping to cook a hot breakfast.

Snack time was on Mica Island (three rock samples added to our burgeoning collection) and then we had lunch just past Kettle Falls. It was a nice little lunch spot; picnic table, latrine, fireplace etc. and we had it all to ourselves. This may have been partly on account of the new sign prominently posted there. It said:

AREA CLOSED
DANGEROUS BEAR

and was signed by the park superintendent. Tina was a little nervous on reading this and got right back in the canoe to eat, but Randy wanted to race up and down the shore yelling to attract the bear. We restrained him. We were tempted to take the sign with us and post it wherever we camped to discourage other travellers from camping with us but thought better of it. Actually there are not that many travellers in this park unless you count the houseboats.

The houseboats were quite a shock at first. There are a lot of them on Rainy Lake and basically I approve. This is a fairly big dangerous lake and vacationers are a lot safer puttering around in those monsters than paddling a canoe. Also since people sleep and live on them they have very little environmental impact. They simply tie up to shore at night. For some reason they reminded me of the diaper days. How nice it would have been to have a big old houseboat to travel in a few years ago. At the time it seemed like the canoe was always full of wet and drying diapers. Actually the boats look fairly attractive to us even now, what with all the windy rainy weather we have been having.

Well the summer is slowly coming to a close. The kids started planning and making lists of all the things they're going to do when we get back. This is pretty much an annual ritual. We planned out the Hallowéen costumes, the Christmas decorations, the elaborate parties we'll probably never have, etc. The most fun though is making up the food lists. We each planned one day's entire dream menu and Tina wrote them all down. It is hard to believe school starts again in only three weeks.

This afternoon we raced black clouds and thunderstorms to a beautiful campsite (and won). The showers swept by, missing us, and we had time to set up and cook supper. Now (7:30) it is thundering and raining hard and we are glad to be snuggled in our tents.

AUGUST 14: RAINY LAKE

Today was finally a good day and we managed to cover another 29 miles. The wind was so strong at 5:30 this morning we debated whether or not to set out but we did, and gradually the wind let up and the sky cleared. It had rained in the night and sprinkled a few times today but all in all conditions were excellent for so big a lake. Today we finally met a ranger and that was the highlight of the day.

The country is very beautiful and quite complicated. The last few days have been like going though a maze with rocky pine islands and peninsulas everywhere. We told the ranger what a lovely park and facilities we thought he had; he replied sort of wistfully that no canoeists ever use it -- just motorboats and houseboats. I guess that is why he came over to chat with us. It's true we haven't seen any canoes for several days now. The lakes (Namakan and Rainy) are just too big for safe canoeing. He did have one really encouraging word. Apparently International Falls is the site of a falls (surprise) but he said the paper company, Boise Cascade, would portage all our stuff around and through the town. It seems that they have built a big plant there obstructing the river and are obligated to aid through travellers.

We continued on till about 8:00 tonight (paddling after supper) and set up camp on a little island about seven miles from town. It will be nice to get off the lake.

AUGUST 15: BOYCOTT

Boy, was today hot! We knew it was only a few miles to town and so we dawdled over breakfast and let the kids take the canoe out for a spin while we broke camp and cleaned up. They set out to paddle around our little island. A half hour later they still hadn't returned though; the wind was picking up and we began to worry. Margie ran over to the far side and then reported back with bad news. The water is so low this year that our little island is now connected by a narrow isthmus to a massive island 3 to 4 miles around. I finished my short swim and Margie was planning to search further for them when we heard a noise. The kids had become aware that something was wrong and had wisely turned around and come back. We were very relieved.

We breezed into the mouth of the Rainy River about 10:00 (cresting along on some pretty big rollers by then) and stopped to food shop at a store the ranger had pinpointed for us. Around the bend we then stopped at Fort St. Pierre (1731), used as a base by La Verendrye. We had a yummy picnic lunch there including a half gallon of cold milk. Then we began picking our way over around and though the log booms down to the massive Boise Cascade paper company complex. We found a little place to land where we could pop out and ask a customs official what to do next. He confirmed the ranger's report, telling us just to phone Boise Cascade and they would fetch us around. Gullible me. I phoned the company and inquired. I must have talked to a lawyer. No, they wouldn't take us around and we better not touch their property. He said they had been to courts several times with canoeists and never lost a case. It has been decreed that the river is not navigable and the company may block it all they want. I was a little surprised to hear this. The river was the main east-west highway to the northwest for the fur trade for 100 years, but I didn't argue. They own the land for about half a mile on both sides of the river around their obstruction so I said I would just canoe down and lift over their dam and be gone. "I wouldn't try that if I were you," he replied and indicated there would be some guards there waiting for us. I told him to make sure that they were well armed and hung up.

What a mess! We began to plan what had now become a long portage, 9 blocks, through the town around their property. It was very hot and we had armloads of boxes and bags of freshly bought food overflowing the canoe. If we had had any inkling of what might happen we would have shopped on the far side of town and saved ourselves a real ordeal. Rather than blame ourselves of course it was much easier to be mad at Boise Cascade. The experience was made somewhat worse when a Boise Cascade truck came by to jeer and honk at us: "Get a horse!" I would have thrown the canoe at them if I had had the strength but I just trundled on. The high point for Margie came when a couple of employees shouted out obscenities as she went staggering by. Eventually, of course, the

131

carry was over and we were on the bank of the Rainy River below their property.

The Rainy River was the recipient of rave reviews from many of the early voyageurs but they would never recognize it today. We were assured that Boise had done a lot recently to clean up their act but it is still hard to describe the water. It is filthy dirty, smells, and has huge floating disgusting gobs floating in it from their operation. It is worse than the Chateauguay and will be unpleasant just to sleep near. We don't want to touch it even with our boots.

Well, we had not been invisible on our passage through town. A reporter was waiting at the end of the carry for pictures and interview; famous again. We were still very disgruntled and complained vociferously about the paper company. The reporter sympathized and related some of the company's other "atrocities". I guess with a company town you don't need to worry about public relations, or anything else apparently. Margie is starting her own personal boycott of Boise Cascade products and is only worried that she might have bought some of their stuff inadvertently earlier this morning. She plans to be as careful as possible in the future.

Well, we hope to get off this dirty river as soon as we can. It is only about 75 miles to Lake of the Woods from here.

Shishkabobs for supper.

AUGUST 16: LONG SAULT RAPIDS

If it hadn't been for the rain we would have done 50 miles today. We left camp about 6:30 and paddled fairly steadily till 4:00 with no portages. The water is low so there isn't much current but the wind was strong and steady behind us. About 2:00 it began to get cloudy and threatening and we had our first shower. By 4:00 it was raining hard and the bad weather had really settled it when we came to a free campground with fresh water. We stopped right there -- 36 miles for the day -- and gave up all thought of continuing late after supper.

We bustled all around setting up camp in the rain and cooking supper, then we settled in to meet our neighbors. They all had trailers and everyone was really friendly. They were mostly retired folks from International Falls, and as nice and helpful as could be. They insisted we try their brownies, use their firewood, etc. A few were impressed that we had shot the locally famed Long Sault Rapids just above camp in the rain without even bothering to look them over. Actually at this time of year they are no more than class II riffles. We saw a snowy (or common?) egret today.

On dark wet nights like this it would be nice to have a flashlight. When it is dark and raining hard and the tent is leaking it would be great to be able to shine around and see that some of the critical little items, maps, bannock, etc. are in a safe dry place. Unfortunately our lights are about used up for this year. Actually I suppose the flashlight is an iffy article for adults to bring. You can imagine times like tonight when you'd like to have one but in practice a light is rarely necessary. The one exception may be with children. Then I suggest you bring $2n + 1$ flashlights where n is the number of children. Even this will probably not suffice.

AUGUST 17: REST DAY NO. 2

Normally we don't take rest days, but today we idled for the second time this summer. Actually it was sort of an enforced rest. It poured all last night, all today and is still raining hard tonight. No one likes to break camp in this kind of weather.

Summer showers are nothing to be upset about, but a cold hard rain can get pretty depressing if you continue to travel. Soon everyone starts getting cold rivulets down their neck and sleeves, then the pants start to get wet. After several hours the fun has gone out of travelling and thoughts turn to home -- dry, warm home. As the trip wears on we are less able to tolerate bad weather before starting to feel the effects, especially the children. Bad conditions are cumulative and as soon as rain starts, it seems as though it has been raining forever. Fortunately good weather will have the same effect. Rain is quickly forgotten when basking in the sun; clothes and gear dry quickly, bodies get warmed, and all is well with the world. Fortunately too, a house isn't necessary to be comfortable in poor weather. A tent and a dry sleeping bag are wonderfully snug at the end of the day, and enough to replenish us for facing the elements once more.

We had a long leisurely breakfast of pancakes and bacon. Then I

133

amused myself by setting up elaborate camp shelters to keep our stuff dry. Next I went out for firewood as we like to keep the fire going all day when it rains. I need a lot of camp chores on a rainy day to keep from getting restless and so I was setting in to cut a "winter wood supply" with the trees I brought back. Just then though our neighbor stepped out with his pocket chain saw and buzzed my logs all to pieces, so I went on to my next project, a long nap. After lunch we took the kids' sleeping bags up to "Screwdriver" Nelson's to put them through his clothes dryer. His wife gave us a giant zucchini that they had grown in their garden. It was late afternoon now, still raining hard of course, and we went back to start baking around the fire. We planned to cook up a storm and return some of the treats the neighbors had been plying us with but we were only partly successful. We sent the stuff over with Tina and she was attacked by their German Shepherd guard dog, dropping her goodies. She'll recover from the bite sooner than the scare I fear.

After supper we stood around a bonfire and listened to the old timers tell stories. Screwdriver was the real expert and later I copied some of his down to plagiarize when I get a lttle older. About then the zucchini came around again. We campgrounders have been passing it along all afternoon. It is too big for even several suppers and no one wants to take the responsibility for disposing of it. Now we have it again.

On days like this I'm glad we have a good toy selection. Gone are the days when a few Cheerios sprinkled around the canoe or tent floor constituted a day's amusement for the children. Now we buy little books, cars, cards, dice etc. and dole out a new gift every week or so. Today we emptied out the toy bag and still the kids got a little bored by supper-time.

Well, it is only another 125 miles to Kenora. We've noticed the leaves are already beginning to turn colors. Everywhere we look are yellow poplars and spots of brown on other trees. We really feel that we have used the whole summer this year. It's nice to think back to starting out last spring when there were just buds and apple blossoms on the trees. Soon the dark green of summer was everywhere, and now the first hints of fall are in the air. Our thoughts are turning to home, school, winter wood supply, etc.

AUGUST 18: RAINY RIVER

Today was bright and blue and the wind was mostly with us out of the southwest. It was an easy day for us and we covered 30 miles before stopping about five miles below Baudette. About 7:30, two 22-foot canoes travelling light and fast (six men each) stopped in to spend the night with us. We offered to feed them zucchini, but were turned down. They are ten days out of Grand Portage and have been chasing us. We talked quite a while, especially as they know friends of ours back home in Marlborough. They are very hard travellers, stopping after dark and leaving before dawn. Perhaps we shall start out with them tomorrow though they will easily outdistance us.

They invited us to leave our gear at their place (south end of Lake Winnipeg) for the winter but we reluctantly declined. We just can't get there in time to be home for September. Kenora will be as far as we can go this summer.

(Margie)

I've spent years in the bow of a canoe but this summer I found that doesn't necessarily mean I can paddle in the stern. We hated to stop for breakfast this morning while the sun was shining and we had a great current sweeping us along, so we decided to take turns eating and paddling. This worked fine for the first half with me eating and Carl paddling, but the second half was a different story. Carl had no trouble eating breakfast; the trouble was with me. All I had to do was keep us moving downstream which in theory sounded simple enough. But I found it is not all that easy to steer our big canoe amid strong wind and current, dodging logs and rounding bends in the river. The experience was enough to make me wonder if I'll ever be ready to take the stern of a smaller canoe once the kids are old enough to paddle. I have a lot of practice ahead of me, that's for sure.

AUGUST 19: LAKE OF THE WOODS

We are really flying now -- another 29 miles today. The end of a trip is always like this as we get hungry to return home.

We left early this morning with the "voyageurs" but only kept them

135

in sight for an hour or so. They were faster than we, of course, but we were additionally slowed by breakfast. We continued the downstream technique of yesterday whereby one of us eats while the other paddles, but the voyageurs had gotten up early and eaten in the dark before breaking camp so they raced ahead.

There was some noise around the packs last night and Margie got up about 3:30 to see what was going on. It was just a little skunk poking around. I told her that if she were to snatch it up quickly by the tail he would be unable to spray but she knows me too well and left it alone.

As the day wore on it became unbearably hot (90 degrees) and we stopped a few times to swim. We were out on the south end of Lake of the Woods and there were many fine beaches. I had expected the water to be clear but it is full of green specks, almost like pea soup in places but clearer in others. I suppose it would be unfair to blame it on Boise Cascade. At any rate we are drinking the water now with no apparent ill effects.

Saw a white pelican today -- first one of the trip.

AUGUST 20: BEARS

Eager to reach Kenora, we started off before 6:00 this morning. It was very cloudy but we chanced letting the kids sleep in their bags for a while and indeed the rain held off until about 10:00. After that we had severe drenching cold thunderstorms for a couple of hours and then straight rain. A couple of times we got off the water and hunkered down under some scrubby little trees while thunder and lightning storms swept by. It wasn't any warmer sitting there but at least the branches kept off some of the rain, which would come down in sheets. Once the worst of the storm passed, we would set out again. At least the rain kept the lake pretty calm. Tina and Randy are understandably tired of all our rainy-day songs and games, but they are anxious to finish the trip now so they want to keep travelling as much as we do. They even help paddle from time to time though I'm not sure if they are trying to speed us along or just warm up. Probably a little of both. It is still raining and right now (it's 7:00) we are safely in our tents, suppered and with tomorrow's bannock cooked. We did another 29 miles today and it should not be more than

136

another two days to go.

Today's highlight was the bear. We found a great big one lying on a rock next to shore. We just couldn't seem to scare her away. When the canoe grounded at the base of the rock she finally sat up, but otherwise wouldn't budge; just sat and stared. This was our chance for a real close up picture but I just couldn't persuade Margie to get out of the canoe. I had to be content with a few shots clicked from the bow and it is probably just as well as the bear was guarding two cubs in the tree above her. We took a few pictures of them too. They were big and furry and determined to ignore us. There was no point in even suggesting that Margie try to climb up and get their attention so pretty soon we went away.

AUGUST 21: FRENCH PORTAGE NARROWS

This was a disappointing day. We only made 11 miles as the weather seems determined to harass us. We hoped to wake to clear skies and with a little luck do the 29 miles left to Kenora. Instead it was showering as we awoke and the sky was covered with clouds. It rained off and on all morning, but a little water I can put up with. Wind is another matter, however, and by noon it was blowing a gale.

This morning we passed through French Portage narrows which have been blasted out so there is no longer a portage there. Surprisingly the water is much clearer on the north side. There are a lot of eagles around here and we also ran across a family of otters playing on a submergible log. They would all pile on and then down everything would sink. Soon the otters would pop up laughing and snorting to wait for the log to reappear so they could climb on again. Great game! The rest of the morning we spent threading our way through the islands, fighting the rising wind at every crossing. The rain finally stopped about 11:30 but by that time the wind and whitecaps were so ferocious we could not continue.

Gradually the sky turned clear and conditions calmed so after supper we went a few more miles. The night seems to be turning cold and still. The adults will sleep out on the beach and the children are already asleep in the tent.

Margie and I went up to sit on a rock and watch dusk come while we squzzled. It has been a great summer -- the best yet. We sat and

137

watched the sun go down and the waves breaking against the rocks, with the children asleep in the tent below. A beaver came out to work in our sheltered cove and a few late birds flapped by. We could hear them creaking and it was clear that their wings needed oiling. The islands glowed green and gold in the setting sun, contrasting beautifully with the deep blue waters. We spent some tender satisfying moments there drinking in the silence and then went down to camp as we began to get cold. It should be nearly a full moon tonight. It is nice to end with everyone so strong, healthy and satisfied.

Randy built the supper fire tonight!

AUGUST 22: ISLAND HOPPING

Slow going here at the end. It stayed starry and bright all last night but the wind never really disappeared. We got up at 5:30 and paddled about two and a half miles but each crossing from island to island became progressively worse as the wind and waves increased to the real danger point. Finally we stopped, spread out the tarp and sleeping bags, and went back to bed. The sun was still not up.

It is suppertime now and we are still here. It has been a bright blue, hot (88 degrees) and very windy day. We sent the kids on a couple of scavenger hunts, but we have spent most of the day lying in the shade. It looks like it may calm down this evening and we are considering a night time run to town. The main thing holding us back is the navigational challenge. People who like mazes will love Lake of the Woods. Picture a squarish lake 65 miles long by 55 miles wide. Now fill in the edges with bays and coves and narrow inlets until you have 65,000 miles of shoreline (more than enough to lap the world two and a half times). Now add some 14,600 islands. Finally place your canoe at the middle of the south shore (Rainy River) and aim for Devil's Gap, a 100-foot wide opening at the north end. Good luck! It's small wonder that the voyageurs were lost more often on this lake than on any other section of the entire trip from Montreal to Lake Athabasca.

Made an interesting discovery today; you don't really need bowls when camping. If you pour (or spill) your food on a rock, it cools a lot faster that way and you can just lap it up.

Well, we did set out after supper and did over nine more miles. The waves were still up but the wind was down and things went pretty smoothly. We set up camp in the dark on a little point a few miles outside town where another couple was camping. The kids went right to sleep and we sat up chatting. We didn't set up the tent since we figured it couldn't rain again so soon, but we were wrong. About 3:00 rain moved in and soon there was thunder and lightning. By then the tent was up and we were all abed once more. We're so close now the weather can't possibly stop us.

AUGUST 23 - 26: REENTRY

At last we reached Kenora! It's always disorienting to come back into civilization after being in the bush a while, and we fumbled around for two hours making nondecisions. Eventually everything was squared away though.

a) We left the canoe at a marina for the winter.

b) We discovered we couldn't afford the bus home since they don't accept credit cards.

c) We found that not having reservations we shall have to settle for first class seats on the train, noon of the 24th. (At least they accept credit cards.)

d) We found a campground, took showers, and went to bed.

The long ride home was more exciting that you might expect. All summer long it seems we had followed the train tracks -- up the Ottawa, around the north shore of Lake Superior, etc. Now here we were sitting in the skydome car rushing headlong back over these same long miles. Seeing Thunder Bay, the Lake, and the long long Ottawa raised memories we'd thought forgotten. We paddled a long way this summer and for the most part we fought for every inch against wind and rain and current.

We arrived in Montreal about 9:00 p.m. on the 25th and portaged through town to the bus station. A bus was just leaving for Burlington, Vermont, and we hopped on. In Burlington we had a seven-hour layover so we crossed the street and slept in the park. Next day the bus ride home brought back more familiar scenes. In particular we drove along the Black, site of so many carries. There was something dreamlike about running the whole trip in reverse at high speed this way.

Then finally, on the afternoon of the 26th we arrived in Marlborough,

139

stepped off the bus, and portaged up the hill to home. It had been a long, satisfying summer.

DECEMBER 28: EPILOGUE OF FIRST YEAR

It is late December now and here in New Hampshire we are in the grip of what looks to be one of the coldest winters in recent memory. It is early yet to be thinking about canoeing but even so we are starting to prepare. Buying new equipment, sending out for maps and typing up our journal all remind us of our venture.

What is it about such an excursion that we find so valuable? It was a full month before we recovered physically from the summer and only recently that we have begun to train again. Why toil so long and hard? I can suggest at least two reasons.

One, we return from such a trip with a refreshed and heightened appreciation of daily life. A sink, hot water, the comforts of home, all take on a new significance. (Perhaps there is in us something of the moron who likes to bang his head against the wall because it feels so good to stop.) But there is a second reason.

Once you have stripped away the insulating complexity of civilization to experience a simpler existence you discover the addictive lure of such a life. There is a special contentment generated by simple life styles. We carry from such experiences an inner peace stemming from a life well lived, which is hard to duplicate. Freed from meetings, carpools, deadlines and other pressures, life is reduced to basics. Your worries are weather, food, and the next set of rapids. The voyageurs gloried in this life and we can too.

It is too soon yet to start detailing next year's plans. The real excitement will begin in March. The spring's first flowing streams release a voyageur's adrenalin then. On the first warm day when the ice-choked brooks begin to thaw, we'll stand and smile and smile and begin to dream. Our trip is not over yet. No, it is only well begun and soon we'll be looking forward to starting out again.

END OF YEAR ONE

140

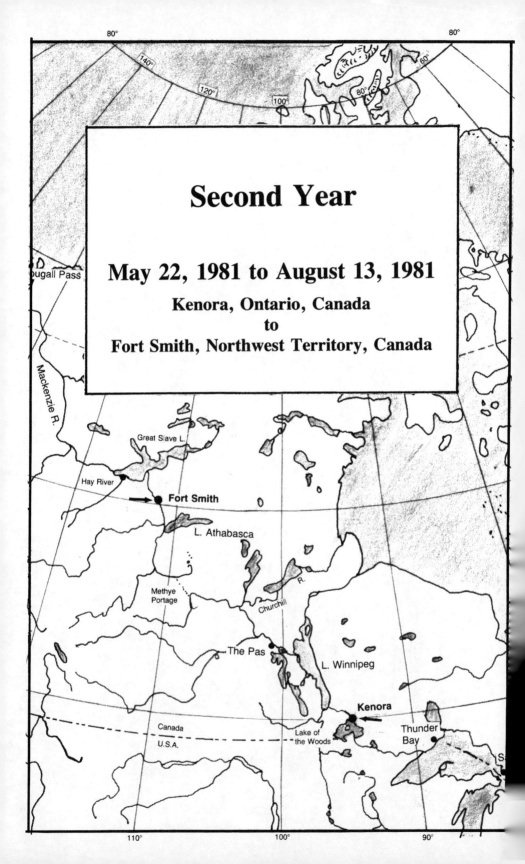

Second Year

May 22, 1981 to August 13, 1981

Kenora, Ontario, Canada
to
Fort Smith, Northwest Territory, Canada

MAY 22: 1981 DEPARTURE

With nine months to prepare for the second leg of our journey we should have been relaxed and superbly organized at the outset, but of course we weren't.

Our departure had been planned for tomorrow morning but by this afternoon we were just too eager to be on our way. We rushed down to pick up Tina at school and then set out from there.

The major tasks had all been accounted for but tonight we are recalling some little incidentals we overlooked in our haste. For instance, our housesitters will have to pay the papergirl and feed the poor cat when they arrive next week. At least we remembered to bring the paddles though, which is more than we did one year.

MAY 23-25: THE LONG DRIVE

There is no way to make a 1500-mile cross country dash in a burdened down Toyota Corolla with two young children sound interesting, so I shall succinctly summarize the last three days; they were trying.

Rather than take the shortest route west to our canoe we decided for old time's sake to follow last year's trip. We plunged into Quebec and were once again struck by the chauvinism of the French. Throughout the English speaking provinces of Canada the road signs are in both languages, but in Quebec the signs are quite pointedly only in French. In fact, on many formerly bilingual signs, their government has crudely painted over the English equivalent!

It rained quite a bit on the drive west but even so there were some good times. One was lunch on the beach where the Sand River enters Lake Superior (a beautiful spot where we had breakfast last year on the morning after our fifty mile dash). A second highlight occurred when we saw four moose standing on the highway. Their long front legs and upward slanting shoulders give them an awkward appearance, but their

GOOD MORNING !!!

SANDERS, '85 ©

142

shape appears ideally suited for feeding from sloping lake bottoms!

Thunder Bay was a disappointment. We drove through before breakfast and it was raining and foggy. The children couldn't see all the freighters they had been looking forward to and a few tears were shed. Soon, however, we were closing on on Kenora and everybody started to get excited. Then just after lunchtime we arrived. Although it was cool (50 degrees) and very windy, the rain had stopped and the children ran down to play on the beach and watch for boats. The parents set up the tents and took a nap! Tomorrow I must retrieve the canoe from winter storage, do some repairs and stash the car for the summer. Margie has the miserable job however. She must do a month's food shopping and packing.

MAY 26: GETTING SET

Today was a beautiful clear day and very busy. Margie shopped while I made repairs to broken canoe seats, rotted gunwales and cracked paddles. I also installed a removable seat in the midsection of the canoe for the children to paddle from. Finally I gave everything three quick coats of varnish. Then we spent the evening packing until midnight when we gave up, still not finished.

We saw a pileated woodpecker and a luna moth today and I collected huge six inch wooden chips as souvenirs from the former. Admittedly, the tree he was working on was a little punky but he could have put a lot of beavers to shame.

MAY 27: THE QUERULOUS MOOSE

This was quite a day and we were glad to get to bed early tonight. For a first day it was a hard one. We got up at 4:30 after less than five hours sleep to finish packing. The canoe ended up being tremendously loaded down with over a month's supplies and by 7:00 we were slowly weaving around the town islands to Norman Dam, the first carry of the summer. There we discovered to our dismay that our mountain of gear required thirteen excruciating trips to portage, three loads each plus an extra.

143

The day was beautiful, hot and clear, but we tired quickly. By 3:30 we were too pooped to continue. We are not in shape yet to push very hard and only covered twenty miles.

We found a nice campsite in a tiny meadow fronted with sloping rock to the water's edge, caught some fish for supper and tumbled into bed by 7:30, hot and sunburned. A good start for the trip, or so we thought. The last molten glow of sunset had just receded and the first grey shadows of night were stealing out of the east. The wind had died and an evening mist was rising off the water. Exhausted, we were lying silently in the tent, cramped muscles and joints slowly relaxing from our first day's paddle, when there was a sudden interruption. Thump, thump, thump, snort, snort, harumph, kerthump. And then, from the children's tent, "Daddy, do you hear something?"

Hear something! Snort, snort, thump, the very ground around us was shaking in sympathetic vibration. By now Margie and I were sitting bolt upright, quaking in the darkness of our own tent. "Go back to sleep kids, it's just a bunny rabbit."

Bunny rabbit heck! Where was my axe? Who had the flashlight? Do you suppose it's an elephant? The stomping and harumphing seemed to be coming from all around us.

Slowly the surge of adrenalin which had shattered our lethargy began to ebb, and reason asserted itself. Our peaceful campsite had been invaded by a congested moose. He was determined to challenge our presence, but to no avail. Cowards all, we sat immobile in our tents. As the night wore on we were to be awakened several more times by his peevish antics and really got very little sleep. His basic strategy was to wait until we had dozed off, then come thrashing out of the woods to stomp around our tent before trotting back into the bushes where he would harumph and make all sorts of dreadful, disgusted noises. It was an unnerving experience and sadly shattered the equanimity of our first night out.

MAY 28: WINNIPEG RIVER

We were awake early and off before 6:00 this morning under a cloudy sky. After yesterday's sunburn, though, the overcast was a welcome change.

The new seat I installed for the children is working well. I put it in as I thought that they might enjoy being able to sit up and paddle and it turns out that I was half right. They love sitting up. This means they really need less room, which is fortunate as they have been getting bigger every year.

The early fur traders would scarcely recognize the Winnipeg River of today. The voyageurs' ''White River,'' so named for its many miles of swift rapids, cataracts and falls, has been almost completely tamed by the great city of Winnipeg. Indeed, so effectively has the great river been robbed of its former liveliness that today the only obstacles are the dams themselves. Now the river is a peaceful (moribund) sheet of water, more like a series of lakes connected together. The last two years have been dry and the dams are all pretty much closed. Still it is pretty. The spruce covered shoreline is clean and rocky, and the area is devoid of people. Of course, it is still too early in the summer for most boaters. In fact, a glance at the budding bushes along the shore confirms it is only spring.

There was only one dam to portage today and our gear seems to have shaken down somewhat, partly because we have managed to eat quite a few of the odds and ends. At any rate today's carry took only eleven trips as opposed to yesterday's thirteen. Another day and almost everything should fit in the packs.

With all the rocky country around we are lucky to be on a sand beach tonight and the children are making the most of it. Even though sand gets into everything from soup to sleeping bags, beaches are sometimes the best places available in the wilderness. They are clear, fairly level, and well-drained. There is usually driftwood around to burn and you needn't worry that the woods will catch on fire. Anyway, as far as our children are concerned, every place else is second best. Their first priority is a good place to dig and run around in and tonight they are taking full advantage of our site. We have had a few showers but nothing bad and the kids have been playing like demons. The grownups' muscles are tired, however, and we are somewhat listless.

MAY 29: STORM ON TETU

Again today we were off before 6:00 under cloudy skies and a light wind. It sprinkled a little at breakfast and afterwards the wind was annoying and steady, but not impossibly strong, as we continued west. At 10:00 we reached the right-angle turn north into Lake Tetu and stopped for a snack in the shelter of the huge rock wall there. Although the northern skies were effectively blocked from view by the wall, we at least had the presence to put on our raincoats while we ate. Thank goodness, as there wasn't going to be a second chance.

At any rate, we turned the corner and conditions deteriorated almost instantaneously. We had scarcely covered a few hundred yards before we were struck by a blinding squall which came racing down the lake. It was as if we had encountered a solid wall of wind and rain and we were absolutely stalled for twenty minutes. It was too rough to land and we spent the time paddling hard, barely maintaining our position some fifty feet off the rocky shoreline. The children sat with their backs to the wind and Margie paddled with her eyes closed against the pelting rain. I would have closed mine, too, but somebody had to steer and the wind was trying to wrest control away from us. We managed to ride over the waves easily at first but then they became increasingly steep. Although the lower segment of the lake is only a few miles long, the whitecaps began to whip up big enough to come in over the bow and the children were soon kept busy bailing out the rain and lakewater.

Gradually, however, the wind lessened and we were able to proceed about one and a half miles up the lake to the leeside of an island in time for lunch. The wind has blown continuously ever since, with occasional showers. We hoped it would let up so we could travel tonight, but it is 8:00 now and the wind is still relentless (also it is raining). Typical spring weather I guess, but it means we could only do ten miles today.

Actually this afternoon was kind of restful, although cool. Tina and I did some fishing, but caught only pike. Then we worked on the children's Rubik's Cubes. Each year we bring a "goody" bag of presents for the children and dole two out every week or so. It was a little early for the first gifts but it was also the ideal day. They each received their own cube and already they are both hopelessly scrambled. They are in their tent now twiddling away and with a little luck their cubes will keep them occupied for the rest of the summer.

MAY 30: EAGLENEST LAKE

Brr! It was clear and cold this morning. The ice on the tents and tarp made it stiff miserable work crushing them into the sacks at 5:30. The metal tent poles in particular were freezing to the touch. After yesterday's half day of rest we were eager to be off though, so we bundled

146

up in winter coats, hats and mittens and set out. By breakfast time the sun had warmed us up quite a bit. Still everyone was eager to huddle around the breakfast fire which was ostensibly built to bake the large pike we had acquired trolling.

The wind, while light in the morning, grew much stronger in the afternoon and we spent the last couple of hours today battling fifteen to twenty-mile-per-hour breezes and sneaking around the lee sides of islands. We are still not in strong paddling shape though and tonight we are pretty tired.

In general, the fishing was excellent today and by supper time we had caught nearly a dozen, most of which we threw back. True to its name, we spied three eagles on Eaglenest Lake. We also saw a turkey vulture and got pretty close to a white-tailed deer.

MAY 31: THE EMERGENCE OF TURTLE

Who is Turtle and where is Turtleland? Have we gone nuts? No, only Randy. If you are not a parent or haven't lived with young children though, you had better skip what follows.

Physically, Turtle is one of Randy's little stuffed animals who is making the trip to Alaska with us. He is also the focus for Randy's alter ego. We don't bring any extra children along for the kids to play with so we compensate by overlooking a little schizophrenia. Raising a split personality is more trouble but the children need all the playmates they can find. Turtle is a little younger than Randy, and first appeared last summer. Now in only the first week of this year's trip he has rejoined us fullblown. He has a slight speech impediment (very annoying) and a distinct personality of his own. Really he is quite a character with a fully developed sense of humor. On the plus side, Turtle is a very good natured little fellow, one that anybody would view with affection. He enjoys big waves and rain and will gobble up the foods that Randy despises. Turtle never cries and is, in fact, never unhappy. On the other hand, however, Turtle never stops talking (absolutely never). At any rate both the children spend a couple of hours a day fantasizing in Turtleland and I suppose it is a blessing for Margie. No longer does she have to make up stories, play games etc. Turtle is fundamentally a far more fascinating and imaginative character than either of us. Margie and I can only stand a continual stream of Turtle-talk for so long, however, before we intervene and snap them out of it. I suppose lots of children have make believe friends but we still find it disconcerting to listen to Turtle and Elly (stuffed elephant -- Tina's alter ego) rhapsodize in the other tent at night. The four of them have a great time though and during their games of hide and go seek it's not uncommon to hear Turtle calling, "Oh, little girl, little girl, where are you?"

Well, the weather was excellent today, in fact too hot. The country is uniformly low, but very rocky, and reminds us a little of the French River. Spring is finally here and today we saw the year's first wee baby duck hatchlings.

JUNE 1: BEARS AND OTHER WILDLIFE

I was up first as usual, around 5:00, and right away spotted a bear a couple of hundred yards away ambling along the shore. It only took a couple of minutes for the rest of the family to get up and we spent a good hour waiting around in the cold morning air watching the bear slowly approach. He was proceeding in a very leisurely fashion, stopping to eat off the tops of the spring clovers, and remained oblivious to our presence. In fact, we finally gave up waiting for him and paddled out from behind the rocks where we had been hidden. We paddled silently right up next to him and then finally the click of our camera frightened him away.

Today was otherwise pretty uneventful. The morning's cloudy sky changed to hazy sunshine by afternoon and the current began to pick up between some of the lakes. In fact, there was even a small rapid to bounce through at Sturgeon Falls. A good wind behind us kicked up little whitecaps and we breezed along. When we came to Seven Sisters Dam about 3:30 we carried around (only eight trips now) and camped in the field below.

I haven't mentioned it till now but there continues to be a tick problem. Ever since leaving Kenora we have been plagued by them. They are small, flat, hard little red creatures with hairy legs (like miniature snapping turtles) and we have never seen anything like them. A couple of times a day we check each other out all over. They are very sneaky and must creep on tiptoes as we never seem to find them until they have crawled under our clothes and attached themselves. They are also

148

devilishly hard to kill, as their hard shells make them very difficult to squeeze to death. It is particularly annoying to be confined in a tent with one. In fact, I have already killed the same tick twice tonight and now he is crawling up my sleeping bag to attack me again. Of the four children, Turtle is the only one who is not afraid of ticks. His hard shell and tough skin are ample protection, and the other three have assigned him the task of shooing the ticks out of their tent each night before they go to bed.

Margie and Tina have problems with sunburned hands and have blisters all over the backs of them.

JUNE 2: LAC DU BONNET

Talk about the sunny prairies! Today was clear and hot, almost more than we could bear, and it looks as if tomorrow will bring more of the same. Tina paddled about two hours today and now both hers and Margie's hands are in trouble. Margie's in particular are very swollen and blistered; even her wrist is all puffed up.

During the morning the wind blew hard in our faces and this, combined with the heat, pretty well drained us by lunch time. Unfortunately we couldn't find a shady place to stop and rest. As partial compensation, however, the heat eventually overpowered the wind and this afternoon we were able to race across Lake Du Bonnet in one unimpeded three-hour surge.

We met people twice today, at breakfast and lunch. Breakfast was spent at a beautiful grassy site with a picnic table. It was marred only by the "Government Nuclear Warning" and "No Trespassing" signs. I was apprehensive about stopping but it was definitely breakfast time and Margie made me. Anyway nobody caught us except for a white coated Dr. gentleman just as we were sliding down the bank to leave. The lunch encounter found us at a disadvantage too. This time we were discomfited by our own New England Puritanism. When it gets hot around here I guess people just strip right down. Fortunately the children were napping and so missed out on meeting some very uninhibited nudists.

We seem to camp mostly at dams. Tonight we are at the MacArthur Dam with about twenty-five miles to go to reach Lake Winnipeg. I got out one of our fiberglass glue repair kits this evening to work on my paddle. It is a super light laminated one made from alternating strips of cedar and white pine that I constructed last winter for flat water paddling. It's light as a feather but is also coming unglued after only one week of use. Anyway I spent an hour repairing it and now it looks fine.

JUNE 3: HEAT

Whew! What a hot day! It was only supposed to reach 81 degrees but it got hotter than that, especially on shore. The daily temperature fluctuations have been tremendous lately. This morning was cool as usual and we were glad to find a large, flat, sunny rock on which to build a fire and cook a hot breakfast. By 10:00 though it was getting uncomfortably warm and the kids, who had been doing some desultory paddling, gave up to concentrate on their schoolwork. They are each missing about a month of school and we have brought along their books and assignments. Each day they do a little work on them -- sometimes very little.

As we paddle our way out onto the prairies, the water has been getting muddier and muddier. Today it finally looked so bad that we didn't want to drink it anymore and so we stopped at a farmhouse to get some we knew would be pure (we have a collapsible five gallon water jug with us). The people were extremely friendly and ended up giving us a dozen fresh eggs as well. It was awfully hot by then but there was no shade around and we decided to push on to the riverside village of St. George for lunch. The last couple of miles into town were so hot and still that we were several times deceived by mirages. The country is flat and the reflections in the water so perfect that we couldn't be sure what was real, especially when we approached the bend before town. There many of the bushes and part of the village itself fooled us by somehow appearing to be on the wrong side of the river.

St. George is a very small town and we were the only ones moving about. Margie did a little shopping (cold soda and ice-cream) and we mailed home some of the kids' schoolwork. Then we found a shady bush and lay there sweltering while we ate lunch and napped.

There were two portages today (around dams) and tonight we are camped on a muddy bank. We stopped early to go swimming and get out of the sun. Later on a couple came by and told us it never rains out here in the summer. Great; I guess. Tina and Margie wore gloves all day and their sunburns seem to be stabilizing although Margie's keeps her

150

awake at night. This evening she is wearing cold, wet gloves to bed to stop them from itching. They are not very conducive to squzzling. Actually I am not all that irresistible myself. I am lying here naked, watching the little rivulets of sweat run down my body and make puddles on the tent floor.

I think there are seven more miles to Lake Winnipeg but I'm not going to try and measure it as I would just get the maps all wet. Although the lake is notorious for its treacherous conditions we are anxious to get there, and neither of us shall miss this river. While the upper sections were rocky, picturesque and studded with islands, the lower stretches have been swampy and not nearly so pleasant. Also, despite the hot weather, spring is a little slow getting here. Some of the trees are only in bud and the shoreline is still brown with last year's dried rushes. Except for the ticks though the insects have not been too bad.

JUNE 4: LAKE WINNIPEG

There was quite a change in weather today. Although we never saw the sun, things started out well and we paddled eighteen miles before lunchtime. Unfortunately that was about it. The afternoon was too windy and then it turned stormy with rain all evening. The exciting part is we are out on Lake Winnipeg tonight and are camped at Sturgeon Point about five or six miles across from Elk Island. Many are the travellers who have worked their way up this stormy lake and we are looking forward to following in their footsteps. We read Eric Sevaried's journal, Canoeing with the Cree, on the car ride west and we have brought along Eric Morse's Fur Trade Canoe Routes of Canada which gives exciting excerpts from Alexander Henry's 1808 trip with the Saskatchewan Brigade. Both those trips took place in August which is when the stormy season really begins. Still it was too dangerous for us to risk going around Sturgeon Point this afternoon.

We were excited to see our first pelicans today. We saw them up around the north end of the Lake and on the Saskatchewan River years ago and have been looking forward to seeing them again. They are suddenly everywhere and it is not uncommon to see half a dozen together. I expect they will be with us the rest of the summer. They are such a comical and pleasing bird to watch. If they are on a rock, as you come

151

near they first jump into the water and try to swim away. As they go they keep turning their heads with those long bills to look back over first one shoulder and then the other. Somehow as they peek back they give the appearance of being extremely guilty of something. When they take off or land they look like little airplanes and in flight they exhibit a tremendous aptitude for "follow the leader". First the lead pelican will flap his wings, then the next and so on down the line. When all have flapped once, like as not the leader will start another row of flaps and so on. Of course their bright white plumage and black wing tips give them a very attractive appearance. Unfortunately about half of them seem to have a huge wart on their nose.

Well, if the weather had held up I believe we would have done thirty miles today. Nevertheless we are content. As a point of interest, this lake has very shallow bays, and today's storm has churned up the muddy bottom. The water is now all full of clay silt, completely opaque, and not very tasty. Also all our gear has gotten muddy, wet and sandy. Complaints, complaints!

Thinking back we both agree that coming out onto the North Channel from the French River last July was much more impressive than today's entry onto Lake Winnipeg. Last year we were coming out of secluded enclosed woods to wide open spaces. Today though we had just come off the relatively open prairies and probably that is the difference.

JUNE 5: WOLF

Strong winds blew the kids' tent fly off around 3:00 last night and sent waves hissing up the beach to lap against our overturned canoe. I got up and managed to square everything away and then we slept in till nearly 7:00 this morning.

There is no question about who has the weakest kidneys in the family and as usual I had to get up first to take the potty paper for a stroll. What a surprise! A large timber wolf was standing right outside our tent. He was nearly black and the size of a very big dog, quite a lot bigger than a German Shepherd. He was the first wolf we have ever met and he just stood there staring. Margie and the kids came out to visit him while I went down to the canoe to get the camera. There is a twenty dollar bounty for wolves and he was understandably nervous about our bustling around.

152

He was less than fifty feet away and our actions ended up scaring him away before we could take his picture. Anyway, we ran over and snapped a shot of his paw prints which were as large as my hand. I never realized just how big a wolf can be.

It was still windy with occasional showers and so we stayed in camp, laying jump rope, etc. with the kids. Finally the lake calmed down a little and we started off about 11:00. We got in two hours of paddling, ad a quick lunch, paddled some more and then had to pull over to let thunderstorms pass by.

At 3:30 we judged it safe to continue and went on for another couple of hours before stopping for supper. Afterwards we elected to paddle further but it soon began to look as if we had made a mistake. First, we ran into one last shower with accompanying winds strong enough to make steep waves two to three feet high. They splashed into the canoe every so often and generally made the paddling unpleasant. Then, we tried to stop at what appeared to be a good beach but in reality was quicksand-like mud. Tina and Randy jumped out first into the shallow water and started running towards the beach. They almost made it. After a few strides, however, they realized they were sinking deeper with every step into seemingly bottomless mud -- a scary feeling. Margie jumped out to help them and then all three were floundering, rooted in the mud. Next I jumped out to save the canoe which was swinging broadside to the incoming surf and so there we all stood, anchored. Of course, with the canoe to hold onto, we recovered, but we sure got things muddy climbing back into the boat.

For the next couple of miles the shore stayed pretty inhospitable with black mud and piles of storm-swept driftwood everywhere. At least the sun came out. It transformed the water into a spectacular frothy chocolate sea. Indeed, it looked as if we were jouncing along on a giant cauldron of boiling mud. Except for the uncertainty of the situation and the lateness of the hour it would have been quite pleasant. Gulls and pelicans flew by, also a heron and a pair of bald eagles, all oblivious to our plight.

Eventually we took a chance on another sandy-looking spot. We surfed in and this time jumped out barefoot to discover a nice firm little beach. The tents are up now and I suppose someday we shall get the mud out of our belongings, but Margie doubts whether she will ever get used to drinking it.

153

The children spent much of the day collecting lady bugs. They like to see how many they can accumulate on themselves at once.

The woodticks are about gone now.

JUNE 6: BLACK ISLAND

We had moderate weather today and progressed another 25 miles. It was very windy when we got up and so we had a leisurely breakfast right at camp. The early morning paddling was slow and exhausting with stiff breezes and waves right in our face. By lunchtime however things began to ease up and the wind gradually lessened.

The bears were the highlight of the day. There were two of them ambling along a sand beach, the younger one kicking up his heels every so often and bouncing around like a puppy. We were able to sneak right in and take several pictures before being spotted.

We tried to continue on after supper but gave up pretty quickly, even though it was finally calm, because it looked so much like rain. The water is getting clearer. This evening we could see down several inches -- but not so far as our stroking paddle tips. Every beach we have landed on lately seems to be covered with tracks -- bear, moose, deer, wolf and smaller things including birds. I guess the shoreline is easier walking for them than back in the swamps. With all the traffic though it is a wonder that nothing has stumbled into our camp in the dark.

The flap, glide, follow-the-leader pelican groups have been working well together lately. Today we saw one group of over thirty heading north in unison.

This is the first night we have really seen mosquitoes, probably because it is the first night without wind. Anyway they are out in swarms and we have popped into the tents a little early.

JUNE 7: CONCENTRATION

You have to be careful paddling on this lake. It is deceptively treacherous. The problem is that it is very shallow and has many barely submerged rocks and reefs. Many of them stick out like long fingers at right angles to the shore and we have to go out half a mile or more to get around them, and not just occasionally either. Because we can't see more than an inch or so down we tend to paddle uncertainly. Although the boat didn't hit anything today, I found myself time and again stroking with unaccustomed tentativeness, half expecting to clunk the bottom. Several times we found our paddles striking rocks but the canoe progressed unscathed. Actually, this was not entirely luck. The wind, which was mostly behind us, seemed to come and go but there were always enough waves and surf to mark the worst rocks with foaming chocolate. Still it was like a giant game of concentration as we stared ahead trying to pick a course and remember between waves just where all the rocks were supposed to be.

Today was our twelfth wedding anniversary and we got to sleep in because it was windy and rainy. It cleared slowly though so we left about 9:00 and paddled pretty steadily till 5:00, stopping only a half hour for lunch and again at 3:00 for a quick dip. We landed on the most beautiful pristine sand beaches at every stop. With no human tracks or sign of people it is easy to imagine we are the first, discovering a new land. The illusion was somewhat spoiled by a bear carcass we passed, however. Obviously someone had been this way before. In fact after supper we met a pair of commercial fishermen who pulled over to chat and dump a pile of fish remains beside our tents. The men were on their way back to camp with the day's haul and they offered us some fillets on ice which we gladly accepted. Their visit gave us a new form of evening entertainment -- watching the gulls and pelicans vie over the discarded pile of fish remains. A pair of pelicans would swim closer and closer, afraid to just barge right into the crowd but unwilling to leave. Every so often the gulls would edge away, however, and the pelicans would dash ashore to snatch a tidbit, then retreat out to begin circling again.

JUNE 8: LOON BAY

Today we rose at 5:00 and travelled hard against wind and waves to cover a grand total of only six miles. The skies were a bleak graphite-gray and we faced a steady northwest wind as we struggled to get out of Loon Bay. It wasn't even eight o'clock before we were hopelessly over-matched. The waves were breaking into the canoe at every stroke and

155

we were forced to stop for what has turned out to be the entire day. The wind will not let up.

We have been on the lake five days now and not one of them has been ideal for travelling. Every morning has been windy (the wind blows even at night) and only one evening has been calm, and that one it was threatening to rain. We are anxious for a break, a good fifteen-hour paddling day. Heaven knows I am beginning to seethe with relentless energy.

Five days may be insufficient evidence on which to base conclusions but it does seem clear that the waves on this lake are far different from those on Superior. This lake is smaller, roughly 300 miles by 50, but it seems to be at least as dangerous, although in different ways. On Superior we could safely negotiate five and six-foot waves as they were generally smooth and massive, even swell-like. Here though, even the three footers are steep, sharp and breaking on account of the shallowness of the water. They don't carry a lot of force but they continually toss into the canoe, so the children are always getting soaked and having to bail. If a Superior wave had ever broken on us then we would have been washed out of sight, but here the waves just smack the canoe with a loud slap and then a bucket of water lands in our laps. Very annoying!

This afternoon we all went swimming in a rocky pool here. The water was freezing and so was the air, but it was time to get cleaned up again. Then we sat around the fire and fried walleye fillets. We managed to eat quite a few and I must say Randy did his share. He and Turtle each ate two.

JUNE 9: THE NARROWS

To say Lake Winnipeg is roughly 300 miles north-south by 50 east-west is a little misleading. Indeed the lake is not rectangular but rather has a very narrow spot two miles wide about half way up and it is this narrows we have been aiming for. The traditional fur-trade route was to come up the east side as we have done, cross at The Narrows and then proceed up the west side to Grand Rapids at the mouth of the Saskatchewan River. Any traverse is a risk, of course, and we were apprehensive about this one in particular. Actually, it is only the first in a tough series of risky crossings. To reach the true west shore will involve traversing a

156

number of substantial bays and hazarding many island hoppings. The exact route we shall follow has not been determined yet but it will undoubtedly be somewhat longer than the traditional voyageur route. We do not have their speed nor their big canoes and are not prepared to tackle the five mile and even longer crossings that they risked. Today's was bad enough.

This morning the lake was finally calm enough to leave early and we were paddling by 5:30. We had great hopes that the small waves would die completely and leave us a flat calm for the crossing. Two hours later, though, we were already experiencing heavy gusts when we ducked into a sheltered cove to cook breakfast. There was a nice beach there but it was already occupied -- by a bear. We debated shooing her off but opted instead to leave her in peace and moved off a hundred yards to a little rocky nook.

Afterwards the waves were somewhat worse but, full of vigor, we decided to don life-jackets and continue battling it out for a while. Mile by mile we struggled up the shore into a strong headwind. Persistence prevailed and by lunchtime we were safely at East Doghead Point waiting for an opportunity to dash across. We lay there resting on the high rocks, staring out to sea, watching for the whitecaps to subside. Eventually our chance came and we hurried off, four paddles flashing. The knowledge that there were over a hundred miles of open water funneling past our canoe and that the afternoon winds could spring up again at any instant motivated even the children, and the canoe fairly flew over the water. The entire crossing took only twenty minutes, and the traverse turned out to be anticlimactic which was fine with us.

The western shore is fronted with limestone layered cliffs, a pleasantly scenic change in topography which we admired as we cruised along the shore. The swells were broadside now and each one imparted a twist to the canoe as it rolled under us to crash against the rocky shoreline. Around 3:30 the wind picked up again though, and soon the waves were steep enough to splash in. Everybody was happy to call it quits (that wind was cold) and we pulled in to the first sand beach we'd seen since breakfast. It's partly facing the wind, but we are safely tucked away in one corner while the wind continues to "blow a gale" out on the lake. It is really howling now and the surf sounds like the ocean. Hope tomorrow is calm!

JUNE 10: CANOE PASS

I guess we are on the right track. The map says we went through "Canoe Pass" at breakfast time which made us feel right at home. We got in some swimming and playing around noon but on the whole the weather was pretty dreary. It was raining when we woke up; it showered all morning, cleared for awhile, and then started showering again about 4:00. Almost simultaneously the wind became overwhelming and the waves just washed into the boat one after another as we tried to get around the rocky southern tip of Little Moose Island. We had to stop immediately and tonight we are camped right there hoping to be able to cross to the mainland in the morning. This is a fine place for a supper fire but as a campsite I cannot recommend it. Nevertheless we have managed to clear enough of the rocks to make two sorry tentsites out near the tip.

JUNE 11: OSTRICH

We left early again today. In many ways the hours before breakfast are the most serene of the day. We get to paddle in blissful silence, see the sun come up, and enjoy the cool calm of early morning. Evening paddling can be fun as well with the sun setting and the kids settling in for a few hours sleep in the boat, but we haven't had much chance to experience the latter this summer.

In any case the children slept through to breakfast this morning by which time we had crossed to the mainland and even paddled a few miles north. The shore was really muddy, but that is not uncommon. It's hard to reach solid ground at such times because the canoe sucks to a halt about twenty feet out and then we have to get out and drag it closer. We seem to sink in six inches with every step and nearly lose our boots, which are too loose for our feet. Then when it is time to leave, the whole process has to be repeated in reverse.

Lunch was on some mud flats just before Passage Point and up till then, disregarding the rain showers, travelling conditions had been pretty fair. As so often happens in the afternoon, however, the wind had begun to build and we hurried to leave while we still could. There was no place to camp where we were (a muddy bank covered with big rocks) and we wanted to search for a better spot around the corner. We had almost waited too long, however. At the point itself the waves were already intimidatingly large. It was hard to get out far enough to clear the rocky spit as we kept losing headway everytime we slowed down to bob over the bigger waves. Finally though we were out there in position to swing about and run in but I misjudged the timing. Huge waves were breaking all around and I guess I zigged when I should have zagged. At any rate two practically simultaneous combers crashed right over us, soaking everything, but then we shook free and literally surfed in to land on a beautiful hard sand beach. This is the best place we have seen in ages. The kids changed out of their wet clothes and are now happily constructing a gigantic sand house. Margie and I went for a little walk down the beach to explore the swamp out back. I saw a huge wading bird there and I am sure it was an ostrich but nobody believes me.

It is amazing what a difference the wind makes. Back in the sheltered swamp the temperature feels twenty degrees warmer. Margie is cold and thought about setting up camp there but it would have meant lugging everything a quarter mile down the beach. It also would have meant lots of bugs, so we stayed put.

We have sure had a lot of rest days (or half days). There is TOO MUCH WIND on this lake. After 16 days we have now been 304 miles for an average of 19 which somehow seems worse that it is.

JUNE 12

I feel like the little piggy who got up earlier and earlier each day so he could beat the wolf to the orchard. Every morning I rise a little sooner trying to get in a day's work before the wind blows us off the lake. Today we were paddling by 4:30 and managed to get in 28 miles before the wind inevitably triumphed. Actually, the weather has not been too bad today, only one little shower so far, although it is all clouded up now. None of us can remember the last day without rain anymore.

The lake is changing character again. It is still shallow and murky but there are fewer rocks and more sandy pebbly areas. In fact, at one point today, the kids were able to get out and run barefoot along a two and a half mile beach. It was a lot faster paddling without them but they still had no trouble outdistancing us by half a mile. Randy nearly didn't make it, however. Tina had raced ahead when suddenly he found himself

159

alone, confronted by a large flapping irate goose which was reluctant to let him by. We've been tearfully informed since then that, "Geese love to gobble up little turtles." I guess it was a narrow escape.

Tina can now paddle a half hour at a time when suitably encouraged and we hold her in reserve for large crossings. Today she helped us cross Kinwow Bay.

For a few minutes there around noon Margie blissfully reported that she was actually too hot all over. Unfortunately, her hands have started bothering her again though. They still haven't totally recovered from those awful early sunburns and today's heat has aggravated their condition.

We got a lot of good sunrise pictures today.

JUNE 13: LYNX BAY

It was windy and overcast this morning and we made slow progress to the deserted hamlet on McBeth Point where we stopped for breakfast. Four Indians had set up their fishing headquarters there and they invited us in for tea. Afterwards we went out to watch them empty their nets. They caught over 1000 pounds of walleye yesterday which at $1.39/lb is a tidy sum. They keep their catch on ice taken from the lake last winter. I shall probably never be able to fillet fish as efficiently as they can.

Later in the morning, paddling around Cat Head and Lynx Point, we were reminded for once of Lake Superior. These are beautiful, massive rocky points and the steady north wind forcing the lake into the cliffs had set up a backwash of choppy three foot waves. We bounced by however, and then crossed into Lynx Bay -- never to get out. The wind was increasing and the seas were running too high to contemplate leaving. We angled in to the southwest corner where there is a nice beach and set up camp in the willow bushes between the beach and a large lagoon-like swamp out back. We landed here in time for lunch and spent the afternoon relaxing and lying around camp.

The wind has not died down this evening; in fact, if anything it is worse. At supper time I looked up and spotted an Indian fishing boat caught in the inshore breakers and ran down to see if I could help. There were three Indians and they had come over from Berens River for an evening's moose hunting in the swamps out back. We chatted over tea (me in English, they in Cree) and then they moved out to hunt (unsuccess-

160

fully). Now the wind is starting to shift more out of the east, the dirty weather direction, and the lake is far too wild for them to leave. They have a big boat but it wouldn't have a chance out there. We all assured each other the weather would be better tomorrow though and then we went to bed. They are down the beach a ways and in for an unpleasant evening as they have no tent or shelter. They thought they would be going home.

JUNE 14-15: STORM

Well, I can't remember the last time I had to spend three nights in the same spot. Fort Chipewyan, our minimum goal for the summer, is starting to look mighty far away. The weather has really outdone itself in its determination to slow us down. It has rained and blown and stormed continually for the past two days and we haven't moved an inch. Neither have the Indians. In fact, I am very much impressed with both their patience and their judgment, but not their foresight. They came over completely without provisions or any kind of shelter and have now spent 48 hours sitting around in the cold rain without complaint. Their predicament has not clouded their judgment in the least, however. They were supposed to be back for work today but as far as I can tell they never even considered leaving with the lake the way it is. They are woodsmen who clearly understand what is safe and what isn't.

The first day the Shepardsons spent sitting around eating, feeding the fire and taking naps in the tents. The Indians set up in a fairly sheltered spot about 100 yards away and spent their time scanning the countryside for moose. About suppertime it finally dawned on us that they weren't eating anything. We checked and sure enough they'd come with nothing so we sent over some tea, bouillon cubes, bannock etc. Interestingly enough they had never seen brown sugar or bouillon cubes before.

Later in the evening they strolled by and I offered them the use of our canoe for paddling though the willow swamps out back. They accepted and we all set out hunting in the rain. Hunting moose, of course, sounds about as exciting as shooting cows. Actually, there is more to it than that. The moose have two advantages. One, they can see over the willows and we can't. They can move pretty quickly too and are not shy about running away. Really, it was like a game of hide-and-seek with both us

161

and the moose haring around the swamp. The second advantage is a little different. Moose hunting can be a little like Parcheesi. The safety zones are the many places one can't retrieve a dead moose from. Moose are awkward bundles to tote around and the first three we spotted were ruled to be inaccessible.

Two of the Indians had assured me that their companion was the best shot in Berens River and I can't argue with them. It was nearly pitch dark when we spotted a fourth moose standing in the willows about 75 yards away. It was raining hard and the moose was nearly invisible but my companion fired twice almost instantly and the moose disappeared. Unfortunately, it was only wounded so we had to follow up the blood trail through the bog on foot. The moose had fallen less than a hundred feet away though and one more shot finished her. It was just good luck she had not gotten too far from where the canoe could penetrate.

The Indians butchered her on the spot and it was quite an experience for me. My part was simple; I got to hold the sharpening stone while they cut her up with their fish filleting knives. So there I stood. It was pitch dark, raining hard with lightning, lots of mosquitoes, and we were standing about knee-deep in swamp. The Indians were talking mostly Cree and it was hard to be sure of what was happening exactly but at any rate the moose butchering procedure seems to be:

1) remove skin, starting at the breast bone. (The skin then serves as a huge blanket to keep the pieces from lying in the swamp.)

2) remove hind legs and one front leg (slice the heel tendons free for carrying handles).

3) slit the stomach cavity and throat, cut the wind pipe and then pull out all the innards intact.

4) cut out the brisket section, cut off the head (use a little hatchet), cut off the tail section and remove the remaining leg.
You now have:

a) 4 legs

b) ribcage and back (cut carrying handles between the ribs)

c) brisket section

d) liver, heart, and kidneys

e) one mystery 30-pound chunk of meat

It was very late before we were finished and we each made two trips to the canoe slogging though the swamp with 100-pound loads of meat. It takes a long time for a moose to cool down and the heavy meat was warm on my back and shoulders as I struggled through the bog with it.

162

We covered the canoe bottom with a blanket of willow branches first to keep stuff clean, then bundled in the meat and Indians. I got in last. Despite the rain it was all very warm work. Also it was quite a load and things were pretty crowded on the return trip. Still, there were no waves in the swamp and we paddled safely back across the lagoons to camp. Once there, the Indians built up a giant fire and started roasting meat, their first real meal since arriving.

Today it was 45 degrees and the storm continued right through till supper but no one seemed to mind. We just sat around eating moose and bannock, but mostly moose. It was delicious! The kids played in their tent all day and we passed in bowls of food every four hours.

The rain, but not the wind, finally stopped about dusk. A lot of stuff is pretty damp and we are sitting around the fire now drying things out. Tomorrow should be a good day? The Indians say they will be gone before we get up. We shall see.

JUNE 16: STURGEON BAY

I was certainly anxious to leave this morning. I got up twice in the night to go down to the beach and stare out at the lake. The moon was up big and bright and the water was calming down. At 4:00 I could stand it no longer, so we broke camp in the dark and paddled off, the children still asleep (so were the Indians).

The sun rose into a nearly cloudless sky shortly after 5:00 and the first few hours of the day went very smoothly. The whitepine and cedar-strip paddle I had last repaired back on the Winnipeg River had continued to give me trouble and during yesterday's storm I had fixed it once and for all. The handle strips had begun to delaminate where they join the blade and I had gotten out a couple of spare carriage bolts. I don't carry a bit brace so I had to improvise when it came to drilling a quarter inch diameter hole through the shaft. First I heated one of our skewer tent pegs and used it to burn a hole through. Then I enlarged the hole by heating a thicker metal rod I happened to have. There were some lock washers and nuts in the bottom of my pack so I ended up being able to really bolt the paddle together pretty securely. Just to make sure though I took a spare roll of adhesive and taped most of the blade. Today the paddle worked fine.

163

As the day progressed the wind began to come up and a couple of miles after breakfast we stopped at Wigwam Point to ponder our choices. We were headed south into Sturgeon Bay and there were two ways to go. The safest option would be to follow the shoreline around the bay. We estimated it would be about 35 miles this way to reach Clark Point which was 12 miles directly west of us. The other option would be to traverse the bay hopping from island to island. There would be four hops: four miles to Inner Sturgeon Island, two more to Tree Island, then two miles to Cochrane Island (which we couldn't see), and finally four to Clark Point which was definitely out of sight in the distance. We decided to settle in for a while and wait on the wind. The kids played on the beach while we rested and then later we all had lunch. Shortly thereafter with the heat of the day it did start to get calmer. We could see clouds building far off in the southwest but still it seemed safe to try for Inner Sturgeon Island. We lit out paddling full speed and with Tina helping we did the first crossing in almost exactly an hour. The clouds were closer now but we decided to push on immediately for Tree Island while we had a chance. Before we got there a shower had swept by in front of us heading northeast, but the waves were still manageable, and with only a couple of moments hesitation we struck out next for the last island -- a dot northwest of Cochrane Island. It was a close race but we arrived there just ahead of the first in a series of thunderstorms. We then spent the next three hours cowering from the storms. It was a small rock island, completely exposed to the weather. The wind roared and the waves crashed but the thunder and the lightning were the worst. The whole island seemed to shake under the onslaught and the rain threatened to flush us away. Margie and I were still recovering from the pressures of the first three crossings -- it is no fun racing the weather across the middle of the lake -- and our nerves were pretty strung out. Nevertheless we dreaded the prospect of staying there for the night. There was no cover to speak of and the island smelled terrible from the bird droppings everywhere. Having just experienced a three-day storm, the last thing either of us wanted was to be trapped there and so we waited for the weather to improve. I got out the compass and map and started figuring out how fast and in exactly which direction the storms were sweeping. They were small but intense and we would not survive being caught out on the water. I knew we could reach the far shore in about 75 minutes though and eventually our chance came. With the large swells our speed was not what it had been earlier, even with both children paddling, but

164

we had timed our departure well. It was clear before we were half way over that we would make it, and gradually the tension eased. At the far shore we were greeted by the sweet fragrance of pine trees from half a mile out. We circled Clark Point, took the first reasonable place we came to, cleared the rocks off two tent-sized spots and leaped into bed to escape the millions of mosquitoes. (We seem to be growing less particular as the summer goes on about what constitutes a "reasonable" campsite. Tonight's is a slanted shore covered with rocks and small boulders, but at least it is dry and in a protected cove.)

The crossings went well today and saved us 23 miles but they represent a kind of pressure we would rather do without. Over the years we have made hundreds of traverses, always in safety. Shrewd judgment comes with experience but on the risky ones there is always that moment of doubt when you ask yourself, "Is this the one?" and then try to paddle even harder.

Tina paddled about ten miles today and was really a big help. Randy burned three fingers trying to save a hot rock from falling into the fire at breakfast.

JUNE 17: MORASS POINT

It wasn't quite raining when we woke up this morning and after a few minutes' hesitation we decided to risk leaving. We didn't get far though before it began to drizzle and now 13 hours later it is still raining. For an hour or so this afternoon it looked as if it would clear up, but it was just the wind springing up and changing direction (into our faces). A little fed up with such adverse conditions, we were glad to stop about 4:00 shortly after rounding Morass Point. This 90 degree turn brought the wind and surf directly broadside and there was nothing for it but to give up and land. Fortunately, there is a beautiful sandy beach here.

The point is well named however as directly behind our fifty-foot wide, two-mile long strip of exposed beach lies a watery morass extending into miles of swamp. Really the place is not that atypical; a gently sloping beach rising perhaps five feet vertically, backed by a brimming swamp seeking places to overflow and gush down into the lake. We have stopped at such places before and as usual there was some difficulty in finding good firewood. There aren't any trees to speak of and any wood on the

165

ground is wet, wet, wet after the days of rain.

With all the rain and cold we found ourselves building fires at every meal today just to keep warm. In fact, thinking back, over the past four days there have been only 2 meals we didn't eat in the rain, and neither was today. What dismal weather we have been having. Everything we own is either damp or wet. Really, the only good thing about today is that it is over and we are all safely in bed. Tomorrow certainly ought to be better.

JUNE 18: DISASTER

Last night was bad. Almost any catastrophe is avoidable, but basically, the moment we rounded Morass Point and were forced to camp on the two mile beach there, our fate was sealed.

At the end of a rather dreary yesterday, we had tossed our gear loosely under the canoe and gone to bed. Neither of us had felt like packing the damp stuff carefully away in the wet packs in the rain so we had just piled it there on the sand with the tarp and canoe on top. Both the canoe and tents were a good twenty feet above the high water mark. Since our position was an exposed one we had taken normal precautions with the tents. The corners were tied down to wooden sticks buried under piles of rocks. And the guy ropes were tied to driftwood logs buried in the sand.

Dusk had come early. The sky was completely overcast and there was steady rain. We retired early, wrote the log, and snuggled down to sleep. We never suspected that at that very moment a gale was roaring across the lake towards us bringing cold rain and winds of 40-60 mph.

It was about 9:00 when we first noticed that the wind was starting to increase. One of the impressive things about this storm was the speed with which it overwhelmed us. We were going to be in trouble before we knew it. It was clear in the first 15 minutes that we were in for a storm but at that point we both assumed it was to be a thunderstorm. In fact we welcomed it. A couple of hours of thunderstorms would be a pain in the neck but they might clear the air and rid us of the oppressive weather systems we'd been saddled with lately.

By 9:30 though things were already beginning to get a little out of hand. I was in my sleeping bag inside the tent (exclaiming it can't last much longer) and trying to hold the tent down by stretching my body flat against the windward floor edge. Meanwhile, Margie was putting on her raincoat and boots to go out and help the children.

Minutes later the children's tent fly began to blow away and then their rear pole sections were whisked away. In self-defense Margie flattened the rest of their tent and sent the children in to ours. They came running in half-dressed to climb into Margie's sleeping bag. Meanwhile I was losing control of our tent and Margie came running over to help hold it down from outside.

About now our comfortable world really started to disintegrate. It was 10:00, pitch dark, raining hard and the wind was still increasing steadily. The lake was beginning to go wild. By now the water had risen twenty feet up the beach and Margie yelled out, above the terrific roar of the storm, that waves were breaking on the canoe and washing away our stuff.

Without thinking (I should have gotten dressed) I dashed out into the storm to save what I could, while she held onto the tent. For long minutes I scrabbled around in the surf pulling the canoe and what gear I could rescue another ten feet up the beach. It was freezing and I knew I needed clothes but by now Margie was in trouble with the tent. I ran to help her but the poles of our two man Timberline just twisted flat despite our best efforts.

I can't adequately describe the appearance of the lake at this point although I shall never forget the scene that presented itself. It reminded me of a hurricane I'd once seen at Cape Cod. In the blackness of the night the "ocean" was frothy white and churned up as far as we could see. The water was flinging itself across the sand and the fury of the huge waves was awesome. The lake was just clawing away at our beach.

Being naked I was very cold and shivering hard. My coordination was becoming impaired and I was aware that I was experiencing the first stages of hypothermia. Action was becoming difficult and surprisingly enough decisions were too. I had to get dressed. Simultaneously however the lake was beginning to gnaw away at the tent and even at the re-positioned gear and canoe. The water was licking around my ankles and I found myself hesitating uncertainly. I had to force myself to choose a course of action.

First the children. They were still in the collapsed (and sinking) tent. Margie took charge of them, getting them dressed and out while I went for the canoe. This time I dragged it up another ten feet and got the

children under it. Then I went down in the surf for the second time to rescue all the gear I could. It seemed forever that I was down there pawing though the debris rescuing dishes, utensils, paddles, fishrods, boots and even Turtle.

Meanwhile Margie dragged the tents to safety. She also got out the pads and our two Polarguard sleeping bags and settled the children into one of them under the canoe. Thank goodness both the kids were still relatively warm and dry. I headed next for the tent to get out my rain gear and boots and found I was shivering so hard I could hardly put them on. Boy was I cold! Finally Margie and I huddled together in the other sleeping bag under the canoe. We just lay there and shivered uncontrollably, determined to endure till morning.

The first slap at the far end of the canoe an hour later was a real shock and I was at a loss to interpret it. It is hard to believe that I could have become that disoriented but when the next wave came licking under the canoe I was jolted back to reality. I had weakened a lot lying there shivering and this time it took all my strength to move the canoe and equipment but somehow we scrambled another ten feet up the beach to safety.

Now we were getting scared. Our beach was disappearing fast and there was nowhere to go. The swamp behind us was five feet deep and there was no way to penetrate it. We couldn't get any rest but we lay there trying (unsuccessfully) to warm each other up and stay out of the rain while we listened to the pounding surf come closer and closer. All too soon we heard the dreaded sound of waves slapping against the canoe again and it began to shift ominously.

We crawled out and began to drag everything up once more, trying not to lose the odds and ends in the dark as the wind whipped them down the beach and the waves tried to wash them away. It was a nightmare come to life. Margie (quite intelligently) wanted to go over the lip onto the swamp edge but I had neither the will nor the strength (even a few minutes effort was sapping me completely) so we moved to the very peak of the beach to lie one last time, but it wasn't enough. The lake was coming over.

This time Margie went out first (she was enduring better than I was) and moved our collapsed tent to the very edge of the watery swamp behind a rise in the sand. We both helped the kids to make the final move. The wind was so strong they couldn't even stand. We could stand but we'd immediately lose our balance when we tried to take a step.

169

Somehow we managed. Then we returned the 15 feet to our belongings. How hard it was to push and drag our gear those few yards! Particularly the canoe. Lift it an inch and the wind threatened to whip all 100-plus pounds of it out of sight. There was no room to place it by the tent and we ended up simply securing all our gear together as high as possible in the grass atop our little rise. Margie went in to the collapsed tent with the kids who were now wet and shivering also and I made a final search of the diminished shore. The tent was obviously overcrowded and I decided to try and spend the rest of the night under the canoe but I couldn't. I was just too cold to make it alone and soon joined the others. We all just lay there drained and shaking uncontrollably from the cold, four of us in a collapsed two-man tent. We were all lying on top of each other. No one could move without disturbing the others, yet it was impossible to stay still we were so cold and uncomfortable.

Lying there we made our last contingency plans. If the lake were to rise anymore we would have to take to the swamp in the canoe, leaving our gear, and attempt to ride out the storm. The exercise of steady paddling would probably restore my vitality but what about the others, not to speak of our belongings? It was as bleak and dismal a prospect as I have ever entertained. We determined to hold onto our remaining square feet of land at all cost. Our resolve was firm but who knows what would have happened if the lake had risen those final inches.

When dawn finally came we took stock of our situation. We were a soaked and cold sandy mess but everything important had been saved -- canoe, paddles, food and tents. The wind was still howling but at least the rain had stopped.

Margie got up first and retrieved a box of granola from our packs that we save for emergencies. Then she dug out a wool sweater, hat and socks for everyone. Only the kids were hungry but the adults forced down a few bites. Then we straightened out the tent as much as we could and lay down shivering to take a nap. The few mouthfuls helped though and in half an hour, this time really hungry, I ate again. I was still shivering but our ordeal was over. Strength was flowing back and I lay there savoring it. Soon I was up for the day. I seized a big log and warmed up by dragging it up and down the beach to restore my circulation. Then I took off my wet clothes, tied them to bushes to dry in the wind and set about restoring camp. It was a full day's work.

Gradually, through the day the wind let up and the sun came out. We spent the time drying our belongings, running scavenger hunts for missing items down the beach and making repairs (there were a lot of tent poles to unbend). As the wind died, the lake receded and after supper it was calm enough to set out.

A few things were irretrievably lost in the storm but very few: a spoon, our grill, a sponge, a tent pole (kids) and a couple of odds and ends of food. A few others were effectively destroyed one way or another, in particular two fishing reels and my ailing woodstrip paddle. I hate to part with a paddle. They come to be like old friends. Just before setting out this evening I sat there mournfully extracting the carriage bolts and then laid the paddle to rest at the storm's high water mark. We all thought back to last year when we had abandoned one of Margie's paddles on the shore of Lake Superior. It was sort of sad and there were tears in Tina's eyes as we paddled off after supper. Don't think all the Shepardsons are foolish sentimentalists however. Randy desperately wanted to break it up for firewood and couldn't understand why we didn't bring it along to cook breakfast over. Nobody had a good answer and Margie told him to keep quiet before Tina began to cry.

Well, it was nice to get out on the water again after a day's inactivity. The whitecaps were gone and there were just a few swells left as the kids settled down to sleep. We paddled on a few hours savoring the sunset and shortly after 10:00 we found a beach to lie on. A wolf peeped out of the bushes at us as we came ashore, but otherwise the beach was ours and we didn't even bother to erect the tents. We ended up going less than ten miles today but no one is complaining.

Margie's hip bothered her quite a bit today and she doesn't walk normally. It went numb last night while we were huddling in the tent with my weight on it and it doesn't seem to be recovering properly. Really though it is encouraging to be reminded once again what resilient animals people are. The children were almost totally unaffected by the storm, except for some bad frights and an uncomfortable night. Margie and I were the coldest, having shivered all night, but now a day later the only reminder is Margie's gait. I suppose there will be "psychic scars." I know it will be a long time before I can totally relax again on an exposed beach. (Tonight our stuff is piled up by the woods.) Really last night was a far more terrible experience than I have been able to relate. There is something devastating about being overwhelmed by your environment.

171

a GUEST

SANDERS, '85©

JUNE 19: LUNCH BEAR

Sleeping out on the beach without tents makes it easy to get a quick start and today we were off before sunup.

The lake was fairly calm until 3:00 and despite a few adverse blows we paddled right along. One of the reasons for the good distance today, 33 miles, (our best of the summer) was the quick lunch stop. With an early morning start we might normally rest as much as an hour over lunch but today we had the misfortune to choose a spot directly in the path of an oblivious bear.

We were barely out of the canoe and were stretching out in the sand for gorp and bannock when a big old bear came strolling along the beach. He just kept walking toward us head down and none of our actions seemed to catch his attention. Rather than wait to be trampled under we decided to step into the canoe and await developments from the water's edge. That was one imperturbable bear! He just ambled on by. Finally our calls and whistles penetrated his reverie. Deigning to acknowledge us at last, he turned to give us a withering glare of disdain then harumphed and ambled into the brush in back of the beach. Since we were already in the canoe we figured we might just as well start paddling again and so we ended up eating in the boat.

Bad thunder squalls forced us off the lake at 3:00. We sat out the showers on shore and then had supper until about 7:30 when it was safe to set out again. This is one advantage of being on the west shore. These west winds and storms barely stir up the inshore waters and an hour after they pass it is safe to travel again.

We continued till about 10:00 and then stopped for the night. There are clouds far out and we have set up the tents as high on the shoreline as we can to avoid any storms.

I wonder if we shall ever have a day when it doesn't rain. Well, we are gradually closing in on the end of this trying lake.

JUNE 20: WICKED POINT

We finally had a chance to catch up on our sleep today as it was too rough to paddle. It began to get windy around 2:30 last night with the waves again working their way up the beach, though not nearly so far as during the last storm. In any case our belongings were piled far, far above the high water mark and our tents were in a sheltered spot. The problem around here though is in finding a sheltered spot. Often the lakeshore is open beach up to a narrow string of willows with swamp behind.

It is really very spring-like still. It was only 50 degrees all morning. Also we have been seeing large clumps of spring violets and clover-like flowers. Today we saw willow bushes just getting fuzzy catkins like they were when we left Kenora. It will be nice to turn west soon and give summer a chance to catch up. It has been a couple of weeks since we felt like swimming and we have all been wearing our winter coats and hats.

We tried leaving after lunch but were a little premature. The waves were still whitecapping and splashed in with regularity. In less than a mile down the beach we put in to shore again at the mouth of a unique "stream." There was a large grassy swamp out back there which was just brimming over and gushing a veritable river down the beach to the lake. In many places this lake is like a sunken tub surrounded by huge, overflowing swamps inadequately held back by little beaches.

Finally, after supper, it really calmed down and we had a chance to get in some travelling. We put the children to bed in the canoe and set out for a delightful evening paddle. There was a fabulously colorful sunset and as we worked our way around the extensive shoals surrounding Wicked Point we were treated to some marvelous sights. Hundreds of gulls, terns, cormorants and pelicans had settled in for the night on the barely awash rocks and reefs. As we passed by, clouds of them would go sweeping into the sky with a tremendous beating of wings. The sun had set for us but a hundred feet up it was still shining, and the flocks of bright white and black birds were strikingly illuminated as they passed overhead.

Finally, at 11:30, we reached a last point. The next step was a three-mile jump over open water to the beginning of Long Point. Since it was far too dark to see across, we stopped to wait for morning. It was almost midnight and all was calm so we just left the kids in the canoe and lay down on the gravel beach in our sleeping bags.

far as during the last storm. In any case our belongings were piled far, far above the high water mark and our tents were in a sheltered spot. The problem around here though is in finding a sheltered spot. Often the lakeshore is open beach up to a narrow string of willows with swamp behind.

It is really very spring-like still. It was only 50 degrees all morning. Also we have been seeing large clumps of spring violets and clover-like flowers. Today we saw willow bushes just getting fuzzy catkins like they were when we left Kenora. It will be nice to turn west soon and give summer a chance to catch up. It has been a couple of weeks since we felt like swimming and we have all been wearing our winter coats and hats.

We tried leaving after lunch but were a little premature. The waves were still whitecapping and splashed in with regularity. In less than a mile down the beach we put in to shore again at the mouth of a unique "stream." There was a large grassy swamp out back there which was just brimming over and gushing a veritable river down the beach to the lake. In many places this lake is like a sunken tub surrounded by huge, overflowing swamps inadequately held back by little beaches.

Finally after supper it really calmed down and we had a chance to get in some travelling. We put the children to bed in the canoe and set out for a delightful evening paddle. There was a fabulously colorful sunset and as we worked our way around the extensive shoals surrounding Wicked Point we were treated to some marvelous sights. Hundreds of gulls, terns, cormorants and pelicans had settled in for the night on the barely awash rocks and reefs. As we passed by, clouds of them would go sweeping into the sky with a tremendous beating of wings. The sun had set for us but a hundred feet up it was still shining, and the flocks of bright white and black birds were strikingly illuminated as they passed overhead.

Finally, at 11:30, we reached a last point. The next step was a three-mile jump over open water to the beginning of Long Point. Since it was far too dark to see across, we stopped to wait for morning. It was almost midnight and all was calm so we just left the kids in the canoe and lay down on the gravel beach in our sleeping bags.

JUNE 21: LE GRAND DETOUR

One thing about sleeping without the tent is you can tell when the

175

wind starts. It was about 3:00 this morning when the first breezes began to whisk across the sand-gravel bar and tease their way into the heads of our sleeping bags. It was cold but at least we didn't get another frost (two nights ago there was a heavy one).

Since it was windy we knew we would have to be off our exposed point early or not at all. It hadn't been a very restful night, but as soon as we could see across the water we started paddling across the bay to the start of Long Point.

With sunup the wind increased and we were forced to land as soon as we reached the far shore. It was a beautiful day -- just too windy to travel, and it was galling to have to sit idly by hour after hour. The kids had a lot of fun though. The seagulls have laid their eggs now and their nests are cleverly camouflaged all over the pebbly beach. Still, with the seagulls sitting right on them they aren't hard to locate. Anyway, the children spent a fair amount of time inspecting the eggs. They come four to a nest, green with dark speckles and are about the same size as extra large chicken eggs.

After supper it was too splashy to lay out the children's sleeping bags in the canoe but it had become safe to travel. As we paddled on conditions continued to improve and soon the kids were tucked in for the night. We were working our way out the south shore of Long Point. This 50-mile detour juts 25 miles out into the lake and is the last serious obstacle before Grand Rapids. The south shoreline is very rocky. It seemed too rough to land and so we just kept paddling, and paddling and paddling. We don't normally like to continue right through the night, but occasionally we make exceptions.

Early in the evening there were a lot of ducks and it being spring they were all paired off. Invariably they would try to outswim us at first, the drake peeking occasionally back over his shoulders to monitor our progress. As we would continue to gain, the female would eventually become alarmed and fly off to circle behind us, closely followed by her husband.

There were two blue herons and in some way they unaccountably annoyed us. Each time we came up they would make a big deal over having to laboriously wing another few hundred yards farther on. This procedure was repeated again and again and again. We begged them to circle behind us but they would have none of it. Eventually it got so dark they figured we couldn't see them and we were allowed to sneak by a few yards out leaving them to their courtship. Stupid birds.

176

A beaver kind of surprised us. He thwumped unexpectedly, soon after dark, right near the front of the canoe and Margie almost jumped into the water. It was like a whale exploding off our bow. The kids slept right through.

It got pretty dark for a while after midnight but about 2:00 the moon rose. I should stay up to see it rise more often. It started out as a spectacular orange subsurface glow far out on the lake, like some super underwater spotlight. Gradually it grew into an orange, then white three-quarters moon. The light helped a lot. It was starting to get windy and we were approaching the end of the point. It was shallow and rocky out there with a lot of submerged reefs and the waves were breaking all around. We were both getting a little nervous. There was a rotating lighthouse beacon there also and the flashing light sporadically illuminating the crashing waves lent the scene a feeling of unreality. Every so often our paddles would touch a rock just under the surface even though we were far off shore and should have been in deep water. Persistence won, however, and in a few more minutes we were safely around the tip of the point. The waves smoothed into swells and the shoreline turned to sand. With this reassuring change in conditions it was easy to continue on till first light about 4:00. By then we had been up 24 hours, and with only four hours sleep the night before our paddle strokes were losing their crispness. We decided to stop and catch a couple of hours sleep before going on and for the second ''night'' in a row we just slept out on the beach. All in all it was a good night. We covered over 30 miles and the bulk of the ''Grand Detour'' is behind us.

JUNE 22

We woke on a beautiful squeaky clean white beach around 8:00 this morning. The sun was shining and the children were running up and down having a glorious time. Heavenly! The wind was gentle and nearly behind us so we ate a quick breafast and jumped into the canoe to paddle from 9:00 to 1:00. The wind got gradually stronger and when we rounded a point to cross the next bay we found it too rough to continue. We stopped for lunch, a swim and a nap and eventually ended up staying for the night. It is a beautiful spot and our tent is perched back in a cozy birch woods. The kids went wading and played on the beach all afternoon.

177

Since yesterday the water has been much clearer. We can actually see rocks under water. The sand is squeaky also -- like cold snow in the winter. We hope for an early start tomorrow and are secretly expecting to arrive in Grand Rapids with a little luck (it is less than 30 miles away).

JUNE 23: MISSION POINT

Apparently there is no such thing as an easy day on this lake. Today was to be our last on its waters and it very nearly refused to let us go. With any luck at all, considering our early start, we would have been in to Grand Rapids by 2:00, but we were hit by a couple of showers at lunch time and then the lake was churned to massive swells. The water seems to be deeper around here and rather than the shallow breaking waves we have grown accustomed to we saw some real monsters. The kids were getting "wave-bumps" (goose bumps from frightening waves) and it really was scary inching along the east shore of Mission Point. It was frightening to be up high on a wave and look down, really down, to see the shore below us. But being in the troughs was worse. The waves were coming from the side and it was hard to believe that a wall of water higher than our heads could slip safely under the canoe. Once in a while we would get pushed in too close to shore where the waves were cresting and then we would have to try and struggle out to a position farther offshore. After nearly three weeks on the lake, however, we were determined to escape its clutches and by 7:00 we had worked ourselves into a campsite right near the town.

We were eating supper (in the rain) when an Indian came over to chat. He wanted to know if we had seen anybody. Three fishermen have been missing from the town since the night of the terrible gale. The community is still hoping that they made it to an island and are stranded there waiting for the searchers.

Note: They were indeed stranded and were rescued a few days later.

JUNE 24: GRAND RAPIDS

It rained off and on all day long today but we could not have cared less. We are off the lake!

178

We spent the whole morning food shopping and washing our clothes at the laundromat. The canoe is heavily loaded again but this time with fresh and canned food, which will disappear more quickly than dried. A couple of days and almost everything should fit in the packs again.

Eventually, we were ready to leave and we paddled out of town, up the Saskatchewan to the Grand Rapids Dam. It is a huge construction and the workers there offered to portage our stuff around (apparently they are obligated to do so by law -- Boise Cascade should see this). Naturally we accepted. Our 20-foot canoe would barely fit in their little truck but somehow we all managed. They dumped us out on the shore of Cedar Lake at a little campsite and here we sit. It is a big lake, all roughed up by the wind, and it is not safe to leave today. (Besides there is a lot of food repacking to be done.)

It is hard to believe that it was only three years ago almost to the day that we came paddling off this lake in our same yellow canoe headed the other way, going from The Pas to Hudson Bay. We were on Lake Winnipeg four days that year and it was a totally different experience. We were on the sheltered northwest quadrant of the lake where the water is clear, the beaches sandy and the wind "never blows". Now, of course, this lake will remain in my memory for years to come as the most miserably difficult piece of water I have ever traversed. By my reckoning it has taken us 20 days to cover some 340 miles of lake. That is a pretty slow pace and yet we found it hard to accomplish even that. Of course family travelling in a big boat with little children is bound to be slow. To show what the voyageurs were capable of, though, I'm inserting some excerpts from Alexander Henry's 1808 journey here as presented in the paperback copy of Eric Morse's "Fur Trade Routes of Canada" which we are carrying. As you read the following notes keep in mind that these incredible men did the entire lake in only nine days.

"August 12th. We hoisted sail and kept on till 2:00, when there was every appearance of a squall from the southwest. We had some difficulty in landing, as the rain fell in torrents and the wind blew a gale.

August 13th. Long before day we were on the water ... The wind blew a gale; however, we coasted along in the weeds and rushes. We made a long traverse to the mainland, where the shore was so steep and rocky that we could find no place to put ashore, and were obliged to push on in the dark. In a short time the wind rose dead ahead from the west, and the swell increased. Our position was decidedly unpleasant; the sea dashed with great violence against the rocks, the night was extremely dark, and the wind seemed to be increasing. Anxious to find any place to land we crept on as near the shore as the surge would permit till, having shipped a great quantity of water, we discovered a small cove. . .

179

August 15th. At 11:00 a.m. everything was dry, and the wind had abated: we hoisted sail ... a sudden squall from the northwest obliged us to put ashore at "Isle d'Encampement where we were detained until 3:00 ... We kept on with double-reefed sail until 9:00 o'clock, when we camped on a fine sandy beach. We soon had a terrible squall ... My tent was blown down and we passed a wretched night, wet to the skin.

August 16th. At 4:00 we loaded, and with great difficulty we got around the reef. As the wind continued to blow hard, we shipped much water ... The swell was so high that, in rounding a point, we nearly filled several times ... We all got wet to the skin, and our baggage was completely soaked.

August 17th. The swell occasioned by the late gale still ran high. After much trouble in loading, we embarked and stood out on the traverse for the Tete aux Pichaux ... The wind increased to such a degree in rounding this point, and the sea ran so high while we were under sail, that at intervals we lost sight of the masts of the canoes not more than 30 yards distant ... We soon found that our canoe could not stand it much longer, as we shipped great quantities of water; and night coming on, we determined to run ashore, at the risk of breaking our canoe ... We ran in close to shore and ... put her about, and kept her stern foremost. Almost every swell washed over her, and as soon as we could find bottom all hands jumped overboard, each taking a load ashore ... We hauled her up with some difficulty, and camped for the night, during which the wind continued to blow with great violence."

No, Lake Winnipeg is not great canoe country. The next section though, from Grand Rapids to Cumberland House, saw heavy use by both the Hudson Bay Company and the North West Company and should be better. In the years immediately preceding the merger of the companys in 1821, this area was the scene of several conflicts and for a place so far inland it is rich in history. Henry Kelsey was by in 1690, LaVerendrye built his Fort Bourbon number 1 here in 1741, and of course the Montrealers were constantly back and forth through here on their way to the Athabasca country. In 1877 the Hudson Bay Company put in an iron rail tramway to portage freight around the rapids for the sternwheelers which were then in use. Today, however, the rapids which necessitated the portages those many years are flooded out and lie beneath the head pond of Manitoba Hydro's Grand Rapids Dam and the resulting lake is a scene of man-made desolation.

The word "Saskatchewan" comes from an Indian word for the river meaning "fast water." The dam keepers told us the river is very high this year due to the heavy snowfall in the Rockies last winter. It should be interesting trying to go upstream. First though we have to get across Cedar Lake.

180

JUNE 25: CROSS BAY

From the time we first conceived this trip a couple of years ago there has been a section that we have been dreading, and here we are. In all the miles to Alaska from Marlborough there will be many challenges but Cedar Lake is the one we have worried about the most. Of course this isn't the first time we have returned to a spot we swore never to visit again, but usually we don't come back quite so soon. The problems we recall with Cedar Lake are:

a) the shoreline. The lake is a man-made swamp and when we were here three years ago there were large sections where the shoreline was barricaded off by 100 feet of floating dri-ki and standing hulks of drowned out trees. We spent one unforgettable day in which we had to paddle right through the night. Come to think of it though, we just paddled through the night the other day on Lake Winnipeg and it wasn't so bad.

b) finding the Saskatchewan River. That's what I really dread. The Saskatchewan empties into Cedar Reservior via a mazed mess. The latest topographic maps are terribly inaccurate there and we had a devil of a time navigating south through the huge delta reservoir area to Oleson Point. Of course last time we did it in the pitch black of night (see (a)), reading the map and compass by flashlight, and so perhaps our recollections are unfairly biased. It doesn't matter. Rational reasoning means nothing. The fact is simple; we have not been looking forward to Cedar Lake. Last time it took us eight days to go from the mouth of the Saskatchewan to Grand Rapids. You can bet we shall try to do it faster this time.

Today started slowly but got better and better as it went along. It rained and blew all last night and was still storming at 8:00 when we got up. We started a big fire, cooked a dozen eggs and stood around till 10:00 when we decided that the wind was no longer making the waves dangerously large. The morning (what was left of it) was hard slow work paddling against the wind and at noon it was still drizzly, but improving.

Late in the afternoon the sun came out and the wind really died away. It was hard to find a campsite (we expected that) and we paddled till 6:30 before locating one we had used three years ago. It was more overgrown than we remembered -- not a real popular spot I guess.

We saw a mink today, running across a log, carrying something in its mouth.

JUNE 26: CEDAR LAKE

We were up early today and broke camp at a furious pace to outrun the mosquitoes. It is hard to find places to stop on shore, but we found a little place for breakfast and a bigger swampy spot with a shady bush for lunch. It was good to get out of the sun for awhile.

The wind, as is so often the case, gave us a very hard time throughout the morning, but shortly after lunch we made nearly a ninety degree turn to the west and began to whiz along. What a change! Beforehand we had had both kids paddling just to help keep the canoe inching forward. Now we were barreling along and the waves were piling up behind us. Unfortunately by 3:30 it was too much of a good thing. The canoe was pitching and twisting as it slid down the face of the bigger swells and we had to call it quits.

It was a lousy spot we had found to stop -- a little piece of rocky willow shore behind some dri-ki, and landing was tricky -- but we were only stopping for a while, or so we thought. We napped in the shade while the children amused themselves by creating a huge grassy "people nest" on the ground in a little clearing in the brush. It was nice that they did. The wind never let up and now we are sleeping there for the night. We are tired of not being able to travel when we want to. In that sense it will be nice to reach river country (even though it will be all upstream).

In regards to the lake, the shoreline is generally inaccessible, though we notice some improvement over three years ago. There are fewer dead trees standing in the water now and more piled up on shore. Someday this lake may even have a real shoreline. Eagles seem to like the area though. Today we saw several of them soaring among the dead trees, and we canoed right by a large nest of sticks in the midst of all this desolation.

Randy lost a tooth today -- natural causes, not scurvy. The tooth fairy certainly has her work cut out to find us though.

JUNE 27: OLESON POINT

Boy, what a grueling day. We only went 21 miles but we worked very hard to do it.

There were thunderstorms in the night and we had to wait till 8:00

this morning before it was safe to leave. The paddling was fine for a while, but by noon the wind had started to increase and we stopped to await developments.

The day was beautiful with bright sun and blue sky. We took a nap and tried to relax but by two we were overflowing with vitality. There are times when we welcome a challenge, and today was one of them. Perhaps we were just overrested but neither of us could resist the chance to "defy" the lake. The waves and wind were bad but conditions were basically safe; that is, it was warm, we would be near shore, and there were no rocks to smash the canoe on. We decided to set out, and for five hours we pigheadedly challenged the lake. It was some afternoon! We paddled and the children bailed. Inch by inch we fought our way along the shore, occasionally losing ground but never giving up. We would set our eyes on a deadhead fifty feet away and paddle till we were by, then zero in on the next. At time we couldn't even control which side of an obstacle we'd pass by on. Basically though our skills were pretty sharp. Time and again we would finesse approaching whitecaps, the combers breaking fore and aft as we skittered sideways across the top of a curl. Strength and endurance cannot be hoarded indefinitely. It is use them or lose them, and today we used them. We were going to Alaska. At 7:00 we reached Oleson Point and there we stopped for the night. With a little luck tomorrow will be our last day on big lakes.

Today Tina lost a tooth. Tomorrow it is Randy's turn again.

JUNE 28: LOST

I knew the Saskatchewan River couldn't be found from this direction and I was almost right. Three years ago we spent a terribly confusing night navigating the swampy delta region where the river empties into Cedar Reservoir. That night we were just trying to find a solid shore to land on; this time the job was harder -- we were trying to find the river. At least it was daytime. In any case I botched it (I'm navigator -- or I was).

The water was almost dead calm this morning from 6:00 till noon and became increasingly dirty as we progressed. At breakfast we filled our big water jug with a two-day supply. We were at the old Cedar Lake Indian Reservation which was flooded out by the dam a few years ago. The Indians have deserted the place and created the new town of Easterville (named for Chief Easter) out on Cedar Lake. Now their old abandoned homes are occupied by duck families which went rocketing out the windows as we entered through the doors.

At least the wind held off all morning and we were able to get through the dangerous crossings without risk. Even this afternoon the wind wasn't bad for quite a while. I don't know if the reservoir has filled completely yet but it is several feet deeper now than it was three years ago and thus much more lakelike. The map 63F (The Pas) is sadly inaccurate however as to the shoreline, size of islands, and the location of the river mouth.

I'm still not sure what the best route through the reservoir is, but having done it twice now I have at least established an infallible route for myself (should I ever mischance to be here again). We followed up the west shore as far as the large point before the former Poplar Point Lake and then launched out for what the map showed to be a six-mile crossing. We wanted to pass from the point across to the new mouth of the river. We were headed for what looked like indistinct trees and land miles away. What looked like far-off substantial land however, turned out to be sunken bushes only three to four miles out. By an incredible piece of good luck though we had arrived at the present (not the map) mouth of the river. Unfortunately, we didn't recognize it for what it was. There was one fleeting moment there when I wondered aloud if that could be it and then we passed on by, following the map, to start hunting through the bushes.

We were expecting to be frustrated and for the next two hours we were. We paddled through the brushy bays searching for a river. We looked in a two mile arc northeast of the actual river, becoming more and more discouraged. Eventually we stopped for lunch although it is hard to quit when you are lost in a watery bushy swamp with no land for miles. When your adrenalin is up you don't feel hungry, and want to keep going. Good sense prevailed though, and we ate and watched the afternoon thunderstorms start to develop. It is galling to realize now that the bushes we were casting about in all that time marked the outside edge of the river channel and that we were just on the wrong side of them.

Right after lunch our luck changed. We spotted a tiny outlet with a collapsed foot-bridge and dam in the bushes ahead of us and turned up it to find the river. The river banks are deteremined by two rows of bushes marching through the lake but it was not till we were between them that the situation became clear. The banks are unmistakeable when viewed from the river but from the outside lake they are nothing more than a brushy jumble.

We got out the maps, stopped on the "shore" and puzzled out where we were. Unfortunately we puzzled it out wrong. With all our weaving about through the morning we misjudged our position by a couple of miles. We were on a branch the map showed as part of the lake. At any rate we headed the wrong way, towards the Summerberry River. What a mistake! Somehow with the wind blowing upstream masking the current and with us getting turned around we continued on a full hour in the wrong direction. Part of the problem was that we hated to turn back till we were absolutely sure of our location.

Anyway, tonight we are camped about ten minutes from where we ate lunch, back at the little broken dam and bridge. At least:

1) we are off the lake (we can see big whitecaps rolling by out there now)

2) we know where we are

3) this is a pretty good campsite for such swampy country. The ground is artificially high here as it is an old damsite and we are several feet above the water.

Tonight we are all grouchy and tired from the long, hot uncertain day. We paddled 30 miles today.

JUNE 29: HILL ISLAND

Now that we are on the river it is not so important to get an early start each day. It can still get windy but there is no danger of being stopped by the kind of huge waves we have been experiencing on the lakes this past month. At any rate we used the change in conditions as an excuse to start off late today (7:00).

While the river is a change, it is also very monotonous. It is swift, in the wrong direction of course, muddy and banked by very swampy shores. About midmorning we came across a dying pelican. It was a good chance to see just how big they really are (huge) and we landed Margie with the camera to go floundering into the brush after him. He could barely waddle, much less fly, and she had no difficulty in overtaking him.

Most of the afternoon we spent with a fascinating Cree trapper,

185

Albert Ballantyne. He's been fishing the reservoir with nets and has a permanent camp set up across the river from Lower Hill Island. It was fun just to sit and chat and we had a great time. Kreuger and Landick, who are half way through their "ultimate canoe challenge", stopped in here a month ago. Albert had maps, news sheets, and other propaganda concerning their trip and was glad to share it with us. With all the discussion it was a full half hour before Albert and I even realized we had met before. He was the moose hunter who passed through our camp one night three years ago, but that is another story.

Albert is a fitness "nut". While ostensibly out here fishing in the bush he has set up his own gymnasium. He has a climbing rope, chinning bar (22 repetitions) and a 1000-yard obstacle course through the bush which he charges along carrying either his 50 or his 75 pound log billet. The camp has a "nuisance bear" so his son runs along the course behind Albert carrying a rifle just in case. Albert also has a huge old poplar tree which he spends half an hour per day on, relentlessly reducing it to toothpicks with his axe. The water is warming up and soon he will increase his regimen by swimming daily back and forth across the river. Really he is out here in "training". He was the King Trapper at last year's trapper festival in The Pas and the town is sponsoring him in an upcoming nationwide Klondike competition. He was anxious to work out with me but I was not feeling very competitive. Tina tried some rope climbing though and finally I did some calisthenics with him and then some chinups (20).

Supper was delicious. We had our choice of moose liver or walleye fillets. Also Albert is the Manitoba Trapper Bannock Baking Champion and he and Margie ran a little competition (he is very competitive). I was judge and she lost -- his is very light and fluffy and she learned a couple of new tricks.

Anyway, it was a wonderful afternoon. He is a very friendly and outgoing person. He used to do construction but gave it up 25 years ago for steady work -- trapping and fishing -- when he got married. Although he had a lot of schooling (ten years) he never got past grade four because of the English requirement (he spoke Cree). Today he says the Cree language is pretty well lost in the area as the next generation speaks only English.

After supper we decided to push on up the river to a spot about seven miles further on where Albert's brother-in-law has a deserted trapper cabin in the bush. It was a pleasant calm evening but bitterly hard work.

186

The river is extremely fast around four-mile-long Hill Island and we worked like dogs. It was nearly dark and the mosquitoes were out in swarms when we finally landed.

JUNE 30: HEAT

The weather inland off the big lakes can be really oppressive and today was hot! hot! hot!

We left early from the cabin and for a while the travelling was pleasant. The current was strong but there was a southwest wind usually behind us which helped a great deal. As the day began to heat up we took half hour breaks for morning snack, lunch, and afternoon snack. There was nowhere to get out on shore so each time we tied up in the shade of an overhanging bush to avoid the worst of the sun. Margie has gone back to wearing gloves all the time to protect her hands and is considering getting help for them in The Pas.

This afternoon the wind eventually died and the temperature rose into the upper eighties. With the swampy shores, there was no place to stop and swim, and we just sweltered along. We rinsed our tee-shirts and put them back on wet. We filled our hats with water and put them on. We took off the rest of our clothes and dunked them also. Nothing helped. Part of the problem was we were so thirsty. We were out of drinking water and didn't quite dare drink the river, it seemed so polluted. Fortunately we were getting near a spot we had camped at before. We knew we would find water there and in fact we have ended up spending the night there.

As it turns out the water here doesn't look as good as we remembered (it is a stagnant green) but no one has gotten sick yet and it has been a couple of hours since we started drinking it. We are sitting here in the tents lathered with sweat, "enduring" till the sun goes down around 10:00 (there are too many mosquitoes outside). The children are particularly hot and miserable -- especially Tina. She wears a body brace for her scoliosis and on days like this she really suffers.

We are quite pleased with our progress up the river, however, and are anxious to reach The Pas tomorrow for a little shopping. Despite the heavy current we have been doing over 20 miles a day.

JULY 1: THE PAS

We arrived at The Pas by lunch time today and it was only then that the significance of the date dawned on us. It is a national holiday in Canada and all the stores are closed. What's more, we can't mail any letters home as the postal workers are out on strike! At least we found an open garage and tanked up on fresh water -- two days worth in the jugs and another day's worth in our stomachs. We felt like camels bloating up but it was good to be saturated once more. Afterwards we sloshed into an open corner store and bought the bare necessities for another few days of travel (mostly comic books). With that done we moved up the river a couple of miles to set up on a little mud bank.

Good camping sites are virtually nonexistent in this country and the mosquitoes are terrible. The morning was hot and sunny but the last few hours it has poured thundershowers and most of our stuff is pretty damp.

We were disappointed not being able to do a real food shopping today. After a week of looking forward to fresh fruit, milk, meat, and a cold drink we hated to leave empty-handed. We even thought about sitting in town till the stores open tomorrow, but reluctantly decided to pass on. It is not much more than another eighty miles to Cumberland House and even though it is a few miles out of our way we shall make a point of going in there.

JULY 2: UP THE SASKATCHEWAN

Today was a wonderful day for travelling and with five weeks of paddling behind us we had the conditioning to capitalize on it. We travelled from 6:00 this morning till 9:30 this evening with only a rest at supper.

Basically it was slow, hot, miserable work though. The current was relentlessly steady against us. The river is abnormally high and swift this year and we found ourselves crossing from side to side trying to search out the weaker currents. Also the water is so high there is virtually no place to land. The willows are standing knee deep in the water and at each break we would simply tie up to the brush and eat in the canoe. We saw a couple of moose and heard several others thrashing in the undergrowth. The biggest problem was the mosquitoes. They are terribly thick. The day was hot and calm and they just buzzed around us incessantly.

188

The current was too strong for us to get out in the middle away from them, and creeping along the shore we couldn't come close to outrunning them. We put on gloves and headnets and plodded on, but it is hard to defend yourself while you are paddling. The children amused themselves by getting out the drinking cups to see who could fill one first with dead mosquito carcasses. We thought a picture of a plateful would make an interesting addition to some of our trail menu photos.

Well, despite my complaints, it was a good day. Steady persistence can be its own reward and today we chewed off 28 miles of river.

We saw a lot of owls today.

JULY 3: TEARING RIVER

Today was a carbon copy of yesterday. A hot, hard, dawn to dusk grueling day in which we covered another 28 miles.

There were more moose, more owls, more mud, more current, more mosquitoes and no place to stop. We couldn't get out anywhere to rest or swim due to a combination of impossible country and hordes of mosquitoes. In fact we even ate a cold supper of Spam, canned corn and cherries in the canoe and just kept on paddling. Eventually we reached a spot of high ground -- an unoccupied Indian camp -- and stopped for the night.

There were some highlights. We crossed another time zone and entered Saskatchewan Province. Tonight we are at the mouth of the Tearing River and with an early start we hope to get into Cumberland House tomorrow. Food shopping at last!

We hope to be out of this prairie mud and onto the Canadian Shield in about a week.

JULY 4: CUMBERLAND HOUSE

We left camp at 6:30 this morning and six hours later we were at the head of the Tearing River, on Cumberland Lake. The river had some pretty swift places and more than once we had to get out and drag up little rapids. The worst though was the bullrushes. I misnavigated in an islandy stretch and poled up through some rapids to a swamplet. Rather

189

than retreat, however, I got out and pulled us through the rushes to the next stretch of clear water. There were about 200 yards of cattails to penetrate and it was decidedly difficult work. They were so thick I could almost walk on them, but not quite. Instead, each step took me in over my waist, and I spent half my efforts in extricating my feet, the other half in lunging the canoe along. Aside from that though the river was quite pleasant. It was surprisingly clear and we greedily drank gallons and refilled our water supply.

It was lunch time when we reached the lake and, despite the wind, visibility was pretty poor. There is a forest fire around here somewhere and a thick haze of smoke obscured the far shore making it hard to see more than a couple of miles.

Despite the wind and waves on the lake we decided to paddle in to Cumberland House to do a little shopping, and we received a few surprises:

(1) Even though it is Saturday all the stores are closed.

(2) They are having a four-day canoe festival here.

(3) Our friend Albert Ballantyne is here for the races and he was surprised to see we had gotten this far already; it was like a little reunion and he introduced us around.

(4) Albert's brother-in-law is here also. We got to meet him for the first time and told him we had spent a night at his trapper cabin. It was just a few days back that he decided to enter these races and a couple of days ago he thought he had better practice. He put 200 pounds of rocks (no gear or food) into his canoe and went out for a little spin. He was having such a good time though that before he knew it he had gone thirty miles downstream and had to spend the night in the bush. I gather the whole thing was a pretty good joke on his wife who thought he had just stepped out for a few minutes before lunch.

This afternoon was very pleasant. It was a chance to put on our sneakers (instead of boots) and walk around on dry land. We watched the races and spent some time talking as word got around where we had come from. Randy took it upon himself to entertain. For a six-year-old he is very talkative and outgoing. He came and got our map of Canada and soon he was spread out on the ground with several Indian families gathered all around. I'm not sure what all went on but he was quite busy for several hours. It was a very agreeable arrangement for Randy as they kept plying him with food and drinks and he somehow came back with $2.00. Needless to say Tina was jealous, but she was slightly mollified with a strawberry soda.

190

Tonight we are camping on the beach in front of the settlement. I wonder how many voyageurs have slept here. Just before we retired the local RCMP drove up and told us not to worry. They would be up patrolling till 4:00 and would keep drunken Indians from bothering our camp. They were being helpfully reassuring but somehow their words had the opposite effect.

We saw two moose today on the Tearing River.

JULY 5: NAMEW LAKE

Today was another hot clear day. The mosquitoes were terribly bad when we got up but later on they disappeared.

We considered spending the day at Cumberland House to watch, and maybe enter, a race or two. We had been offered the use of a racing canoe and it would have been a good excuse to stay till Monday when the stores open. In the end though we decided to spend our energy getting one day closer to Alaska and we were paddling out the channel to Cumberland Lake by sunup. We retraced the three miles to the Tearing River, then turned northeast heading for Sturgeon Landing thirty miles away at the mouth of the Sturgeon Weir River.

We paddled through several miles of shallow, weed-strewn lake and gradually the country began to change for the better. We crossed Cumberland, Cross and most of Namew Lake and the swamp and bullrushes seem to be pretty much behind us now. We saw a lot of huge limestone outcroppings and stopped twice to go swimming, once at some beautiful clean ledges where we could dive directly into the water. The water is the clearest we have seen all summer and we even see occasional stands of spruce now. Just a few more days and we shall be on the Canadian Shield.

We paddled 33 miles but didn't make it to Sturgeon Landing. Somehow we left Margie's hat on an island and had to double back for it later. Still we are on a point only four miles from the river and shall pop in early tomorrow.

191

JULY 6: STURGEON LANDING

Today was disappointing but restful. It started raining and blowing last night and it wasn't till late this afternoon that it was safe to leave. We slept late, played in camp and napped. We almost never have regrets but it is a shame we couldn't do the last four miles of Namew Lake yesterday. It would have been nice to spend today ascending the Sturgeon Weir River rather than watching the breakers crash along our lake shore.

A herd of rabbits ran wild all around our tents last night. Leaping and thumping they would zig-zag through our campsite and it was very entertaining. Unfortunately, come morning, there was one little baby bunny huddling in the bushes all by himself. He was only four inches long and must have gotten left out when all the other bunnies were put to bed. Anyway, the children had fun cuddling him. They tried to feed him milk, carrots and wild strawberries but he wasn't having any.

The children were all set to bail as we paddled into Sturgeon Landing this evening and were a little disappointed by our "masterful" handling of the canoe. Pretty soon they got tired of waiting to be splashed and dropped off to sleep. Naturally, an uncontrollable wave took just that opportunity to break all over them and bring Tina splutteringly awake (we felt guilty).

Sturgeon Landing is not a town -- it is a campground and a store. We were going to splurge and pay to stay but rules were "no fires". We don't carry a stove so we ended up having to establish ourselves for free 150 feet across the river where we built a little bonfire (it was drizzling a little). There were some Americans at the campground and we took the chance to send out a packet of mail with them since the postal strike is still on. The children are still irresistible I guess and each managed to acquire a big bag of candy from well wishing campers, so they are well-supplied for another week. The store was pretty small but Margie was able to pick up a few (expensive!) odds and ends of food. I tried to get information about the river from the residents but no one had anything helpful to say. We shall be on the river for the next 140 miles and frankly it looks terrible from here. I mean it looks nice but not for canoeing. Down here at the mouth it is not much more than a big stream and as far up as I can see are shallow rapids. I was told people have come down it but the idea of going up it to the source was a new one on them. How times change! One hundred fifty years ago this river was part of the highway north to Lake Athabasca. According to Eric Morse the voyageurs refererd to it as the "Riviere Maligne" and Mackenzie characterized it as "an almost continual rapid". I wonder how long it takes to wade 140 miles.

JULY 7: STURGEON WEIR RIVER

Today we started up the Sturgeon Weir. It must be a beautiful river to come down -- it's all rapids. We started right off wading the first few miles and waded off and on all day long. The first wade of the day is always the hardest. My body rebels at getting into the cold water in the early morning. Soon though we were sweating hard as we worked the canoe along, and the first dunkings were forgotten. Really it was a pretty good day to be in the water, hot with only a few showers. The rapids were many but they were mostly "navigable" and there was only one long one above the junction with the Goose River that we had to portage. We are expecting about 100 more portages though between here and Fort Chipewyan.

The country is continuing to improve. Tonight we are camped on real rock beneath spruce trees, a very nice site. There is a little rapid out front and we are having walleye for supper. Tomorrow we expect to reach Amisk Lake which marks the beginning of the Canadian Shield.

The children were very good today. We found a nice place to swim early in the afternoon and they had fun splashing around in the gravel and fast water. Swimming in moving water is still a new experience for them and their unexpected bouyancy added to the fun. The rest of the day they entertained themselves with their accumulated books and games. Later on we staged a picture. We set Tina out on a rock with the camera and then laboriously waded the canoe up the rapid past her. Documentation for our photo album.

JULY 8: AMISK LAKE

It was cold this morning and once again we were reluctant to get out there and start wading. Instead we had breakfast in bed and waited for the sun to get up over the trees so it would at least look warmer.

There was a strong wind at our backs which enabled us to pole and paddle up the first set of rapids, but it wasn't easy. We would be paddling furiously and pushing against the bottom to maneuver between the rocks and progress against the current. Then we'd get a sudden gust of wind and the rocks would appear to leap sideways at us, or even "move" upstream. Margie felt disoriented and it was only by glancing at the shore that she could tell how much we were moving or in what direction. At least we were gradually moving upstream, but our luck couldn't last. We were wading by 7:30 and for the next three hours we alternated wading and paddling till we reached Amisk Lake. It was a cold morning and the water coming out of the lake was really frigid. The river bottom was good walking -- a flat limestone shelf -- but the water numbed our legs and we were uncomfortably cold by the time we reached the road terminus at the beginning of the lake. At one time the road crossed the river there to an old mining camp in the bush a mile or so west. Now, however, the settlement is gone and the bridge with it. There is a commemorative plaque and picnic shelter at the terminus and we stopped there to rest and wait for better conditions before attempting to cross the lake.

The weather was windy, cold and sprinkling, and before the day was over the wind had increased until it was gusting over 40 mph. It is no more than twelve miles across the lake to the next segment of river but even large motorboats would have been hard put to go out there today. We were in a poplar grove and by midafternoon the wind was starting to break them off. Popping poplars! With a sound like a gunshot, they would just snap off about twenty feet up and fall at our feet. This happened three times this afternoon and it was quite disconcerting. The fallen tops were over a foot in diameter and wreaked havoc with our nerves. We had never experienced anything like it.

Margie gets hurt every year and today was the day. We are headed into a stretch now which will probably total 100 portages in the next month (one of them 13 miles long) and today she sprained her ankle at our rest stop. What bad luck. Technically we were still on the river (although we could see the lake) and the water was very rocky and swift. I knew I couldn't launch and load the canoe alone in such a turbulent stretch so after supper we packed up and I portaged everything half a mile down the road to Dean and Bonnie Tait's Cabins on the lake. With all my running back and forth the kids and I still got there well before Margie who was having a pretty miserable time of it trying to hobble-hop down the road with the paddles as crutches.

194

Once there we got a tremendous welcome. The Taits wouldn't let us pay to use their campground and offered us hot showers and homemade ice cream. There were two nurses there also and they inspected Margie, confirming her diagnosis and congratulating her on the fine bandaging job. Those first aid courses pay off again.

Now for the best part. Dean gave us the finest souvenir one could ever hope to see -- a birch bark chewing by Angelique. She is quite possibly the last practitioner of this ancient art and lives on an island out in Amisk Lake. She takes a square of birch bark and with her teeth chews it into a beautiful design. Ours is a six inch square containing a fully detailed symmetric flower. In the old days these chewings would be temporarily sewn to a garment as a pattern for bead-work. Once the beads were on, the pattern could be ripped away. They serve no practical purpose now of course, but their delicate beauty is an entrancing reminder of things past.

Later on we were invited in for wine and to hear the weather report. "Moderate" winds are forecast for tomorrow and the Tait's suggest we leave very early, or not at all.

JULY 9: SPRUCE RAPIDS

The wind was strong again today but at least the poplars weren't snapping off anymore. This morning they lay on the ground everywhere as testimony to the power of yesterday's storm; with so much manna from heaven the beavers will be able to rest their choppers for weeks to come.

Although the wind had moderated it was still bad enough that we could barely progress. Despite the difficulties, however, we managed to cross the lake by noon, at the expense of a few extra miles, by snuggling along the shoreline. It was really quite a long stint though as we had started out from camp at 4:30.

After lunch we paddled up against the current as far as Spruce Rapids, the first portage, where we have stopped for the night. For the first time this year there is real evidence that others have passed this way. There is a good trail, fireplace and tentsites. Also a lot of garbage. The fishing is pretty good though and we are having walleye for supper.

I tend to forget how much Margie carries on the portages until

195

something like her sprained ankle comes along. It really zapped my stamina to have to make four to five round trips this afternoon.

JULY 10: SCOOP RAPIDS

There is good news today. Although Margie's ankle is still swollen all around she reports it is beginning to feel a little better. She is hoping it will show big improvements in the next few days.

It was a grey day, mostly overcast, and blissfully calm compared to the last two days. This morning's obstacle was Snake Rapids where we portaged about a mile to avoid three rapids marked on our map. It was a nice trail, level, and well-used. Still, no portage that length is easy.

This afternoon we were paddling steadily, fighting our way up against the constant current, when we met two fairly well-loaded canoes drifting down the stream. It looked like fathers and sons out for a few days' paddle. They had a lot of new equipment and I gather it was their first wilderness trip. They were lazing along and frankly they could not have chosen more beautiful country for such an outing. The river is narrow and steady, hemmed in by steep rock walls and stands of spruce.

Tonight we are camped at Scoop Rapids which seems to be the local hangout for birds. It is like a little falls here and it's fun to watch the pelicans go bobbing through the standing waves at the base to join their buddies on a rock across the river.

We found a nice new four-man tent and a bottle of bug spray here almost hidden in the tall grass at the end of the portage trail. We presume the people we met today somehow forgot them. If so they will spend an unpleasant night as the mosquitoes are out in force. We are betting though that they will not have the heart to retrace their miles upstream to fetch them back.

JULY 11: CORNEILLE LAKE

Another nice day today. The weather has been really pretty good the last few weeks. It has started to turn a little cooler and the mosquitoes are nowhere near as bad as they were back on the Saskatchewan. The

196

country too is pleasing, rocky and picturesque. Really it is only the wind and the current which gives us trouble. With respect to the wind we gather it has been a highly unusual month in these parts with strong breezes virtually every day. The current of course we knew about before we came. We have hundreds of upstream miles ahead of us though and we shall cope as did those who came before us.

Today we pushed on another twenty miles, occasionally against stiff little rapids. We lined once, portaged twice and tonight we are camped on the carry into Corneille Lake. We like to camp on portages whenever possible since it eliminates one unloading. If the portage is short, you hardly notice that you have done it as you go about setting up camp, swimming, etc. Gradually we are forcing our way up the Sturgeon Weir and tomorrow we hope to reach Pelican Narrows. Two more days after that should bring us to the stagnant swamp where this river originates. There we shall "hop" across Frog Portage to the Churchill River.

The fishing is very good here and we have pulled in about a dozen pike with each of the children catching a couple. Next year though they have to learn to take them off the hook.

JULY 12: PELICAN NARROWS

We got up early and paddled on to the next portage where we stopped for a leisurely two-hour break to fish in the rapids, portage, and cook breakfast. Since the storm on Lake Winnipeg we have been travelling without a grill and all our fish are baked on green sticks nowadays. It was Tina's turn to start the fire and she used up the accessible matches, which gave me the chance to practice with my metal match. I carry this flint-like device with me always in case of emergency and it is amazing how easy it is to strike a fire with one. Still it is good to practice once in awhile.

Before carrying the canoe across Margie and I went out to dipsydoodle around in the lower rapids. There was a destroyed canoe lodged midstream on the rocks out there and we wanted to get a good picture of it.

We stopped later on for a couple of swim-rest breaks but otherwise it was a pretty busy day. We stopped in at Pelican Narrows about 4:30 but it is Sunday and the big Hudson Bay Company store was closed, so we settled for a small variety store. (We have never had such a bad streak

197

of luck with stores.) Afterwards we continued on to camp at the Medicine Rapids Portage around 9:30. This evening I think we paddled through some of the most beautiful country I have ever seen. It was a glorious sunset and the contrast with the gem-blue lakes and rolling spruce-covered hills was breath-taking.

Margie's ankle is slowly improving.

We saw a deer today -- "springers" the Indians call them. We also covered another 27 miles.

JULY 13: FROG PORTAGE

The disadvantage to sleeping at a portage is that travellers may pass through your camp at any time. We are used to that but still it startled us to be awakened long before sunup by some partially sober Indians. Our surprise guests had left Stanley Mission yesterday afternoon in their motorboat and were now headed in to Pelican Narrows in a marathon 80-mile, nonstop jump which appeared to disregard such minor inconveniences as portages, darkness, and particularly confusing waterways. Apparently their sole misjudgment was in not bringing adequate provisions. Their beer had run out shortly after midnight and now we were faced by some extremely thirsty Indians. We couldn't help but be a little in awe though of these people who so casually leap a distance in the dark which will surely take us three hard days going upstream by canoe.

Well, thanks to our visitors, we got off to an early start today. We completed three portages before breakfast even (a new record), and by travelling hard managed to cover 28 miles. It was a beautiful day with the wind predominantly from behind and we breezed along with occasional stops to swim and eat.

Tonight we are off the Sturgeon Weir and onto the Churchill. How we have looked forward to reaching this mighty river! We have thought and read about it so often that its very name evokes for us images of a grand and glorious past when it was part of the trunk route west. Now we have 400-plus miles of upstream work ahead of us to reach the infamous Methye Portage.

We are camped tonight in the little clearing on Trade Lake which marks the north end of historic Frog Portage. The carry itself is only about 350 yards long. It traverses the shallow height of land joining the swampy source of the Sturgeon Weir to the Churchill watershed. The carry has a log railway and cart which we used to get the canoe and a couple of packs across. Truthfully it would have been easier just to pack everything across on my back but the novelty of the thing was just too much to resist, especially for the kids. It is not easy though, pushing a heavy little rail car uphill on uneven log tracks.

Well tomorrow we start up the Churchill at last. I believe this is the portion of the summer we have been most looking forward to. The river is by and large a series of lakes connected by intervening rapids and falls. There will be many places to line and portage but we are finally starting to feel that we are getting somewhere. Also Margie can walk on her bad ankle now and in a few more days she should be back to normal.

It is a little rainy this evening but worse than that the kids have taken to teasing and arguing with each other over nothings. Randy in particular is being an annoying mumpsimus, oppugning every statement, and is driving his sister crazy. I guess they are both tired from the very long day. Normally we let them sleep in the morning.

JULY 14: KEG LAKE

Today we changed direction and so, incredibly enough, did the wind. It breezed out of the east and we just sailed along. It was cloudy and gray this morning but no one really minded. We were having too much fun just being on the Churchill. Long before we reached the west end of Trade Lake we could see the flickering white from the waves of Grand Rapids. The fishing turned out to be excellent there and we ended up staying for lunch. The rapids marked the end of the easy travelling though for today. This afternoon was less pleasant as the wind switched more into our faces and we had to wade up some little swifts. It was cold splashing around waist deep in the water and the kids were huddling down in the boat to stay sheltered out of the wind.

Tonight we are camped on the day's fourth portage at the west end of Keg Lake. Navigating upstream is always more difficult than coming down. Going with the flow it is simple to stay with the main current. When you are working your way up, however, it is much harder. It is all too easy to get sidetracked by accidentally going up a tributary (something that can't happen to downstream paddlers). It's also easy to end up

199

in a dead end. Surprisingly enough this second is almost quite likely. As you work your way along, the natural tendency is to always seek out the path of least resistance. In an effort to avoid the worst of the current, you can work your way right off the main flow into the dead water of a lake arm or more likely into the wrong "side" of what was supposed to be an island. We were faced with just such a choice this afternoon. Our map showed the main flow of the river passing through a major rapid with a long portage on the south shore. It also showed a hair-thin blue line of a channel going around the rapid and connecting to the east end of Drinking Lake just above the portage. We decided to detour and risk the narrow channel which is perhaps three to four miles long and hope that it was navigable. Tonight we are sleeping at a little falls about one mile along the way and are confident we made the right choice. The Indians have blasted out a rocky defile around a falls here and made a skid-pole portage for boats so obviously we are on the beaten path.

Until it started to drizzle we had a lot of fun here. We were teasing the walleye and pike. The idea was to see how far out we could cast and not catch one. We were jerking and skittering our lures back across the water trying to keep them away from the fish which would go crazy lunging after the bait even to the point of grounding themselves at out feet. We weren't totally successful, however, and ended up having to eat five walleye for dessert.

JULY 15: STANLEY MISSION

Today was cloudy and overcast with occasional light rain but still in all a good travelling day. Our "hair-thin" channel brought us out above the major rapids at the east end of Drinking Lake as expected. There was still another mile or so of swift current and minor rapids to ascend but, by ferrying back and forth across the "lake", we managed to get by everything without wading. Really, it is a funny river, supposedly lakes separated by falls. In actuality though the lakes too have current, and even little riffles at the bends. You would hardly notice them going downstream but going up is another matter. Drinking Lake is a case in point. They must indeed have been drinking to call the thing a lake for the lower end is only a widening in a fairly quick river and we were forced to paddle hard to make it up at all.

200

Drinking Falls separates the west end of the lake from Nistowiak Lake and the last half mile of lake (rapids) before the falls is very tough padding for upstream travellers -- too tough for us. We got out and waded the canoe up against the swift current to arrive dripping wet at the wilderness lodge marking the portage by the falls. It was already a cold and drizzly day so the extra soaking (it was chest deep between the rocks) was not really an added inconvenience. We packed up and squished across, then stopped in at the lodge to visit. By the time Margie and I got in there the kids were chatting away with some of the staff over lemonade and granola bars -- a real treat. Kreuger was through a few weeks back and the owners were still excited. They had copies of all his literature to impress us with. We enjoy hearing about his trip from everybody we meet but find it hard to manifest the awe with which he is generally regarded. Still, he has got to be one heroic paddler.

Late this afternoon we paddled in to Stanley Mission. Today is Wednesday and all the stores (both of them) were open. Food at last! The post is also the sight of an historic gothic church, which is very beautiful with all its stained glass windows. It was the first church in Saskatchewan and we spent half an hour inside and out, taking pictures etc. We were reminded of the early missionaries who braved the loneliness and hardships of this wilderness to live with the Indians. They must have been unusual men. Afterwards we turned northeast up Mountain Lake for nearly an hour till we reached a beautiful sand beach for tonight's campsite. Unfortunately it is only a few miles from town and the Indians have littered it terribly -- they can be such slobs.

For the second time this summer we seem to have paddled near a forest fire. Many of the hills surrounding Drinking Lake and even some of the islands were freshly burnt over. The smoke was fairly thick and waterbombers (helicopters carrying a gigantic bucket of water precariously suspended) were flying all around. It makes me nervous to have one pass too closely overhead but the children love it.

Well today was good. We saw mink, eagles and deer. We portaged several times and waded others but still managed to progress another 23 miles. We believe that even going upstream we can average 20 miles a day and we shopped accordingly. We bought about two weeks of food to carry us the approximately 250 miles to Ile à la Crosse, but even this amount has loaded us down as a lot of it is canned.

You don't see many paddlers out here but today we met a couple just below Stanley Mission headed downstream. Of course, we stopped to talk. They were the counselors for a co-ed camp group. Embarrassingly enough they have lost their charges (a good half-dozen canoes) and don't know where to find them. They asked if we had seen them (negative) and then they decided to push on to their next portage to camp. Hopefully the group has not become lost on Mountain Lake with all its confusing arms, islands and channels.

JULY 16: GREAT AND LITTLE DEVIL

It was very hot today and as usual the heat took its toll. There were a lot of long portages and Margie's ankle is still only good for one trip across. In addition the packs are heavy from yesterday's shopping. At any rate tonight I am dirty, hot, and tired from the day's exertions and so is Margie. By this afternoon the mental effort involved in loading and unloading, picking up, and carrying the packs and canoe was almost as bad as the physical effort. It must have been ninety degrees, before the thunderstorms struck.

We got off to an early start with the kids still asleep in the canoe. The early morning wind calmed down and the day grew hot and humid. There was still smoke in the air from the forest fires and the sky was hazy enough to make distant points and islands indistinct. The water-bombers were choppering all around but gradually they fell behind.

There were five portages today but the last three were the worst. The third, at Otter Rapids, was well over a third of a mile and we did it in the heat of the day. There was some momentary entertainment though as we portaged along the bank. A green capsized canoe came pinwheeling down through the rapids followed by a thrashing swimmer. We usually like to talk to fellow canoeists, but he was very busy plunging through the big drops and standing waves out in the middle, chasing his canoe, and did not stop to chat. He seemed to know what he was doing so we did not disturb him.

The next carry was a half mile one at Little Devil Rapids. About this time it started to cloud up and threaten rain but we decided to race for Big Devil Rapids and the long portage there. Our timing was not good -- we arrived in the middle of a thunderstorm. Margie stood around cooking supper in the rain while the kids and I made one trip across to set up camp. By the time we returned Tina and Randy were really tired

202

from all their hiking. Still there wasn't much we could do about it; their beds were on the other side now. After supper we had to load them up again, like little donkeys, and send them trudging off down the wet muddy trail to their tent, nearly a mile away. We stayed to clean up from supper, then repacked and carried across to join them at the other end. By then it was getting dark and time for bed. This was a long hard day -- 24 miles -- but the children stood up to it well.

Late this morning we met a bunch of misplaced canoeists, a large camp group of co-ed youngsters. Interestingly enough they had lost their counselors! We told them where as of last evening their leaders were waiting (ten confusing miles and three portages away). We got out the maps and explained carefully but they were overwhelmed. They are going to sit there and wait for the counselors to find them. I wonder which group will give up waiting first!

Tina got stung by a bee today.

JULY 17: 1000 MILES

Another taxing day. We did nineteen miles, six portages and crossed the 1000 mile mark for the summer.

It was very pretty in the morning. The day was to be clear and hot but the early morning hours were calm, cool and misty, and we took several nice pictures. It is very hard to navigate in a thick morning mist but we enjoyed just paddling and floating along the shoreline while we waited for it to clear a little.

The travelling was quite varied. There was lake travelling, hard upstream paddling, lots of portages and quite a bit of wading along pulling the canoe. We met a lot of canoeists coming downstream today and it was exciting to have them come rollicking through the rapids on either side of us as we hauled our way up the river, waist deep in the swirling waters.

We tried to finish the series of little portages ending at Trout Lake so we wouldn't have to start off by wading tomorrow, but we didn't quite make it. Each portage had a campsite better than the last and we finally succumbed. Tonight's spot is really outstanding; a wide open pine grove with several flat tent sites beside a little falls. There is also a large fireplace with log benches and even some blueberries around. We were still unloading our stuff when we noticed another group a few hundred yards upstream at the next portage, headed our way. Immediately we ran around strewing gear trying to simulate the appearance of a large group. Perhaps our bluff worked. At any rate the other group decided to camp where they were. We had stopped early so we had plenty of free time before supper. The kids made moss beds, Margie did some washing and I went fishing. Later we had the fun of organizing the food packs to see exactly how many meals are left.

Everybody's boots are falling apart. We all bought new ones to start the trip but now seven out of eight have leaks. Mine is the worst with a ten inch gash and it flops around my ankle. Actually it hardly matters for Margie and me as we are generally wet to the waist from wading anyway.

Tina is getting good at whittling marshmallow sticks and firestarters.

JULY 18: VISITING DAY

It was warm and sunny today and we spent a lot of time visiting with other travellers. We got off to a fairly early start and it didn't take long to go the few hundred yards to the next carry. The party we had seen there yesterday was camped all over the portage trail and still sound asleep so we decided to drag up through the rapids and not disturb them. We snuck quietly by undetected but the next group was not so lucky. There were 23 of them camped at Rock Trout Falls. There was no way to line up those rapids so we had to land. We had everything unloaded and were just sneaking through their site when something woke them up; it might have been me when I lost control of the canoe trying to tiptoe over their darn fishing rods. Anyway, it turned out for the best. They were extremely gracious and invited us to breakfast. The kids in particular enjoyed all the attention they received.

We reached the south end of Trout Lake in time for lunch and this time we invited ourselves to eat with a group of four men from California. They shared their trail mix with us and told us some of their adventures. This is their first canoe trip and I guess they are really enjoying themselves. They have their own plane and flew up here to try paddling. They are travelling through an outfitter who has sent them out on a week's loop, and I guess they had a little difficulty navigating at first. Leastways sometime on the second day they were astonished to round a corner and find themselves back at the outfitter's dock. This time the outfitter pointed them off in the right direction a little more carefully and here they were. Today they were resting as yesterday they overextended themselves with six terrible portages (we can identify with that).

After lunch they got to watch us take our inauspicious leave wading out of sight up the next set of rapids headed for Birch Portage. This portage skirts the falls marking the outlet of Black Bear Island Lake. This huge lake is loaded with islands and is a real navigational challenge. We stopped early for supper and then decided to push on afterwards. It is fun to meet people, but with all our visiting we hadn't really got much work done. The lake was calm so we put the children to bed and then paddled on till after sunset. Tonight we are sleeping perhaps one-third of the way up the lake's central channel. Black Bear Island Lake has three channels and each of them is shown by our map to be blocked by a rapid (stupid lakes). Anyway we have elected to work our way up the shortest, central route.

JULY 19: SANDFLY LAKE

Cooler temperatures make quite a difference when it comes to travelling. The day was mostly cloudy and overcast and even though we took a nap at lunchtime we got a lot of work done. We travelled from 6:00 to 6:00 and passed over three portages, ascended two rapids and paddled 27 miles. We also passed what seemed to be a village of Indians on the move. There were perhaps 75 of them in about 20 of their huge motorboats and they were moving east, some from as far away as Buffalo Narrows.

Tonight we are camped on Sandfly Lake (sandfly is a euphemism for no-see-um) and are in pretty high spirits. The raspberries and blueberries are becoming quite plentiful (blueberry bannock for the second day in a row tomorrow) and the weather is clearing off. We are perched on some high rocks at Needle Rapids and it is very scenic. For a while the kids had acquired an old Indian who was too drunk to stand up but then some other Indians came by and took him away from us.

Just by chance we spotted some Indian pictographs today. They were very faded and must be pretty old.

JULY 20: SNAKE RAPIDS

The steady upstream travel has been gradually wearing us down and this morning we were sort of dragging. What with one excuse and another we didn't get off till 6:30. We decided to travel hard and stop early so we could get a good rest. So much for good intentions. Unfortunately 3:00 found us at the bottom of Snake Rapids. Now there is nothing less relaxing than setting up camp at the base of a long rapids. You know that first thing in the morning you are going to have to get out and start wading while it is still cold and the impending misery preys on your mind. There was really no excuse not to continue while it was warm and sunny, so reluctantly we did.

There must be very few things as difficult as wading our heavily loaded 20-foot canoe up through powerful rapids. It may take more sheer strength to shoulder the canoe and portage with it, but in the end nothing is more tiring than wading. We spent three hours wading three long miles. First we had to be so careful. There were stretches of very heavy water that even teams of experts would want to look over carefully before shooting downstream. It was a very bouldery stretch and it took all our strength, balance and agility to pull the canoe along with the water sucking around our waists. One misstep and all could be lost, and those rocks were slippery. Hanging on to the ends we would slip and stumble as we lurched a few steps forwards, being careful not to get a foot wedged between underwater rocks that we could scarcely see. Often to move the canoe at all we would have to brace ourselves against the current before tugging it a few feet farther on. If the bow had gotten swept out or if we had stumbled we would have lost control of the boat in an instant. This process had to be repeated over and over. It wasn't safe for the kids to be in the canoe so they walked along over the boulders on shore, keeping ahead of us easily. We were still being careful of Margie's ankle and in the worst stretches she would go along the shore holding the fifty foot bow line taut as a safety measure. Actually, we must have looked a little funny as we were naked except for our boots. It was a warm day and we wanted to keep our clothes dry. Well, like I say it was tiring work; but by the time we reached Sandy Lake at the top our legs were quivering with exhaustion and our backs ached. Still we had avoided what the map showed to be miles of portaging.

We found a nice sandy beach campsite on the lake near the head of the rapids and the kids went swimming (we'd been). The day ended well, but it wasn't the restful one we had envisaged. We covered another 29 miles on top of yesterday's 27. Tomorrow we stop early, no matter what!

Everybody is sunburned from too much overexposure this afternoon.

JULY 21: KNEE LAKE

What a beautiful streak of good weather we have been having. Ever since the windy day when we left Amisk Lake (288 miles and 13 days ago) it has been excellent. Again today it was hot and clear. Knowing that we were going to stop early I just paddled all out from sunup onwards. It is fun to test your strength and endurance against the current to see how long it lasts (till 3:00).

We only had to wade one rapids, but the current was consistently strong. The river stretch between Degler and Knee Lake in particular is long and fast and those miles took us five hours. The country is slowly changing as we begin to work our way off the Canadian Shield. There is less rock now but more swamp and sandy beaches.

We got in at 3:00 and spent the rest of the afternoon swimming off our sand beach, lying in the shade and picking blueberries. The kids went swimming six times today.

I just measured the map. We did another 27 miles.

JULY 22: PRIMEAU LAKE

It is starting to get exciting. I don't know how many portages we have left to do this year but I bet it isn't more than a dozen. There is a series of rapids above Knee Lake but by keeping to the right side and working hard we managed to paddle up most of them, only wading once. It was exciting inching past the shoreline and paddling up the vees between the rocks and it went much better than expected. Knee rapids involved a portage of 500 yards and then just a couple of miles farther on we reached Crooked Rapids in time for lunch. This was a long carry (three quarters of a mile) and we were barely started over when we were subjected to drenching thundershowers. The others got pretty wet but my 20-foot umbrella kept me nice and dry until the end. Packing up to leave was a

207

problem though. We are surely off the shield now and virtually all of the rock is gone. It was a very muddy launching site and it was tough to carry the packs and children out to the canoe without embedding myself in the mud. The worst was yet to come however. Once Margie and I were in the canoe it was enough weight to solidly ground the boat and we couldn't push off. It was very frustrating as we could get no purchase with our paddles -- they simply sank into the mud bottom as far as we cared to push them. By stepping on matted grass and pieces of driftwood though we slowly inched the canoe forward and managed to escape.

The change in the country has brought further difficulties as well -- campsites are suddenly very scarce. We paddled quite a while hunting for one in the rain this afternoon and finally had to backtrack a mile or so to a mediocre spot we had turned down earlier.

Everyone is in bed now and the rain seems to have stopped. A nice blueberry bannock is baked for tomorrow and we are hoping for a return to sunny weather. A few good thunderstorms really get us wet but at least the kids don't complain, a nice change from when they were babies. They dried out a lot by the fire and now they are wearing damp clothes in half damp sleeping bags in a wet tent. Nevertheless, they are talking happily and ready to settle down for the night.

JULY 23: GLASSES

It was cloudy and rainy all day today. We got up late, travelled slowly (against the wind) and quit early. We only had to wade once but that was enough. All our boots leak now and Margie and I have had wet feet for what seems like two straight weeks. I gave up wearing socks days ago.

It was pretty confusing finding our way through the swamps west of Dipper Lake but it is certain that we are on the right track. We just met another Indian carrying Kreuger's handout flyers. Really the man must be travelling with his own Xerox machine. Every Indian since Cedar Lake has had a few copies. Seriously though, Kreuger must have run into trouble. First he seems to be following an abbreviated route, not the longer northerly loop outlined in his advertisements. Secondly he is not pulling ahead of us the way he should be. In our own leisurely way we are almost creeping up with him.

Tonight we are camped on a blueberry-coated portage at Dipper Rapids. Margie is not in the best of moods. Due to a complicated set of circumstances beyond her control involving three Indians, tall grass, and a portage skid pole rail cart, she lost her glasses on the carry. Despite the rain and hordes of black flies and mosquitoes we have searched the trail diligently twice to no avail. Tina broke hers weeks ago and so now both the girls must do without them the rest of the summer.

NOTE: Kreuger did run into difficulties later on. He and his partner, Landick, didn't make it over the Chilkoot Pass before winter set in and they had to wait for spring.

JULY 24: DEER, LEAF AND DRUM RAPIDS

We may be coming to the end of this river but it is sure not getting any easier. A full day's work and we only covered 14 miles. That is the distance from Dipper Rapids to just above Drum Rapids. Every one of those miles is against swift current and there were many long sets of cascading rapids to overcome.

It was very cool today, sunny in the morning and then intermittent showers all afternoon. At times this morning with the strong wind and powerful current I felt like just laying my paddle down across the gunwales and calling it quits for the day. Actually that was the good part of the day. The afternoon we spent frigidly wading and portaging. It seems unfair when we are wading up to our hips that the canoe is still scraping rocks. The wading is so poor here, with slippery boulders and deep water in between. (With hundreds of miles of experience we are getting to be wading connoisseurs.)

Tonight we are camped at a well-used Indian site on a high bluff. There is a nice clearing and fireplace but it is pretty trashed up. I am weak tonight but it is probably because I am sick. We must have drunk some bad water someplace. Everyone's stomach is upset. It is hard not be excited though. I think the next 150 miles has only one portage and no wading. After tomorrow we shall be home free.

We saw a deer today, just before Deer Rapids.

JULY 25: PATUANAK

It was like October in New Hampshire today; crisp and cool in the morning, hot in the afternoon, and then cool again in the evening. We got in to Patuanak shortly after breakfast but then wasted two hours looking for a place to shop. It was Saturday and the stores were closed but the manager of the Hudson Bay Company store took pity on us and let Margie in to do a little shopping anyways. It is only a couple of days to Ile à la Crosse so she just bought some odds and ends.

We expected to portage Shagwenaw Rapids which mark the beginning of Lac Ile à la Crosse and were pleasantly surprised to find that we could wade instead. It is funny how much colder the water is just below a big lake though. We were reminded of the set of rapids below Amisk Lake; clear and cold.

Just a week or so ago we were seeing canoes every day but until this morning we had gone days without seeing one. The country is pretty accessible but I guess it is not too attractive for canoeists. We are definitely into swampier country, although there are nice sand beaches occasionally. Also of course the lakes are getting big again. It is over thirty miles down this first stretch of lake till we turn right up the Aubichon Arm. In breezy weather like we have been having the water can kick up pretty rough. In fact the canoeist we met today has been windbound for the past two days.

We continued until about 9:00 tonight and are now camped just below Halfway Point. We paddled 29 miles today and expect to reach Ile à la Crosse tomorrow. It has been a long time since we have seen a moose but there are tracks all around here.

JULY 26: AUBICHON ARM

Today was windy all day. Noon hour we spent resting on Sandy Point opposite Ile à la Crosse. We stared forlornly over at the post but it was just too dangerous to cross the lake arm so we finally decided to pass up our visit and head directly for Buffalo Narrows; it is only a couple of days away. Unfortunately, even Aubichon Arm was more than we could handle. The waves were splashing in from the left hindquarter and the children kept busy mopping up. At last we found a fairly sheltered cove to land in. There wasn't any beach but we cleared some tent sites back in the woods and tonight everything is cozy. We picked an awful lot of raspberries today. Now we would all like a big glass of cold orange juice.

Back on Sandy Point Randy got a chance to do a little sword-fighting. Some Indians were living there and the children came over to play and everyone had a good time.

JULY 27: MacBETH CHANNEL

We stopped at 3:00 today to go swimming and ended up establishing camp because it looked so stormy. Sure enough, once everything was under cover it began to thunder, and now it has been raining for a couple of hours.

Tonight we are so near the top of Macbeth Channel that we can almost taste it. By straining to look around the corner we can practically see Churchill Lake, the top of the Churchill River. There will be just one more upstream to paddle, the short La Loche River, then pop across Methye Portage and it will be downhill for over a thousand miles. I can't describe how exciting a prospect that is, or how much we have been looking forward to it. We feel as though we have gone up every river in Canada, and we have the muscles to prove it. We have nearly forgotten what it is like to go downstream. Perhaps we shall try to break our record fifty mile day from Lake Superior. In fact we are fantasizing about doing a hundred miles in one day on the Mackenzie. Twenty hours of paddling with a good current should do it easily (daydreaming is such fun).

Margie is planning to buy ten days worth of food tomorrow at Buffalo Narrows to take us across the carry and down the Clearwater to Fort McMurray at the junction with the Athabasca.

We saw a deer up close today. We can also hear wolves now, howling across the channel from us. The fishing has been pretty poor lately.

JULY 28: BUFFALO NARROWS

We were so excited about finally getting off the river that we got

211

up and did the eight miles into town before breakfast. It was fun to be in a real town and we took advantage of the opportunity to go shopping and visit a laundromat. This was our first chance in over a month to wash clothes and Margie just tossed them all into the tubs without even checking to see how dirty they were.

I'm not sure I would like to live in Buffalo Narrows. It is not that we had any trouble there, I was just uncomfortable. Once in awhile you find a settlement where race relations are strained. That may not be the case there but still the atmosphere felt awkward to us. Maybe I have just been in the bush too long. We did meet some very nice people, particularly the Airways people. Randy spent all morning watching their water planes take off and land.

The weather was only fair and after lunch we paddled on about four and a half hours in the rain. Eventually we came to Sandy Point which marks the beginning of a beautiful sand beach which is at least six miles long. We set the tents up under the shelter of some willows and piled the gear under the overturned canoe. It is still raining but really everything is quite dry.

It is not like us to travel without a margin of excess food but this time we are pared down to the limit. We have counted and recounted the miles to Fort McMurray and brought provisions for exactly ten days. The problem of course is that we don't want to carry a single excess crumb over thirteen-mile-long Methye Portage. It is hard to imagine how we are going to get everything across though, especially the canoe. Margie and I practiced carrying it together earlier this summer but it didn't work that well. She finds it easier if I do it alone.

JULY 29: PETER POND LAKE

A lot of the lakes are pretty big up here. Everybody knows about the giants (Athabasca, Great Slave, and Great Bear) but even a lot of the others such as Churchill or Peter Pond would pretty well dwarf anything in New England. We paddled another 27 miles on Petrer Pond Lake today and still the end is a ways off. It is a fat lake, miles across, and with all the wind we were lucky to progress as far as we did. The wind was particularly difficult in the morning and we stayed in camp for breakfast. Afterwards we paddled all out just to cover 7 miles in three hours. The effort so exhausted us we stopped an hour and a half for lunch. The country is pretty scenic, the Grizzly Bear Hills are just west of the lake and for people who haven't seen mountains since New England they are very impressive.

Tonight we paddled until just after sunset and for the first time all summer we are averaging over 20 miles a day for the trip. Our campsite this evening is a small and very buggy glade of waist-high grass. We haven't seen mosquitoes like this since the Saskatchewan River and we dread getting up in the morning unless it cools down somewhat.

JULY 30: METHYE RIVER

In the course of spending a summer in the bush we unconsciously acquire an enhanced awareness of our surroundings. At home I am practically oblivious to changing cloud patterns, temperature fluctuations and variations in wind speed and direction. Living outside, however, sharpens our sensibilities. Last night it was a difference in the noise of the waves breaking on the rocky shoreline which drew me out to survey the beach. It was only a harmless switch in wind direction which had aroused me but I was grateful for the occasion. It was very cold, the bugs were gone, and the northern lights were on display. There was an unusual amount of green mixed in with shimmering white curtains and flaring streaks and I woke up Margie to admire them as well. Having someone you love there to share an experience with makes it that much better. It is this dimension that soloists such as Kreuger are missing from their trips.

The lake was calm in the morning and we found the Methye (la Loche) River without difficulty. We paddled up it slowly but steadily, doing some nine miles of it by lunchtime, when we reached the junction with the Kimowin. We were pleased with our progress, although the last few miles had been uniquely difficult. The river is almost choked by weeds. The canoe would lodge in the growth at times and it was hard to take a paddlestroke.

Once past the Kimowin the river became much smaller and the water plants were less thick. We paddled up a relatively clear, narrow, brush-lined channel for fifteen minutes. Suddenly though, we turned a corner and our hearts fell. Our little river had abruptly changed to a rocky mountain stream. There had to be some mistake. Could the voyageurs

213

have paddled 3000 miles to face a series of steep, shallow rocky rapids? The stream was so small I could spit across it and I couldn't believe that they had brought their big canoes through there. It was with grave misgivings that we got out and began to wade. The one encouraging sign was that, despite the shallow rocky appearance, the canoe somehow slippped up the central channel of the rocky shallows and little rapids without scraping. That could not be chance. Sometime someone had gone to a lot of work to clear away the rocks necessary to allow a large canoe such as ours to pass unobstructed. We spent the next three hours wading, paddling and poling up rocky riffles at what had to be a snail's pace. By 4:00 the fun was going out of it and the sudden appearance of a large beaver dam was another blow. We had to unload the canoe, then teeteringly drag it across and reload. Slowly things began to improve after that. There were still rapids but they were less severe and we increasingly found ourselves able to pole up them. In another hour we stopped at a rough campsite under the pines.

Tomorrow we would love to reach Lac La Loche. We don't know how long it will take though because we are not sure how long the river is with all its bends, nor how fast we are moving, nor even where we are.

JULY 31: THE TOP

The La Loche River is behind us now. Ten hours of paddling through winding swamps and wading little rapids brought us out to the sandy shallow lake where we are camped tonight. We have a beautiful site, a big sand beach, and we are nestled back in the dunes among some birches. The weather was great today -- very cold in the morning, then hot and sunny all day long, and now there is a beautiful sunset across the lake. There are abundant quantities of blueberries here and we picked over a quart. We had a blueberry bannock with supper; then peaches and blueberries for dessert, and tomorrow morning we shall have blueberries and cold cereal.

The mosquitoes are really humming back in the woods this evening. As we picked up camp the sound grew louder and louder and we popped into the tents as soon as possible to avoid the swarms.

Well we are finally here. Paddle the twenty miles across the lake, carry the thirteen miles across infamous Methye Portage, and then it will be downhill "forever".

214

AUGUST 1: LA LOCHE

Lac La Loche is peculiarly dirty. As far as we can tell the entire lake from top to bottom is filled with suspended greenish brown particles. Last night we cleared a couple of quarts of drinking water by straining it through some pieces of gauze taken from our first aid kit. Then this morning we breezed into town early in order to get more clean water and learned that our precautions were well taken. In fact we were told to not even swim in the water as it would cause severe itching. We can't imagine what the particles are. We also took advantage of the chance to get rid of some gear. We threw away

    a) all our boots

    b) the children's ground cloth

    c) some workbooks and other toys the children no longer use, and

    d) a few well-worn items of clothing.

Anything to lighten our loads!

It took us a few hours to get down to the end of the lake but we found the portage without any trouble. A mining company has set up a temporary camp there. We used their latrine (it came fully equipped with large magic markers for graffitiizing the outhouse walls) and were told the carry starts right at their camp. Don't you believe it. We didn't. Instead we got into the canoe again and pushed up a very overgrown winding little stream for another half mile to where the trail crossed over. I'm sure that we saved ourselves a quarter mile of swampy portaging as well as a nasty stream crossing.

Methye Portage may be the major carry of our lives and we spent an hour getting prepared. Everything had to be packed as comfortably and economically as possible. It is twelve and a half miles across and we wanted to be sure to cover it in only two trips. Actually there is a natural break at Rendezvous Lake, a puddle two-thirds of the way across. It was at this lake that the Hudson Bay Company's Mackenzie and La Loche Brigades would meet each summer. The Mackenzie Brigade, coming from the north end of the carry, would portage in their year's collection of furs and exchange them for the tons of supplies brought out of the east by the La Loche Brigade. After exchanging loads at the lake each would return back the way they had come. We aren't carrying the tons of supplies they did, but on the other hand we are trying to get our canoe across, a problem they didn't face.

It was about 4:00 when we finally topped off our water jug with two gallons of water (sixteen pounds) and started out. We had studied the map and knew that it was just over eight miles to the lake and I had estimated it as 16,000 paces. It is easy to become discouraged on a giant portage and I determined to count my steps as I went along so as to have a good idea at all times as to our position. Arbitrarily dividing 16,000 by 800, I decided to try to cover the eight miles to the lake in 20 hops.

For me a hop consists of first shouldering the canoe and then counting out 800 paces. Margie follows right behind with a very heavy 75-pound pack and the kids straggle along with their loads (pack and paddle). They stay with the canoe to pick blueberries and fight mosquitoes while Margie and I go back for our second loads. For her second trip Margie takes another pack, tent and paddles. This is my "easy" trip, although it is actually somewhat heavier than my first. I carry two of the Duluth packs, one balanced on top of the other. I am quite hunched over but at least my hands are free to deal with the insects. There is nothing like a good sweat to attract mosquitoes.

The trail started off beautifully; level, wide and a little sandy. The country is very open and the children were able to pick lots of blueberries. We made three hops and then stopped to cook supper on the trail (literally on the trail, for fear of starting a forest fire anywhere else). We hated to part with any of our precious water to put out the fire and were fortunate to be hit by a passing shower just as we were eating. Afterwards we packed up and did two more hops for the evening. We are camped tonight in a little blueberry glade that we estimate is two miles (4000 paces) along the carry. We are all a little tired but glad to be part way over. We plan to try and do the next six miles to the lake in time for lunch tomorrow. Our drinking water will be about gone by then.

We noticed several old campfire spots along the trail tonight where others have had to stop. I don't imagine we shall meet anyone though. The kids are holding up well although the blackflies and mosquitoes were very thick, especially after the rain.

We ate a can of cherries when we got here, to lighten our load. Yum, yum.

AUGUST 2: RENDEZVOUS LAKE

I can already see that this portage is one I shall never forget. Twenty-five years from now I'm sure that Margie and I shall still be raving about our sufferings. Everyone is still alive but the physical strain of today's hike exacted quite a toll.

First, we got up a little earlier than expected. What can you do though when it is not even 6:00 and Randy is standing outside your tent already dressed, wearing his pack, clutching his paddle and anxious to start! We got up and started carrying before our eyes were hardly open. Margie and I were stiff and sore for the first two hops but then we began to loosen up. At least it was cool, and the bugs weren't bad that early. Later they were to become abominable.

We portaged pretty steadily, with a few minutes off here and there, from 6:00 till 3:30. That may seem like awfully slow progress but remember Margie and I had to cover eighteen miles to progress six, and we took time out for breakfast and lunch.

The kids really didn't have that bad a day; they were able to wear headnets for the bugs and pick blueberries along the trail. For Margie and me, however, it degenerated into an ordeal. At least the trail was good, straight and level (pretty much). By noon though we were running out of water and tiring quickly. We nibbled at our sandwiches and savored the last of our oranges. The afternoon hops weren't as easy as the early ones had been. It was hot work. We were out of drinking water and growing very thirsty. After each hop we would have to drop to the ground for a moment's rest in the shade before continuing. With the water gone the kids wanted to go on alone to get some more and wait for us at the lake. Finally at 15,200 steps we said go ahead and gave them a water bottle. In the next hop I moved the canoe down to 16,000 and when Margie and I returned with our second loads we found a quart of water and birchbark note from Tina. It was only another three hundred paces to go! Our first glimpse of the lake was the most exhilarating moment of the summer, and we practically ran the last hundred yards to camp. Really tonight's campsite is an excellent one, but we are unable to fully take advantage of it. It is open and parklike but we can barely hobble much less play frisbee with the children. The area is landscaped with blueberry bushes however and Margie and I sat out amongst them eating while we stared out at the beautiful lake.

Well, tonight we are nearly crippled -- aching feet, hips, back, shoulders and legs. It is hard to believe that a single day could so demolish us. By the time we reached the lake we were limping awkwardly and we just stumbled in for a soothing swim. Tonight we are lying in the tents wondering if we shall ever be able to walk again. Besides our blisters, our feet and joints just ache deeply. Fortunately tomorrow's carry is scarcely more than four miles. There have been lots of thunderstorms go by but so far all have missed us.

One of the interesting things about today's trip was all the wolves. We never saw any of them, but at one time Margie and I were pretty worried. We had gone back for our second load when we could hear them howling back where the kids were. Nothing happened but after that we made them keep their whistles handy and we tried to hurry whenever we were separated.

Margie and I have been talking it over. We don't begrudge carrying the necessities but perhaps we should have whittled down the children's rock collection. The problem is it took them two months to amass them all and so naturally they hate to part with a single one. Still, as I hobbled along today I couldn't help recalling our early backpacking days in the 60's. We used to saw off our toothbrush handles and clip away the tea bag labels to lighten our loads. Now we are staggering along with loads that would have a donkey down on all eights, and a distressing portion of it is rocks, rusty bottle tops, discarded baggie ties and other delightful collections.

AUGUST 3: THE CLEARWATER

Well, tonight we are across the carry! I am sure that it will be at least a week before any of us can walk normally again but our problems should be behind us. On the other hand the map shows seven portages for tomorrow, the longest over a mile; but nothing can be as bad as the last two days.

Early this morning we paddled across the lake and began the last part of the portage. Our blisters forced us to walk gingerly at first but soon we got into the spirit of it again. The worst for me was the back of my neck and shoulders. Our oaken center thwart has tenderized me in a line across the top of my shoulders and it was a good deal more painful to persist a full 800 paces today than it was yesterday. Then too the trail was nowhere near as level today. From the lake we climbed steadily for the first couple of miles. We did three hops and then stopped for breakfast. This time we had plenty of water from our recently filled jug.

218

Sometime in the early part of our third mile we finally reached the view we had heard so much about. The valley of the Clearwater is nearly seven hundred feet deep and after portaging eleven miles it is a stupendous sight for sore eyes. From a spot near the top, the land suddenly drops away to reveal a tremendous view of the valley, perhaps as much as thirty miles, with the Clearwater winding along the bottom. The early explorers were enraptured by this view and after paddling well over 3000 miles to get here I can easily see why. There is nothing like it between here and Montreal. As can be imagined, the seven hundred foot descent to the valley floor is a steep one. Before long our knees were wobbling and the center thwart was threatening to decapitate me. I cannot imagine someone portaging up that awful hill.

The trail which had been so good so long finally gave out in the last half mile of thick growth in the valley bottom. There have been a number of windfalls and blowdowns over the years and the trail split into several lesser paths. We chose to stay with the old original, crossing several mudholes and small streams along the way. Soon we were bursting through the last of the willows to a clearing on the banks of the Clearwater. Hallelujah! We did it! We fished out a confetti package and sprinkled it into the air, then we fell down to rest. It was already 1:30. We had spent almost two full days in coming across and Margie and I had walked nearly forty miles.

It was a beautiful spot there -- a small field, sparkling river and tall jack pines. It would not have been unreasonable to spend the night. Yet after a half hour rest we found ourselves being irresistibly drawn down to the water's edge. At times we seem to have an almost irrational determination to keep moving. It was still early and we packed up the canoe to paddle across the river to a nice sand beach. Everyone enjoyed a good swim and had a chance to rinse out their sweaty clothes. Afterwards we set out for a couple of hours paddling before supper. Really there had only been that one short paddle across Rendezvous Lake in the last two days and it was nice to get back into the canoe again.

The river is beautiful. The valley is deep, wide and winding and it was very scenic drifting along between the tree-covered slopes. The water is fast and clear with a nice sand-covered bottom. We were probably drifting at nearly four miles an hour and if it weren't for impending thunderstorms we would have continued right through to Alberta. For people accustomed to toiling upstream the bottom of the shallow river was flashing by at a dizzying rate. We simply marveled at our speed and the picturesqueness of the setting. Anyway when we came to a sand point with some overhanging willows we stopped to set up camp, and barely in time too. We had scarcely settled in before a storm broke.

It has rained off and on for the last few hours but now all is clear. Despite our happiness at being on the Clearwater though, we are not looking forward to tomorrow. Our joy is somewhat tempered by the imminent prospect of seven more portages. It hurts to stand up, much less walk, and our shoulders are destroyed.

The land is slow to recover here in the north but even so the heyday of the fur trade can scarcely be discerned at Methye Portage. There are still clearings at either end of the trail, but no hint of the buildings that once were there. Peter Pond was the first white man to cross this carry (in 1778). The fur trade was close behind him and throughout the next century the area fairly bustled with activity. There was a full wagon trail across where now there is only a sandy path. Sledges and oxen were used to negotiate the terrible slope at the end. Now all is gone and at the end the trail is nearly obliterated. Today we walked a forgotten path, attuned to the silent echoes of those who passed before and vanished without a trace.

AUGUST 4: WHITE MUD FALLS

Watch out for White Mud Falls! It can be a dangerous spot. The government has gone all out to make it safe, however. Well before you turn the fatal corner there is an extremely well marked (orange metal sign) portage trail on the right. But since the falls were still invisible, and we were determined to make the carry as short as possible, we passed it up. No problem, the government knows how foolish some people can be and was determined to save us from ourselves. A short ways farther on they had established a second equally outstanding landing site for the foolishly persistent. I passed it up too. The falls were still not in sight and I was determined to paddle every inch. So we zipped around the corner and THERE IT WAS! Really I felt as though we were on the lip of Niagara, it was so disconcertingly close. We immediatedly hugged the right shore and were borne down to a last little island. Sure enough, there was a third and final portage opportunity and this time we took it -- there was no survivable alternative.

220

We had managed to cut the carry down, but it was still a good five hundred yards. There had been a lot of mist on the river early in the morning but by now it was sunny and warm. The government had placed picnic tables, latrines and fireplaces at the falls and we spent a couple of pleasant hours fishing, picking blueberries and cooking breakfast. The portage itself ended up being almost painless.

The next portage was at Pine Rapids. The carry is 1100 yards long and we simply got out and did it. Afterwards it was time for a long swim and lunch.

In the afternoon we passed up the remaining portages and ran all the rest of the major rapids on the Clearwater (Big Rock, Long and Cascade). Really they are not much and I did them all standing up. There were a few shallow spots and ledgy drops where the canoe almost scraped but otherwise we just riffled through, the canoe bucking a bit on the bigger waves. In New England they would have been classified as II's and III's, which present little problem for a large canoe such as ours. The rest of the summer should be easy now -- there are no more rapids or carries for hundreds of miles.

Well, today was a beautiful day; pleasant, sunny, relaxed and warm. We travelled easily and scarcely covered twenty miles. Really it was a chance to recuperate from Methye Portage and that is what we have done. We stopped early and I expect tomorrow we shall go a little farther.

AUGUST 5: CLEAR SAILING

The Clearwater is a beautiful river and this was another great day. The weather was perfect and the scenery terrific. There were still five-hundred-foot hills on each side of the valley and many open meadows along the shore. Sand banks were plentiful and the river bottom too was mostly sand and we all went swimming more than once.

We continue to marvel at the swift current, especially in little rapids where the shore seems to fly by. Downstream is great. There is really nothing as pleasant as standing idly in the stern, keeping an eye out for obstructions and feeling mile after mile of riffles bubble under your keel. This is a pleasure that necessitates a long paddle (to avoid stooping and cricking your back) and is the chief reason the stern man should bring one along that is a few inches taller than he is. It is also the reason my

VIEW from AFT

SANDERS '84

canoe has no thwart aft of the center. I like to have plenty of room to stand and move around in. I realize that many people seldom practice standing up, but that is the down-east way to deal with rapids (at least through class II). Of course it helps to have a big canoe and be accustomed to poling, which is excellent training for this activity. Tonight we are camped at the mouth of the Cristina River and are starting to see occasional tar deposits.

AUGUST 6: FORT McMURRAY

Another beautiful day. We set off before breakfast and once the morning mist had lifted we stopped to eat on an island and warm up in the sun. We could hear wolves howling back of the river's south shore and a few minutes later a moose came thrashing out of the bushes and bulled his way across the river below us. Although we were in plain sight less than a hundred feet away, he was so intent upon his business that he never saw us. We were on a very small island and it turned out to be the first of many good chances to examine tar deposits. A whole section was paved over with broken lumps much like an old crumbling parking lot. The kids collected big chunks which were indistinguishable from the material coating our driveway back home. Later, canoeing downstream we passed over ridges and ledges of tar lining the river bed. It was like a road passing a foot beneath our keel.

It was noon when we reached Fort McMurray and we stayed till nearly 4:00 accomplishing our chores. First we did our last shopping of the summer (in a real supermarket), then we spent the rest of the time acquiring bus, train, and plane schedules and prices. The time had finally come to start thinking about returning home. After weighing all the alternatives we have decided to paddle to Fort Smith, then take the bus to Kenora to pick up our car. This plan has several advantages:

i) it is far and away the cheapest;

ii) Fort Smith is in the Northwest Territories which we are really anxious to reach; and

iii) Fort Smith is roughly three hundred miles away which is about the right distance for the time we have left. I am supposed to be at work by the twentieth of August and this leaves us fourteen days to paddle three hundred miles and then drive 4000.

223

Tonight we are camped on the Athabasca, another beautiful river. It is big, wide, and swift. It is also silt laden (about the color of Lake Winnipeg) and we brought water from town with us to drink for supper. The river's most impressive features are its massive banks of sheer tar, rising over a hundred feet almost vertically out of the water. On a hot day like today it smells like a melting city street when you pass near shore.

AUGUST 7: THE ATHABASCA

This was a long day. We travelled from 6:30 a.m. to 8:30 p.m. with a couple of stops to swim and two hours off to cook supper. We also made stops to get drinking water from side streams as the river is full of silt and tar deposits. (I suppose we could drink it but we would rather not.)

The Athabasca is a very wide and shallow river and the Coast Guard has marked the channel with buoys and markers. A couple of times we tried to shortcut the winding channel at the corners but it was a mistake. With the chocolate colored water it was impossible to read the depth and we ended up running aground on sunken mud bars. The Coast Guard seems to know what they are doing and we finally resolved to follow the channel wherever it might lead.

At suppertime a Coast Guard tug out of Fort McMurray overtook us. It was checking the channel and replacing damaged buoys and markers and we hustled out to race. We were slowly outdistanced, however, and by the time we stopped for the night he was out of sight. I guess he will reach Fort Chipewyan long before us.

It was hot again today. A breeze came up around noon which cooled us a bit but Margie is not sure she wants it again tomorrow since it was out of the north in our faces. Even so the swift current more than compensated for the wind and we continued progressing without serious difficulty. In fact the kids paddled alone for two miles at lunch today sitting in our seats while we stretched out for a nap in the middle. It was fun for them to try and steer the slalom course of channel markers back and forth across the river. They are eager to try it again tomorrow and we are anxious to let them. It was kind of nice lying in the sun realizing we were being chauffered to Alaska. Too bad the summer will be ending so soon. We paddled 53 miles today, which is a record for this trip.

AUGUST 8: COAST GUARD

Another beautiful day; hot and clear with the wind not too bad. We got off to an early start and snuck by the Coast Guard tug while they were still asleep (they had moored to the bank for the night). We only stopped for a couple of swims and a long supper break and ended up covering over fifty miles again today. Most of the day's excitement was supplied by the Coast Guard. All day long our two boats played leap frog along the river and it entertained the kids no end to have the four of us paddling as hard as we could to keep up. Again today the tug pulled into the lead for good when we stopped for the evening sometime after supper. I suppose we may see him again in the morning. The children want us to lift them (asleep) into the canoe early before sunup again tomorrow so as to get a good start.

The country gradually changed today as we raced along. Early on there were still tremendous mud cliffs towering hundreds of feet and coming down almost sheer to the water. By tonight though the country had flattened out a great deal and this evening we are sleeping on a mud bar about a foot above the water. Heaven help us if it rains. There are no stones, tar, or even hills anywhere around here although occasionally a mud bank will still rear up a hundred feet. The water is not getting any cleaner.

The highlight of the day for Margie and me came early today before the sun was even up, while the kids were still asleep in the canoe. We spotted some wolves running along in the dark shadows of the far shore. We tried to take some pictues but I am afraid it was too dark.

Well, these big rivers are really kind of a pleasant change from the upstream months. Still, after racing the tugboat all day long, we are scarcely well-rested. We set another new distance record today.

AUGUST 9: FORT CHIPEWYAN

Today's report could have been called "The Monster in the Night" but Fort Chipewyan is just too significant a title to pass up. The fort was the western terminus of the old fur trade route and was about as far west as it was practical for the voyageurs to headquarter. Any farther and the annual brigades would not have been able to get back before the ice

225

formed in the fall. The area was rich in provisions (whitefish, moose, etc.) and it was a fairly central location from which to tap the furs of the Mackenzie, Liard and Peace River valleys. Even though there are no roads (or railroad) into Fort Chipewyan today the community is still active.

Anyway, late last night our sleep was rudely interrupted. A tug and barge had been approaching upstream while we slept, but its progress had been so insidiously slow against the current that I guess our senses had discounted the mounting noise as harmless background. When the tug finally churned around the corner to come abreast of our mud flat though there was no dismissing it. The thudding of its huge engines shattered the night and we looked out to see what appeared to be a prehistoric monster bearing down on us. It was all lit up and topped off by piercing searchlight eyes which pinned us to the bank. It gave us quite a start and we were some time trying to get back to sleep.

The morning started out well enough. We got off to a quick start and paddled hard trying to catch the Coast Guard before they started off for the day. A few minutes before 8:00 we spied them nestled along the shore where they had spent the night. We whisked by them, then laid down our paddles to collapse into the bottom of the boat for a well-earned breakfast, while the canoe continued to drift along in the strong current.

It wasn't long before the Coast Guard was bearing down on us though and the kids were ready for the day's races to begin. I guess the crew could restrain their curiosity no longer, however. The captain had a loudspeaker and he hailed us alongside. We chatted for awhile and the captain described some of the channel options up ahead. The cook brought out cold cans of orange juice to go with our Cheerios and we had a little picnic. I believe that they were impressed that we had kept up with them so long. Today, however, they were going all the way to Fort Chipewyan. They said to look them up whenever we arrive and then they revved up their diesels. They were really humming today and there was no way we could match their speed, even for a few minutes.

We saw a moose shortly afterwards and took a belated snapshot. Slowly the day was heating up. It got hotter and hotter and soon was over ninety. We stopped frequently to swim and then gave up early for supper at 4:30. We cooked up a big tuna rice casserole but it was just too hot out to even eat; we ended up putting everything back in the canoe untasted and paddling on. Later about 8:00 we stopped in the shade of the willows and ate cold casserole with a can of applesauce for dessert.

The Athabasca is a huge river with many channels leading out to the lake, and as per the captain's instructions we had picked up Fletcher Channel and then branched off it onto the Embarras River. This little shortcut was used by the voyageurs and saved them several miles of paddling on dangerous Lake Athabasca. By now the river shoreline was very swampy with alder bushes and cattails, and no good stopping place presented itself. Today is my birthday and we finally decided to celebrate by paddling on into Fort Chipewyan. It would mean a fairly long day (65 miles) but it would be fun to see the Coast Guard again.

It was just about then that we came upon a forlorn group of six Indians sitting in a motorboat alongside the shore. Our Athabascan is not good but we managed to make ourselves understood. There was Grandpa (70), Grandma, two folks our age, a girl and a little baby. The myriad channels leading out to the lake are confusing and especially shallow this year. The Indians had spent six hours trying to find a way back to the Fort and had finally run out of gas. Night was coming on, it was starting to chill down, and the baby was crying. We offered to paddle someone into town for gas (it was only seven more miles or so across the lake) and Grandpa accepted. Unfortunately he was a little deaf, spoke no English and was quite arthritic. He could not fold himself into the middle of our canoe. Sighing to myself I had him and Margie trade places, giving him the front seat and putting her in with the children. It pained me to do this; there is a limit to my endurance and I was fast approaching it. We have gone over 170 miles in the last three days and I did not relish a solo seven-mile paddle though the gathering darkness across ever treacherous Lake Athabasca in a heavily loaded canoe. Tired as I was, the venture had all the earmarks of potential disaster. Was I in for a surprise!

That Indian was incredible. He fiddled around amongst our paddle collection, picked out a big one, looked back at me and grinned. Then he started in. It was amazing -- the man was a paddling machine, a real professional. He dug in with short powerful strokes and the canoe began to hum along. I had to really dig in myself to maintain the proper rhythm. He could feel the added thrust as the canoe began to surf and again he looked back to smile. I smiled back and then we were off to the races. As soon as he began to tire on one side he would switch sides without a pause and continue on. The first such switch caught me by surprise; Margie and I never alternate and I wondered what to do. I considered switching also to accommodate him but then decided he probably wasn't going to look back again anyway. (Really so long as the stern man has

227

a full sized paddle it makes little difference which side the bowman paddles on in a big canoe. It just takes a little more snap in the wrist as you lift the paddle out of the water when you are both on the same side.) Anyway I continued stoically, apparently oblivious, lost in silent contemplation of the sun setting behind the mountains across the lake, or so it seemed. Actually I was in trouble. I'd already paddled some fifteen hours today and my muscles were protesting. If he wanted to race though, I was not going to disappoint him. There is no way that I have come 3500 miles to be done in by an aging arthritic septuagenarian. It was a gorgeous evening and the lake was very beautiful. The sky was all aglow with a peach pink haze from the setting sun and the water was flat calm. I set the canoe to rocking with that smooth rhythm that comes from a consistent stroke, then turned off my mind to stare into the distance. I knew it would be over in less than two hours.

Actually, it ended sooner than I dared hope. Another motor boat came by and my Indian waved it down. His pal took him back to gas up the boat and we were free to continue at a more sedate pace, but not for long.

Thunderclouds were coming and we were going to be hard put to reach safety before they arrived. About then our Indian came back with his refueled boat and insisted on towing us the rest of the way into town. He was very concerned about the approaching storm and we wisely acquiesced, arriving just as it was getting fully dark.

We made it the first order of business to drop in on our Coast Guard friends. Were they surprised to see us -- we felt as if we had set some kind of speed record. (We didn't tell them about the tow of the last couple of miles.) They pointed out a good campsite and invited us for breakfast. We can hardly wait -- fresh food.

The local teenagers turned out to help us set up camp. The Indians were very friendly and spoke excellent English. Really, they were like so many excited puppies in their eagerness to play with the kids and be helpfully underfoot. They tried to unload the canoe, get out the tents, put them up, and get the beds ready. It was too dark to see though and everything was total confusion. They asked questions nonstop and with their help everything took us about three times as long as normal. We were grateful just to tumble into bed shortly after midnight, alone at last.

Tonight I have my annual gripe with Timberline. We bought a new tent this year but now the zipper has worn out already and the mosquitoes are terribly thick. This has happened before so there are two spare four

228

foot heavy duty zippers at the bottom of one of our packs, but this is not the time to set up for a major sewing bee.

AUGUST 10: RIVIÈRE DES ROCHERS

After three record-setting days in a row (190 miles from Fort McMurray to Fort Chipewyan) we finally lost momentum. The Coast Guard doesn't serve breakfast until 7:00 and we began the day by sleeping in till 6:30. When we finally trooped over to their boat, however, it was well worth the wait. They fêted us with eggs, bacon, toast and jam, apple and orange juice, and milk. Then we were given a quick tour of the boat (which has a crew of eight) and finally sent off with a bag of goodies -- cookies, oranges, and chocolate bars. At 8:00 sharp they left for Uranium City at the east end of Athabasca Lake.

Afterwards we toured Fort Chipewyan, which is getting electricity and plumbing this year, and did some shopping. Of course we met the inevitable natives carrying Kreuger fliers. We are well-accustomed to this by now though and find their presence everywhere a source of amusement.

It was nearly noon before we set out around Mission Point for Rivière des Rochers. It is a strange area geographically. The terrain seems to consist of huge rock islands surrounded by dismal swamps. Still these huge rock outcroppings (100 feet high or more) give the otherwise monotonous wetlands an oddly scenic appearance and are visible from miles away towering above the swampy grasses. The river current is very weak and we battled a strong head wind out of the north for much of the afternoon. In fact, we were lucky to cover the twenty miles down to the portage at Little Rapids where we are camped tonight.

Somewhere nearby is the worst fire we have run into all summer. This afternoon the smoke was so thick it made breathing difficult and now the sun is so obscured that it is just a red dot through the smoke. The prospects of a raging forest fire make us a little queasy but it is a big river and we are camped on an island in the middle.

Despite its color we are drinking the water. Margie is baking my birthday cake. We are a day late with it but it smells delicious!

229

AUGUST 11: SLAVE RIVER

Another slow and windy day. The highlight of the morning came when we used our accumulated woodcraft to sneak up on a moose that turned out to be a tree stump. At noon we reached Slave River and had a lengthy lunch stop on the huge sand bar there which marks the confluence of the Peace River and Riviere des Rochers.

The Slave River is huge and fast, really like nothing we have seen before in terms of power. Every so often the current will swirl in whirlpools and giant boils which leave the paddler feeling almost helpless.

Today was hot and the children went swimming but the water was far too cool for us. Later on we saw a bear out swimming also but we frightened him away. The river banks are high and muddy and tonight we are camped directly in their shadow on flat mud at water level. Fortunately, it so seldom rains around here that the ground is baked dry and hard, and is fragmented by a honeycomb of surface cracks. Tina and Randy have been collecting flat chunks of mud which they have cleared off of the boulders nearby. They have also been for a walk down the beach and reported tracks of moose, bear and wolves.

AUGUST 12: HAILSTONES AND OZONE

Last night after we went to bed the wind shifted and soon the forest fire smoke became so thick that it was acrid breathing even in the tents and we all found ourselves coughing. Then about 1:00 the sky started to streak with lightning, thunder echoed, and we were treated to a succession of storms which kept us in the tents till 9:00 this morning.

The storms brought quite a change of weather. For the last week or so it has been in the eighties but today it was cool enough to see our breath. Nobody felt like swimming. The high clay cliff had protected us from the winds in the night but the rain had made the walking pretty greasy and packing things up was a slapstick comedy as we slipped around in the liquid mud.

It was strange weather today, with lots of wind, smoke and storm clouds as well as the surprising coolness. About 3:00 we pulled over and barely got stuff tumbled under the canoe before we were hit by a real humdinger of a thunderstorm. For several minutes we were pelted by a flurry of marble sized hailstones and the lightning was cracking so near around us that the smell of ozone persisted for several minutes. Fifteen minutes later though it was over and, somewhat shaken, we loaded up to continue on. For the third straight day the wind was powerfully against us and we battled whitecaps and rollers that were driving upstream. If someone had told me at Fort Chipewyan that after three more days I would be less than seventy miles away I would not have believed it, and yet here we are.

We stopped early tonight and the weather now is very cold, windy and rainy. Supper was an unpleasant affair. Margie hunkered under the tarp mixing the bannock between downpours, and the children kept warm by tending the fire. Our narrow shelf of mud was very slippery so just to get a drink or brush our teeth at the water's edge was to risk falling in. Now, however we are comfortably ensconced in a handhewn clearing amongst some pine, high atop the bank overlooking the river. It was quite a trick climbing up here, but well worth it. Safely settled in our eyrie we sit here watching the rolling dirty Slave sweep irresistibly by. The rippling boils and eddies are irrefutable evidence of its raw power and their rhythmic surging has mesmerized us. The north has claimed us and each year we must return. Eventually perhaps we shall have had enough but by then there will be a lifetime of rich experiences to look back on and no one can ask for more.

AUGUST 13: FORT SMITH

We paddled thirty-five miles today and now Year Two has ended. This morning it was sunny and nearly calm. We slid down from our campsite high on the bank and set off at 7:00.

It was nearly suppertime when we reached the ghost settlement Fitzgerald, where we stopped to eat while we pondered our next move. Ever since Fort McMurray we have been warned about the thirteen miles of class six rapids between Fitzgerald and Fort Smith. "Don't go around the corner" has been the universal cry and so we stopped to consider the situation while we ate supper.

Soon a truck pulled up to say hello. The Jewells had come over from Fort Smith to check on their boat and you can't imagine a nicer couple. They offered to drive us into town, to keep our gear for the winter, and even arranged for us to catch the bus out tomorrow morning.

231

So here we are, our first and last night in the Northwest Territories. It is exciting and a little sad. We would love to keep going, but know we can't. We are going through our all too familiar withdrawal symptoms; saying goodbye to one world, and hello to the next. It takes a few days to adjust. Soon though we shall be back in New Hampshire. For the next eight months I shall tick off the days till spring on my office calendar exhibiting the prison mentality that my colleagues so deplore. Eventually though the snows will melt, school will end, and we shall come roaring back to complete our dream. It will be Alaska at last!

END OF THE SECOND YEAR

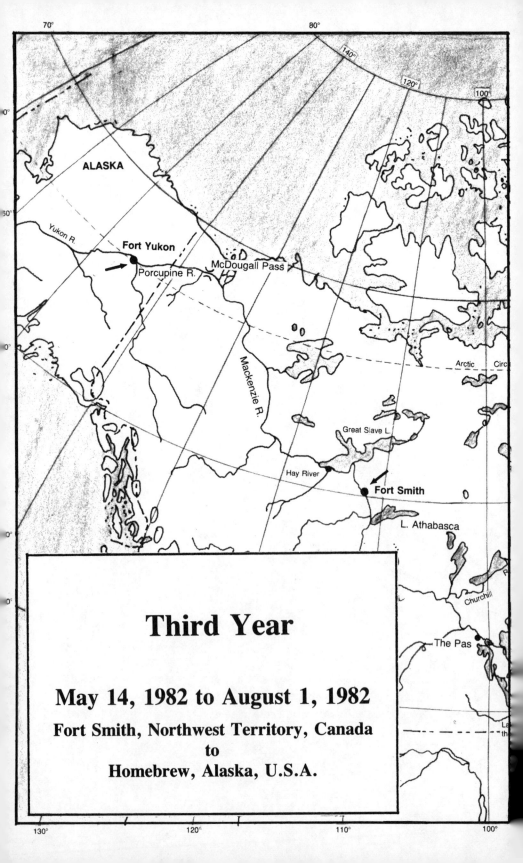

Third Year

May 14, 1982 to August 1, 1982

**Fort Smith, Northwest Territory, Canada
to
Homebrew, Alaska, U.S.A.**

MAY 14, 1982: DEPARTURE

Tomorrow we leave. Margie got up early this morning and phoned our radio weatherman. Then we lay snuggled down, luxuriating a few final moments in our comfy bed, while we awaited the answers. A few minutes later a puzzled announcer had the news, "It is 8 degrees and snowing hard in Fort Smith, NWT." Brr, that's cold!

Perhaps we are leaving too soon, but we are absolutely committed to the date. I have given up my job for next year and we have leased out the house. The tenants move in tomorrow. Our belongings are scattered amongst relatives and friends and the cat has gone to the SPCA. The children have withdrawn from school -- there will be lessons for them in the canoe this summer -- and we have given away our car. We have piled gambles on risks, acting with complete assurance despite the uncertain nature of our venture. Many a traveller has failed in an attempt to cross the Rockies via the route we have chosen but as with the early Klondikers our commitment is almost total. We are not exactly sure where we shall end up next year, but we are on the way!

MAY 16: NIAGARA FALLS

We have been on the road two days and have perhaps another ten to go. A colleague offered to drive us out to Fort Smith where our gear is cached and after some hesitation we gratefully accepted. Four thousand miles is a long ride for five people in a pickup truck and we were worried that he might not be able to stand us so many days.

We wanted to show the kids Niagara Falls and the visit was a great success although it reminded us of how late spring is. Above the falls a steady parade of ice floes tumbled along continuously to spill into the steaming depths, while down below, the gorge was completely choked for several hundred yards by contorted ridges of piled and jumbled ice.

Nevertheless, the day was warm and we all came away with a little sunburn.

MAY 25: ANTICIPATION

We have driven over 3000 miles in the last ten days, stopping only occasionally to visit the scenic wonders that tourists frequent across the top of the nation. This morning we finally changed direction and the day became one of mounting anticipation as we headed due north. Mile by mile it seemed to get colder and we began to worry about the increasingly winterlike conditions. Glacier Park had been all but closed on account of snow and as we headed north out of Calgary the temperature dropped from 57 at midmorning to 47 by midafternoon. The leaves began to wither back into buds and disappear and when we reached Lesser Slave Lake our worst fears were confirmed. The eastern half was completely ice-covered and the western half only beginning to break up. We have a long ways north to drive yet and it begins to look as if we should have brought a sled. Tonight we are camped at 56 degrees north latitude and that is precisely double the present temperature.

MAY 26: ICE

Today's temperatures quickly rose into the forties and then declined from there. We reached the town of Hay River in time for supper and are camped tonight on the shore of Great Slave Lake. We were disappointed but not surprised to find that the lake is still covered by ice.

The temperature is only 27 degrees here but the sun is shining brightly. It is 11:00 p.m. and we should not see darkness again until the middle of August! Tomorrow we reach Fort Smith.

MAY 27: FORT SMITH

The wooded drive into Fort Smith changed some in our absence.

Late last summer a forest fire raged northwards over the highway simultaneously threatening the three communities of Hay River, Pine Point and Fort Smith. Local opinion now has it that the best idea in such a conflagration is to stay in your vehicle to avoid death by heat radiation and oxygen starvation. (Plan instead on going up with your gas tank if such be your fate.)

In Fort Smith we went to the museum where we learned more about the history of our route, particularly about Albert Johnson, "The Mad Trapper" who led the Mounties on an incredible winter chase up the Rat, over the Richardsons and down the Bell. In one three-day blizzard he managed to cover ninety miles and when the RCMP finally trapped and killed him they discovered each of his hand-made snowshoes weighed ten pounds. That is about what each of our water-filled rubber boots will weigh as we struggle up the Rat river in his path but I suspect our pace shall be a little slower. We also learned that pelicans have the world's slowest wingbeat, 1.3 seconds, which is at least part of the reason they appear so majestic in flight.

Well, today was not all play and, despite the recent low temperatures, the mosquitoes were surprisingly thick. We reclaimed our canoe and spent much of the afternoon working hard on it. I replaced a two-foot section of rotted gunwale and added a couple of screws to the other, which had broken the night of the moose hunt when the wind slammed our overloaded canoe into the Indian's boat. The cane seats were shot also and I started weaving new cane and webbing combinations which I'll finish tomorrow. The old paddles received a little sanding and a lot of varnish. Although I had to give up on adding another layer of cloth to the canoe bottom (it is just too cold for the resin to set), there is still a lot to do. Also tomorrow is shopping day. We plan to start out with supplies for over fifty days, a very heavy load when combined with all our other gear. (We have tried to bring almost everything that we might need to carry us through next winter. I persuaded Margie to leave the electric skillet but I think we still must have thirty pounds of books.)

Well, the 29th is the big day. We are aiming to push off before noon. It snowed south of here yesterday but so far our weather continues fair.

MAY 29: WE'RE OFF

What beautiful weather to start the trip; sunny, warm and calm till noon. We had clear sailing all morning, marred only by the swarms of mosquitoes following us downstream. We never expected to see so many so early in the year and lunch was in the canoe to avoid the worst of them. It was hot enough that I could smell the back of my shirt baking and Margie donned her gloves to prevent a recurrence of last year's burns.

Early this afternoon the wind began to hinder us but with the help of the current we continued to progress although at a slower pace. At least the breezes kept the bugs down and cooled us off. The canoe was very crowded, so much so that the kids could scarcely lay down to take naps. They each paddled a couple of hours instead, which could, I hope, become a habit. Later on the wind picked up in earnest and we encountered a miniature typhoon. It sounded like a rushing rapid as it came closer and closer, skittering back and forth across the river about one hundred yards behind us. It was a first experience for us but apparently of no concern. As suddenly as it came the whirling column dissipated before our eyes.

The river is far less attractive for camping now than it was last August. There are big hunks of dirty ice along the edges keeping the shores slick and muddy, and all along we hear continual splashing as eroding chunks of mud tumble down from the undercut banks. We spent two hours searching for a campsite, investigating steep muddy banks one after another, and finally settled for a small clearing in the bush high above the shoreline. The mosquitoes are just frightful and unloading the canoe turned out to be miserably difficult with the deep soft mud. In fact, we had to leave the largest pack right in the canoe which we left afloat, tied to a bush for the night. The pack was too big and awkward to remove and there was no room on shore to put the canoe. Up on top we erected the tents so that the kids would have a bug-free haven in which to play. Margie and I ate a quick supper in the smoke of the fire and the kids dined at leisure in their tent. Afterwards, we popped right into bed. As Tina said, we should be allowed to break in gradually and not be hit with such difficulties so early in the summer. Really, the kids behaved well today under very confining conditions. They managed to spend long hours painting with their new watercolor sets and were otherwise very helpful.

We saw a bear and a beaver today, the first ones of the year. The Slave River is extremely muddy, even more so than we remembered,

236

and we are carrying our drinking water with us. With such flat and muddy country though we wonder where we shall be able to resupply. Also a minor catastrophe was revealed tonight when we discovered that somehow we have left our axe in Fort Smith. Unfortunately, I have always believed an axe to be the one indispensable tool on any wilderness trip. Let's hope I'm wrong and that it doesn't rain enough this summer to make fires difficult. Well, we have survived the first day and are driving for the finish. Alaska, here we come!

MAY 30: SWANS

Today was what we assume will be a very typical day this year. We did 38 miles, heading north, paddling with the current and against the wind. There is no sand, gravel or rock anywhere and after only two days everything we own is covered with a thin film of dusty dried mud, even the dishes. The water is so dirty that a cupful looks like coffee with cream and we can't really clean anything. The shore is wet and muddy due to the melting ice and the inside of the canoe is coated with a greasy quarter-inch layer of mud from all our stepping in and out.

Last night it was impossible but this evening I did manage to get the big pack out of the canoe. It is very ungainly and weighs over a hundred pounds. I had it out but began sinking in the mud before I could take a step. Margie floundered to my rescue and tried to help by pulling up on one of my hind legs but then the other one only sunk in deeper. It was very comical and fortunately I was in too deep to lose my balance and topple over.

The mosquitoes have outdone themselves this year, really the best crop we have ever seen. Whenever the wind dies they just light on us like little leeches and at times our pants legs are completely covcered by their bodies. They are so thick that when we slap with our hand it actually squishes and comes away wet.

The two new lightweight strip paddles I made before leaving home are working very well and may be the best we've ever had. They were made by alternating strips of fir and mahogany and are quite beautiful besides being so light and functional.

Well, the first few days are always tough physically. We paddled ten hours today and by this afternoon my mind had started to dwell on my aches. Margie, however, is doing very well. She is wearing gloves for sunburn and taking aspirin three times a day to prevent the recurring shoulder aches that give her problems. She has brought along 600 of the coated ones (coated to prevent disintegration) which should be a full season's supply.

The weather was intermittently sunny all day long with occasional clouds and a light shower. The children played happily by themselves. They did schoolwork in the morning then played cards and painted with watercolors in the afternoon.

Today we saw our first swans and also several eagles. Two of the latter were sitting in their nests but were quick to pop away when we tried to photograph them. A third was likewise camera shy and played leap frog down the riverbank ahead of us always just out of camera range.

MAY 31: FIRST HUNDRED

Only three days out and we have already done a hundred miles! This is easily the quickest start of our three year trip. Actually, however, today was pretty poor for paddling. It was cold with a stiff breeze out of the north making a chill factor that was decidedly uncomfortable. The kids needed mittens to play and Margie's feet never did warm up. This afternoon there were whitecaps coming upstream forcing us into the slower water near shore. By 4:30 we were exhausted and stopped for the night on a relatively dry mud bar.

Today we saw two muskrats and a gray goose with a yellow bill that we were unable to identify. We also found some fresher water. The stream coming in from Hook Lake is relatively clear, about like dirty bath water, and we replenished our drinking supply.

I am having a hard time adjusting to the endless daylight and am unable to sleep effectively for more than a few hours each night. Perhaps I am just not tired enough yet.

The children went wading and sliding in the mud at our campsite this afternoon, then we all changed to clean clothes.

JUNE 1: TYPHOON

This river has some peculiar weather. Twice this week we have seen little typhoonettes mysteriously spring up. Today's was a rip-snorter and we were pretty apprehensive for a few moments. At first it sounded like the whir of ducks taking off, then the noise built to a rapids-like roar. The swirling column pursued an erratic course off to our left for a few hundred yards and then veered off to crash into a high mud bank with a whomp. I don't understand how such mild weather manages to rip up an otherwise placid, fast flowing river and send it twisting into the air. I'm not sure what our best defense is but it is nothing to experiment with. Today's waterspout certainly hit the bank with a real shock.

Well, today was pretty normal otherwise. It was hot and calm. The further down the river we come the more ice there is along the banks, and it is very muddy and sloppy climbing up to camp. Several times a day there is a resounding crash as a major portion of riverbank falls into the water, and we keep well back from the overhangs. Also we are hoarding our drinking water as there are no clear tributaries and the river is filthy with colloidal silt. We use river water for cooking and washing.

We are seeing more and more birds which are new to us, particularly large groups of swans, small grey geese, and almost-white ducks.

The children, on account of the insects, have adopted a new travelling style and we scarcely see them anymore. During the day they hide out under the tarp in the canoe where they sit and play wearing their headnets. Then, as soon as we hit the shore, they set up their tent and disappear inside until morning.

Tonight a new breed of mosquito has appeared. Until now we had been dealing only with speedy little ones with a high-pitched whine. This evening, however, some big ones with bright green eyes have found us. They sould like humming birds, are surprisingly agile and are possessed of great strength. I did manage to catch one in my left hand but he pried my fingers apart and escaped before I could crush him.

JUNE 2: END OF THE RIVER

We are keeping a lot of items lying loose in the bottom of the boat this year to lighten the packs and make it easier to lift them out, but we are still having problems. The mud is so sticky that even with our lightened loads we become mired and in trying to free one foot we invariably trap the other. The worst though is when a boot is sucked right off and we trip directly into the muck. At least we haven't buried a pack yet though, so perhaps our strategy is working.

Tonight we are camped on the outskirts of the Slave delta. We have a nice dry accessible site with trees instead of brush and we stopped early rather than risk venturing out to the lake late in the day. Today's weather was cold and mostly cloudy, but whenever the sun did break through the temperature shot right up. As a result, we spent an unusual amount of time donning and doffing layers and changing hats and mittens in an effort to stay comfortable.

Three Indians from Fort Resolution dropped by about supper time. They said we should have taken Nagel Channel and saved some miles. (The delta is fairly complex and we chose to stay with the main current in Steamboat Channel.) We also learned through observation that the water is safe to drink. One Indian gulped down a cupful and an hour later he was still okay.

After supper the Indians put on a miserable display and had poor Tina in tears. They were after a beaver in the channel and spent most of an hour firing away with two rifles as they cruised up and down the waterway in their motorboat chasing the animal each time he surfaced. It was a pretty pitiful spectacle. Bullets were riccocheting all around as they fired at every suspicious ripple. Beaver are out of season now and these were not treaty Indians, but give some people a motorboat and rifle and they think they are hunters, no matter how inept or illegal. Poor Tina was in the tent all upset long before it was over, only wanting to know after each shot whether the beaver was dead and if we thought he might get away. He didn't.

JUNE 3: FORT RESOLUTION

What a welcome to Great Slave Lake. We thought that we would zip right in to Fort Resolution for breakfast. Instead it took six hours. The river mouth was clear, except for the hundreds of swans and other water birds in the shallow bay there, but the problem came soon after.

Mission Point guards the bay on which the village lies and ice had jammed up there as far out as we could see. We spent at least three hours on one half-mile stretch alone. We were both out on the ice trying to mush the canoe along while the children watched from shore. The ice was about two feet thick but honeycombed so badly that occasionally we fell right through. It was hard risky work, and cold too. The bottom of our canoe took quite a beating and I chewed up one of my old paddles hacking away at the ice. We are going to have to be a lot more patient in the future.

Once past the Fort we were able to continue another seven miles into Resolution Bay before the ice closed back in. Again the kids got out to run along the shore while we alternately paddled, poled and waded through the drifting floes. It never got above fifty degrees today and even working hard we were chilly. Thus it was with some surprise we looked over to see the kids playing barefoot on the beach and wading out amongst the floes up to their knees. For some reason they were wearing their boots on their hands.

Although the woods are deep with snow here, there is one major improvement over yesterday -- the water is clear and cold. It is excellent for drinking and good for washing too. Tonight the mud is nearly off of our belongings.

JUNE 4: FIRST REST DAY

Tonight we are sleeping at the same campsite again. We woke up at 3:30 this morning to a hard rain and found the wind was blowing our ice-free lagoon up under our doorsteps. In fact, we were on two-inch waterbeds and our packs were almost floating. Last night we had risked erecting the tents on a low sand beach and now we had to move. Fortunately the land in back was mostly tussocky hummocks of grass and snow. Also, even at 3:30 the sky was fully light so we were able to reposition without trouble.

It rained all day and stayed very cold (upper thirties). Occasionally we would pop out for food or for books to read, then run back to bed. Everyone was damp but we survived quite well. Later this afternoon the rain began letting up and we went scrounging back in the alder bushes for dry wood. In such conditions, without an axe, it seemed an almost hopeless task, but nevertheless we soon had a roaring fire going. No one felt like playing in the drizzle so we simply cooked a hot meal, dried our sleeping bags as best we could, and went back to bed. Tonight though the rain really does seem to be ending although the sky is still heavily overcast. There are whitecaps on the lake and the thermometer reads 34 degrees. At least the ice-pack has blown about a mile offshore and we should have clear sailing in the morning. It is only about eighty miles to Hay River and perhaps we can get there before it blows back in.

The snow in back of camp didn't melt much today.

JUNE 5: SNOW

I'm not sure that we are hardy enough to be "Territorial Trippers". Yesterday was miserable and today was hardly any better. It rained some more last night but, good news, by morning it had stopped. The bad news is that it was snowing instead -- not much of an improvement with the wind howling and the temperature in the twenties. With all the inclement weather and nothing but wet driftwood and alder bushes around, it was again hard to start a fire. I really miss my axe. Still I managed to accumulate dry wood by using my knife to split some little logs and soon we were standing around a bonfire contemplating our position. It is more or less a family rule that we don't canoe in the snow and we had to wait till noon for it to stop. Afterwards, we tried paddling with mittens on, but they were little help and our hands quickly became numb. The ice pack drifted back onshore almost immediately and even though the sun was out the temperature stayed near freezing. It was 34 degrees at suppertime and it is 28 degrees now. The afternoon was spent wading through ice, poling and hauling, and we made only a few miles. Tonight we are camped on a rocky point. Out back the snow is two feet deep and out front the ice stretches from the shore to the horizon in every direction except for the narrow little path we hacked out from the east.

Randy can be so exasperating. Somehow all his wool socks and both his mittens are soaked from playing in the ice and snow the last two days. At these temperatures it is a little hard to dry them. This is canoeing?

JUNE 6: MOOSTLETOE

It was 23 degrees and snowing hard when we got up this morning. There was no way we were going canoeing. The lake had frozen solid. All the little interstices between the floes and the narrow strips of water in the shallows were glare ice. When you toss boulders onto the lake and all they do is bounce it is a safe bet that you won't be paddling for a while, and we ended up staying -- rest day number two. At least the snow eventually stopped and the sun came out.

Actually the day was not a total loss. In the morning the kids did a little school work and whittled a lot of sticks. Margie got out her brushes and bottles of oil paints and decorated the canoe. All around the outside just above the waterline she painted the names of the major lakes and rivers along our route, so now we are a moving travelogue. I spent the time staring out at the ice hoping for it to melt but I may have overdone it. For awhile I could have sworn there were two new islands which have since disappeared.

In the afternoon the kids got into Margie's paints which are apparently a lot more fun than their watercolors. It was not the disaster you might imagine. We have always encouraged the children to be creative and today they were. They began by painting miniature Easter eggs and jellybeans for Turtle and Elly. They have been collecting dessicated spheres of moose turd and a few daubs of color on each was all it took. From there they went on to Christmas presents. I have some very fine wire in my tackle box and we used several of their best eggs to fashion earrings for Grandma. Although these wilderness concoctions may not be to everyone's taste, we made several bright and delightfully exotic pairs. We have plenty of materials and there seems to be no end of possibilities. This evening we are branching out. Tina is working on a necklace and I have made a sprig of "moostletoe", something no door-jamb should be without come Christmas.

JUNE 7: REST DAY NUMBER THREE

Another day in the same place. At least this is a beautiful spot and we have established a comfortable schedule. In the morning we get up and heave rocks onto the clear ice that froze the night before. Then we

the CROSSING

SANDERS, '85 ©

244

sit and watch the rocks melt through. This takes several hours, say till 10:00 a.m., and is the subject of much spirited discussion as we speculate on which ones will sink through first.

The days are clear blue, really bright and sunny. With so much ice everything sparkles all the way to the horizon. By noon the ice is really starting to melt and we run up and down the shore poking at it with sticks. By 2:00 all of last night's new ice has melted and real progress begins. This is the exciting part of the day but it is over by 4:00. We spend those two hours wondering whether enough has melted to allow us to push the canoe along. At 3:00 I even take the empty canoe out for a little test spin and get about twenty feet, wading and poling, before I am hopelessly jammed up. Maybe tomorrow. About 4:00 everything has finally loosened up to the point where the on-shore breezes can crunch the ice pack in another ten feet and pile it up along the shore. From 4:00 to 6:00 this new shore ice begins to melt. After that it starts to harden up again for the night. There will be several more hours of sunlight but the sun is too low in the sky to be effective. Although the sun feels hot all day, we keep a driftwood fire going right along and the thermometer shows the temperature has never gotten out of the thirties in the shade. Another good day for cooking pea soup.

Well, the kids did schoolwork today, ran scavenger hunts, and read. Margie and I went for a walk, napped in the sun, and played Scrabble (thereby concluding that canoeing is an agathokakalogical activity). All in all it was a second idyllic day in what could be an endless chain for all the progress we can see.

JUNE 8: REST DAY NUMBER FOUR

Today I got out the mirror and watched my whiskers grow. I believe the white threads were the fastest. Another day here and I shall be climbing the trees.

JUNE 9: REST DAY NUMBER FIVE

We are starting to think of being here in terms of weeks rather than

245

days. On the fifteenth one of us shall start hiking out to prevent search parties from being launched as our Hay River late-date approaches.

Last night I was determined that no matter what, we would leave today. If necessary I was going to load the canoe on the ice, then sit and watch it melt through. Next, I planned to pull it up on the ice a little farther west and repeat the process. We would have proceeded at a slow but steady clip, but, unfortunately, the weather did not cooperate.

This morning was bitterly cold, just 18 degrees when we arose. Then, on top of that, the whole lake began unaccountably to move. There was not even a whisper of a breeze and yet it was the most spectacular action we have seen here. For over an hour the ice just ground ashore, coming in at the rate of about one foot per minute, piling up deeper and deeper as it jammed against the rocks. After that, of course, the plan was hopeless. We shall be days just melting back to where we were.

There have been many new sounds and noises this year. Living in the bush seems to improve our hearing almost without limit; soon we should be enjoying the clashing of individual molecules. On the river we had the distinctive plops of eroding banks and the whooshing of waterspouts. Now there are the many ice noises. Two days ago it sounded like wind chimes as the breezes tinkled the floating shards together. Since then there has been the constant background rustling each day as the ice shifts and slumps into slush under the steady pressure of the beating sun. This morning though was all pops and groans while the ice creaked its way up over the rocks. Then all was silent. It was rather eerie with the still, white expanse stretching out of sight, until the familiar melting rustle began again a few hours later.

Naturally, we have discussed portaging along the shore. It is about 100 miles to the Mackenzie and normally we would set out to carry as far as necessary, but for once it is simply not practical. Knowing there was only one short portage in the entire distance from Fort Smith to the Bering Sea (we're not going that far), we decided to bring along a few extras this summer: a second towel, a bigger pot, etc. They add up to quite a load and would entail many trips. Also, I am hesitant to even try carrying the canoe. The shoreline is all rocks and boulders and it would be only a matter of time till I fell. Our poor old canoe is really not up to many more hard knocks. So here we sit.

246

JUNE 10: AT LAST

This morning it finally happened! The sky was bleak and gray when we awoke and then around 9:30 the wind began to shift offshore. It was only a few hours more before big cracks and leads were opening up a half mile out. After lunch we packed up and carried everything 200 yards along the shore to a more promising spot and sure enough, at 2:00 p.m. we were paddling out a newly opened channel. Free at last! We paddled steadily till suppertime and then on till 10:00. The breeze remains steady offshore so things look promising for tomorrow. Two more such days and we shall reach Hay River.

It was fun to be out on the water again today, and a little awe-inspiring. The floes and ice chunks appear to have been pushed up by giant bulldozers, sometimes ten to twenty feet high.

The sky cleared late this afternoon and the ice shone white against the deep blue waters, making the submerged portions of the bergs a watery green. It was as if by magic we had been transported to a summery arctic coastline and only the seals were missing to complete the picture.

JUNE 11: SULPHUR POINT

What a grueling day! We were up before 5:00, anxious to be off while conditions remained so good, and the children slept the first two hours in the canoe. We were covering almost three miles an hour, exulting in the glorious conditions as we paddled in and out amongst the giant bergs, when the wind began to shift. We were determined to eke out every inch and made it half way across the final bay to Sulphur Point before the incoming ice began to hem us in. Turning shorewards, we managed to wade the shallows to within a mile of the rocky point before progress became impossible. There we faced a solid sheet of ice and snow which was jumbled house-high onto the shore. This was the last big point between us and Hay River and it appeared the ice could well be there forever, or at least until July. The time had come to portage.

We cooked a hot lunch and then started out. The walking was better on the ice than along the brushy shore so we portaged over the slanted shore-bound bergs, warily avoiding the deep crevices between floes. There were many trips to make and by supper we were scarcely two miles

247

along. The children were exhausted though and we set up camp on a tiny grass clearing amid some driftwood. Afterwards I portaged on alone.

It is nearly midnight now but I believe the end is in sight. Two-thirds of our belongings are up at Sulphur Cove and just beyond there I saw clear water before turning back to camp. We shall make an early morning portage and then perhaps we'll be free again. I saw a lot of wolf tracks along the shore this evening and Margie found a kildeer nest near the tents.

JUNE 12: FISH POINT

For the first time we can remember, it did not freeze at night. In fact, the lake continued to melt while we slept and today was bright and hot. Unfortunately, this meant that the hordes of mosquitoes we experienced earlier have returned to bother us.

The morning, as expected, began with the long carry to Sulphur Cove. Then the rest of the day we paddled except for the last few hours. By then the ice was forcing us into the shallows and we had to wade to keep the canoe from grounding. Tonight we are camped at the little creek just beyond Fish Point where Randy has caught us an excellent pike for supper.

Great Slave Lake lacks the grandeur of Lake Superior but it is striking nonetheless. The sloping stacks of ice layered 20 feet deep upon the inshore rocks and beaches are the most spectacular feature but we are also impressed by the fact that there are no leaves and hardly any buds on the shrubs fringing the shore. It is still so winterlike. Indeed each day we marvel at the cold air streaming shorewards off the ice. It is distinctly visible as a low and moving layer pulsing toward the land, distorting all that lies behind. Viewed against a distant point it creates shimmering mirages; close up it is an invisible breath of cold.

The ice itself has many aspects. Much of it is so hard it would bounce an axe. In other places, however, two-foot vertical shards cling precariously together, forming fragile floes ten feet in diameter. At the slightest touch these latter starburst into a glittering fan of icicles like some giant flower unfolding. Even so slight a disturbance as our passing wake will send them cascading musically apart, the colliding shards becoming nature's wind chimes.

248

JUNE 13: HAY RIVER

Today was another hard day. It stayed warm last night and the mosquitoes were so thick when we arose that we decided to escape with a cold breakfast out on the water (a box of Cheerios and instant breakfast drink). We planned to arrive in Hay River for an early lunch but once again the ice delayed us. In fact we had to wade, dragging the canoe, and even make occasional portages along the beach for the final six miles. Eventually we stopped to cook lunch over a driftwood fire. When we finally did arrive we were amused to see that even the Coast Guard is frustrated. The ice is late to leave this year and they had three powerful tugs out trying to push the ice back from around the mouth of the Hay River. They were pretty successful but now that it is evening they've gone home and the ice is starting to drift back in. In general, the ice is less than two feet thick now, say about fifteen inches.

We are intrigued by the occasional eagle we see sitting forlornly out on the ice. I suppose they too are waiting for spring and open water. It is a wonder that their toes don't get cold. Of course the yellowlegs (we call them ice-pipers) can run around pecking on the ice all day long. It is cold again tonight.

JUNE 14: SWIMMING

This morning was all business. We did a little food shopping in Hay River, then visited the post office and laundromat. We were pretty dirty and would have enjoyed a hot shower before putting on our clean clothes, but the closest thing available was a sponge bath at the local campground. For a dollar each we could dip hot water out of their sink and pat ourselves down with a warm washcloth. Of course, prices are high up here, but that was ridiculous. We held our breaths and took the plunge into the lake. Actually it was a delightful swimming spot with a nice sandy bottom, and we even washed our hair. Still the next time we feel the urge to clean up I hope there won't be so much ice in the water.

We left town in the middle of the afternoon and tonight we are camped just beyond Pointe des Roches. There have been thunderstorms since suppertime and the mosquitoes are unbelievable. We jumped into the tent as soon as we landed, not even bothering to eat the dessert of

249

canned peaches we'd been saving.

Margie's hands are a wreck again this year. In Hay River two people tried to offer her unsolicited first aid. She has been wearing gloves but they didn't prevent blisters, or itching and swelling for more than the first few days. We are almost positive now that it is not just sunburn. Anyway, a week of first aid (pills, salve, and "Second Skin" taped on) and preventing exposure to either heat or cold seems to be helping. The swelling and itching are almost gone and we hope that in another week the sores will be healing too. As it is, everything from cooking to packing is quite a chore for her with mittens on.

Outside Hay River we saw an Indian church whose steeple was made from flattened tin cans back in the days when metal was scarce up here. Beer cans, I suppose.

JUNE 15: MACKENZIE RIVER

The weather has sure turned. Tonight we are lying in our tents just dripping with sweat. It is so hot!

We started with a rush this morning. First, we were aroused early by a wolf padding around the tents. Then, because it was so buggy, we just dragged the tents down to the shore and threw everything into the canoe. It was a quick start to what should have been a great day (the ice was way out), but soon we were paddling directly into a strong wind and the hours from 7:30 to 12:30 passed with agonizing slowness. We did get our first close-up look at a coot, however. He was entangled in a fisherman's runaway net and I had to hold him in my lap to slash away the cords that were cutting into his feathers and trapping his feet. He did not act particularly grateful though. Once free, he plunged into the water and disappeared.

Well, it was an exhausting paddle, but tonight we are off of Great Slave Lake and parked a few miles down the south channel of the Mackenzie, just before it opens up into Beaver Lake. Now that Great Slave is totally behind us I can conclude that the southern shore is really quite miserable canoe country. The area is low and swampy with shallow rocky waters extending far offshore. Except for isolated beach areas near Fort Resolution, Buffalo River and Hay River, the shoreline is unattractive and makes pretty poor camping. Actually, the first few miles of the Mackenzie are not much better. Also the mosquitoes are fully as bad as we experienced on the Saskatchewan last summer. Today we wore head-nets, gloves and raingear to help us survive through supper. We had a couple of small pike as the main course and afterwards I took a few more practice casts while Margie put away the dishes. We were in a hurry to get into bed away from the bugs but I ended up having to spend another hour out there. Fishing is a perverse enterprise and now when I least desired it, I found myself battling with a real monster. I have a special lure for my after dinner practice casts, one with a single barbless hook, so I was sure he would get away soon. But we were both unwilling to release the lure so the tug of war went on and on. Eventually I tricked him into swimming onto the beach where I could measure him: 40 inches, a huge pike. We snapped his picture and then slid him back into the water where he swam away. I'm sure he weighed over 20 pounds.

Well, we are in the tent now and the only sounds are our dripping sweat and Tina's shouts. Despite the bugs Randy has suddenly decided to go outside and practice casting, and typically Tina is giving instructions -- from inside their tent. Fortunately he is independent enough that he can ignore his "second mother" much of the time.

There are only scattered piles of ice along the river bank but back on the lake we can still see solid ice, and floes have been drifting by all evening in the current.

JUNE 16: BEAVER LAKE

When a duck takes wing in the early morning stillness it seems like you can hear his squeaky flapping for a mile. When a whole flock takes off it sounds like a jumbo jet. This morning was a veritable international airport with crowds of ducks coming and going constantly.

The day was flat calm and we were treated to some unique canoeing as we proceeded down the length of Beaver Lake. This lake is miles across and has a central channel of river current perhaps 100 feet wide which might not normally be discernible. This time of year, however, particularly on a calm day, the channel is choked with an amazing river of floating ice while the remainder of the lake is totally ice free. We were following a trail of silver across a 20-mile-long mirror of blue.

The morning was misty and cool and enshrouding fog made it hard to see even a few canoe lengths, so at first we followed down the middle

RANDY with PIKE

SANDERS, '89

of our icy highway to make sure we didn't get lost. Unfortunately it was too much like running rapids handicapped by moving "rocks", and after a continuing series of bumps and bangs we edged off to the side. Later when the mist burned away we could see the sharply defined channel of ice stretching miles ahead into the distance.

Tonight we are off the lake, camped on the point before Fort Providence. The water was extremely swift the last few miles, in fact so much so that it was hard to land here. Indeed the final stretch was quite unsettling, the water boiled around us so. The worst though was the ice. It's fine when it is moving but when a big 50 foot floe snags up on an underwater ledge or rock, it suddenly stops and appears to come surging towards us as we bear down on it. And the noise! When such a floe grinds to a stop and the rushing water begins to rip away one chunk after another, it sounds as you might imagine the colliding of ships.

Well, the sun was intense today. Every one of us has sunburned lips. Now I understand why the rest of the family is always using all those chapsticks.

Randy lost a tooth today -- the second since leaving home. Tonight he will leave it under his pillow for the tooth fairy, who is able to find us no matter where we hide.

It is a little cooler this evening and there seem to be fewer mosquitoes.

JUNE 17: MILLS LAKE

Today was one of those shoulder-cracking, muscle-knotting days against the wind that leaves your arms so tired and cramped in the evening. The last four hours crossing Mills Lake in particular were the worst. Late in the summer I enjoy a good blow. Now, however, we have only been out a few weeks (much of it sitting on shore) and we are not in very good shape yet. Today after only a couple of hours out on the windy lake the ache of straining shoulders started to set in. Times like that my world focuses inwards. Instead of watching a distant point, I stare at each little rock along the shore and count the strokes it takes to inch by. Still in all we are coming along nicely; a few minutes rest is sufficient to restore us and I am sure that in another week we shall be almost tireless.

Tonight the black flies are out and the children are spending a lot of time in the haven of their tent. This evening Turtle is in with them, being forced to sit through yet another reading lesson. Poor Turtle! For a three-year-old he can be very precocious but when it comes to reading he is a slow learner. Again tonight Randy is having trouble just getting him through the alphabet when only yesterday it seemed he knew it. Still, Turtle works hard and Randy is very patient. Elly helps too and I have no doubt that Turtle will be reading all of Randy's books before long.

We stopped in at Fort Providence today. It did not strike us as a very friendly place. Some night I shall write an essay, "Why Indians Don't Wave," but it needs a little more research. The basic theme, however, is that whites wave and Indians don't -- even when waved at first. On the other hand Indians are prone to invite themselves to dinner, something whites seldom do.

We saw some large brown birds on shore today. They were about 3 feet tall with long legs and neck, and they walked along pecking at the ground. We have tentatively identified them as sand hill cranes.

JUNE 18: SIXTY MILES

Today we paddled 14 hours and drifted a couple more. The current was a little disappointing but it is hard to quibble. We covered 60 miles and expect to do even better tomorrow as the river narrows and quickens up ahead. There has been some very nice shoreline lately, gravelly banks and little beaches, but there are bugs everywhere when the wind isn't blowing and we shall probably put in a series of long days to avoid them.

Despite the many hours in the boat the children rarely complain and in that respect today was typical. In fact, Turtle and Elly spent most of their time watching television. They carry an imaginary TV with them and like to set it up on the packs. It has 100 channels. The summer shows are mostly reruns but it is not too annoying as Margie and I missed many of the original episodes and the children are obliging enough to lower the volume during the commercials.

We saw two barges today. They leave huge swells in their wake which seem to go on forever, rocking our canoe and making paddling precarious.

JUNE 19: FORT SIMPSON

Now, today, the current was really fast. The river was narrow with high cliffs and the channel buoys appeared to be racing upstream toward us. They sent up surprisingly large bow waves and from a distance resembled water skiers zooming along on a single ski.

By 5:00 this afternoon we had already reached Fort Simpson, a distance of 70 miles! We could easily have done a hundred before the day was over but decided we had better shop instead and then spend the night. The fort lies at the junction of the Liard and Mackenzie and is the oldest continuously occupied settlement on the Mackenzie. Originally built by the North West Company in 1804, it was taken over by the HBC in 1821 when the companies merged. Now it is a very pleasant community linked by road with the outside world. It would be possible to reach Alaska by branching left here up the Liard but there is a better way. We shall continue down river and later go up the Rat.

We saw a very young moose calf today. It bleated like a lamb and was barely mobile. The mother stood her ground between us and would not move at all. We have never seen that happen before as once the calves have any size at all the family just dashes into the brush. We also saw the year's first baby ducklings. They were still all yellow and fuzzy and they stood on the shore afraid to get their feet wet.

Well, the current was really something today. Whirlpools boiled up everywhere and in places the canoe had a mind of its own. Indeed at times my paddle hardly had the purchase of a wire wisk. The canoe would suddenly twist to one side or change speed as whirlpools, boils and other current quirks materialized beneath us. Everyone remained conscious of our balance as we rocketed along.

JUNE 20: NAHANNI RANGE

There were thunderstorms last night and then today was calmly humid and much too hot. The current, while strong in places, was nothing like that we saw yesterday. In fact, stretches were lake-like and the mid-day heat seemed to drain us. By late afternoon we were glad to stop on a mudbar island where we swam and set up camp. The countryside is higher here and we see real mountains up ahead. There is a narrow fringe of green along the shore and then the snow-streaked Nahanni Range rises up, gray and bare, into the blue sky. It is very picturesque and it is easy to imagine the excitement Mackenzie must have experienced. For twenty miles he paddled west toward the cut ahead and he surely must have felt it would lead him to the Pacific. It looks so promising as a way through the Rockies and he could not have known about the approaching Camsell bend where the river angles sharply north to head once more for the Beaufort Sea.

Tonight is one of those terrible evenings when the sun seems to beat right through the tents and we are wishing now that we had drifted on. It would be cooler out on the water, but we were just too tired to continue.

The river has been very muddy since its junction with the Liard and we expect to fetch our drinking water from side streams the rest of the way.

JUNE 21: THE OLD BUCKET TRICK

If you tried to imagine how bleak and poor a day on a far northern river could be, you'd probably come up with something like today. The wind was steady out of the north and west and whitecaps were working their way up the center of the river, forcing us to the side. The sky was darkly overcast and the temperature was a steady 52 degrees. As we rounded Camsell Bend gray clouds streamed like liquid smoke over the barren Nahanni peaks and came pouring down their sides to spill out over the river. Lightning flickered in the darker patches while squalls ranged the valley. With no attractive alternative we simply paddled on in the shadow of the Camsells, and 36 miles was our reward come supper for ten long hours of hard work. It was pouring rain when we finally stopped by a stream, caught some large pike for supper and settled into bed on the east bank of the Mackenzie.

Across the way showers still stride down the peaks sweeping them from view as they pass by, but at the moment we are dry. Actually we expect a good night's sleep; cold and no bugs.

Rounding Camsell Bend today we were really struck by the appearance of the shore. The massive weight of the winter ice has forced the rocks into the mud flush with the ground, and swept everything else from view. The beach resembles nothing so much as a finely cobbled street, perfectly flattened and smoothed.

Again, today, we were able to use the old bucket trick to advantage. On large rivers such as the Mackenzie and the Slave this trick is a useful addition to any canoeist's repertoire. Indeed, when travelling downstream against the wind there are times when it can actually increase your speed. The idea is to simply lay your paddle down and throw out your bucket (make sure it is tied to the bow). The current will seize the pail, pulling the canoe downstream against the wind and at the same time keeping it in the main channel. We have only lately become aware of this useful trick, but on the advice of Eric Morse we are using it quite successfully this year, particularly when we wish to snack or eat a meal. Between times, however, we always paddle. Our constitution is such that we'd rather paddle no matter how slow the pace than watch our bucket do the work while we sit idly by.

JUNE 22: ELYSIUM

If every day could be like this the country would be deluged with sightseeing voyageurs. Rarely have we paddled through such picturesque settings as we saw today. Five-hundred-foot wooded ridges rose up on either side and rocky mountain ranges patrolled in back. Every bend revealed new vistas and every break in the ridge framed a view of the higher mountains behind.

Only the weather could have been better. The morning started cold and cloudy but by suppertime there was sunshine and blue sky. The wind which had bedeviled us early on let up also and after supper we paddled on in a tranquil, almost euphoric mood.

We had wild onions with supper tonight.

JUNE 23: SIZZLING ALONG

Another gorgeous day! The current was strong once more and we sped along with the occasional (mealtime) aid of our bucket. At times we were going so fast that the canoe was making a sizzling noise. This is the second time lately that we have noticed this weird phenomenon. For miles at a time the water simply sizzles as the canoe passes by, bursting the millions of tiny bubbles boiled up by the swirling waters.

In the afternoon the wind was too strong for us to profitably continue so we napped while the kids played. There is a lot of ice on shore and in places it is piled in mounds over twenty feet high and fifty feet across. Elsewhere it lines the shore for hundreds of yards, still ten feet thick. Anyway, the children played hide-and-seek amongst the room- and even house-sized blocks of ice that littered the point where we had stopped. Afterwards they played in the mud, trying to dam the myriad streams which flowed down the bank from the melting chunks of ice and snow. Playtoys for the kids; the ice is a problem for us though in that it keeps the banks wet and muddy, and we paddled ten more miles after supper searching for a dry campsite.

Tonight Turtle is in the doghouse. A heavy cloud of suspicion hangs over him as he was the last to brush his teeth. Tonight we found the tube of toothpaste without its top and toothpaste squeezed out all over the carrying case. What a mess!

The valley and mountains were beautiful again today. Drinking water is becoming a problem though. Even the tributary streams are getting too silty for our taste.

JUNE 24: SUSAN

This morning we had scarcely paddled half an hour before we spied a canoe and tent perched up on shore. These were the first canoeists we had seen all summer so, despite the early hour, we angled over to wake them up and say hello. Meeting strangers can be exciting, but imagine the thrill when we discovered it was Margie's sister Susan and her boy-friend, Joe. We had a grand reunion around a breakfast fire, then we spent the day together and are camped side by side tonight. They are on a leisure trip. They started from Fort Simpson on the fifteenth and travelling in tandem today it was easy to understand their different pace. Our canoe is just too big and heavy for them to keep up. We try to stay in the main current and because we are so heavily loaded the river is able to push us right along, drifting almost as fast as they care to paddle. We may travel with them tomorrow and then again we may not.

Today was another beautiful sunny day, this time with the breeze behind us, but by common consent we stopped at 2:00. It was an enjoyable, relaxing day and the shoreline passed by at a dizzying rate. Even at lunchtime when the two canoes were rafted together we seemed to drift at over four miles per hour. In the afternoon we spotted two moose and a black bear. The latter posed on his hind legs to eat some high bush berries while Margie manned the camera and Tina and I did some fancy upstream paddling to close right in on him. We should have a good picture this time.

Tonight's campsite is almost ideal. It has good tent sites, good swimming, good drinking water, and no bugs -- but alas no fish.

Sue has a bird book and we positively identified some past sightings as whistling swan, sandhill crane, coot, roughlegged hawk, bank swallow, least sand piper and Arctic tern.

This year Margie is making bannock a quicker way -- mixed right in the frying pan. It's easier with Teflon coating but should work with any pan. Although the order of ingredients doesn't matter, the simplest way seems to be: pour in part of the flour and all the other dry ingredients, cut in solid shortening with fork or fingers, then stir in measured amount of water (1-1/4 cups for maximum size in our pan). Finally, work in enough flour for soft dough and pat evenly over the pan; bake as usual.

JUNE 25: FORT NORMAN

We paddled with Sue and Joe for a couple of hours this morning, then pulled ahead when they stopped to cook breakfast (we tossed out our bucket and ate in the canoe). We were in a hurry to cover the 55 miles to Fort Norman in time to do some shopping and we agreed to rendezvous below town later in the day. By paddling without a break we managed to reach the Fort by 2:00 and I'm afraid we ended up not leaving very much in the store for Sue. This was our last big shopping day of the summer and we just plain cleaned the place out of many items. Eventually the manager even brought out his truck to start driving stuff down to the river. It was like he was provisioning a barge. Anyway the canoe is heavily loaded once more and we have food for 40 days. It is hard to estimate that far ahead accurately but we believe it is enough to carry us over the Rockies and down to Fort Yukon in Alaska.

When you are in a hurry on a big river as we were this morning it is important to ride the strongest current. The thing to remember is that the shortest way is not the quickest. We invariably save time by forgetting about distance and weaving across the river however the current dictates. With practice you can tell from the shapes and placements of the islands and shoreline indentations on the map where the fastest water will be. The way to really learn the best path though is to go with someone else. Don't follow them, but stay out to their side and experiment to see who is drifting faster. In that respect, yesterday was a great opportunity and I spent several hours silently comparing our two speeds as I tested the different distances from shore. To reliably follow the river-within-a-river that marks the fastest course I need to repeat these experiments every few years. We have been coming into the cut banks too soon and leaving them too early. Of course, even with a cut bank you shouldn't get too near shore. In fact, frequently the first few feet of water may be flowing upstream, particularly if any kind of brush has fallen in. Besides watching the cut of the shoreline, the sternman must keep his eye on both the grain of the water and the riffling effect of the wind. When the wind is blowing upstream you can spot the fastest water by where the waves are roughest (not in the flattened swifts near shore). Unfortunately, there is danger in big river waves and often a compromise route must be chosen.

Well, it has been an almost perfect travelling day, calm with light breezes, but it is 9:00 p.m. and Susan still hasn't appeared. I guess we shall gradually leave them behind from here on out.

Fort Norman would not sell us a toothpaste top without the tube.

JUNE 26: DANCE OF THE SANDHILL CRANES

It is really tough to keep small children in footwear. Randy has already worn holes through his new spring boots but there were none the right size to replace them at Fort Norman yesterday. Today when we reached Norman Wells we decided to try again. It is a losing effort though. True, we did get new boots, but while Margie and I were talking on shore Randy took off his only shoes to go wading, and somehow in departing we never thought to check that he had them. Anyway, now he has boots but no shoes -- they are back in Norman Wells and we are not pleased. Still he and Tina are both growing up. It is hard to remember back to when they would cry and we would have to guess why. Later when they began to talk it was a little easier but we still had to do everything for them. Now they show some independence and we have stopped looking after them every minute, so much so that now they can get into the canoe leaving their shoes behind and we don't even notice. It has its good and bad points.

Last night Sue pulled in around 10:30 but we were already asleep. Early this morning we woke them to say goodbye and talk about their plans. They had considered flying in to Summit Lake from Fort MacPherson to join us on the Porcupine but now they have decided to limit their trip to the Mackenzie. They have plenty of food and time and should have a wonderful trip down to Inuvik. We tend to be loners but the two days we spent with them were a lot of fun.

Today was clear, hot, and fairly calm. In fact this evening's paddle was almost perfect and without really trying we seem to have covered another 60 miles. This is an amazing river. Day in and day out we paddle over fifty miles at a clip and yet still it stretches hundreds of miles ahead.

There were lots of ice piles along the banks again today, but the evening paddle was really the highlight. There were nice beaches along the shore and almost everywhere we seemed to see more sandhill cranes. I'm sure now that they are the bird I mistook for an ostrich on Lake Winnipeg last summer. They are large, ungainly brown birds which specialize in exotic dances along the waterfront. Tonight we saw three together doing the hokey-pokey. They were hopping and jumping into the air where they would flap and wiggle their wings and toes. Really very comical.

JUNE 27: SAN SAULT RAPIDS

Another beautiful day. What a fantastic river to canoe this has been! The conditions and the scenery have been gorgeous. At supper we took a three hour layover just to relax and enjoy our surroundings while the children played. They like to dam up little streams whenever they get the chance. They discovered the pastime some while ago and have been perfecting their abilities all month.

After supper we girded ourselves and the canoe for the infamous San Sault Rapids. We have been warned about them for a thousand miles (since Fort Smith) and we were ready. The children were poised with bailing buckets and the ship was tidied for disaster. We kept along the left shore (the safest route) and, as is so often the case, all was anticlimatic. In fact, half way through we got out the camera and took some pictures.

We saw another waterspout today. They pursue a very erratic course. We dodged and twisted all over the river but then at the last moment it managed to elude us. (I have had a change of heart and am determined to catch one.)

JUNE 28: THE RAMPARTS

The good weather just continues. A cooling wind blew pretty strongly for a few hours and slowed us down this afternoon, but the rest of the day was calm and hot. Such warm weather is unusual for June and we are making the most of it. The kids spent a couple of hours swimming earlier and now the adults have just completed their dip. It is 11:00 p.m. but still 80 degrees and the sun is high in the sky. It is early in the summer though; at Fort Good Hope the first food barge of the year has not even arrived yet and their shelves are pretty well depleted.

Today we passed through the Ramparts. They are marked by an abrupt narrowing of the river and sheer but colorful rock walls. Mackenzie must have been apprehensive there as the river gives every appearance of heading for a major rapids or even falls at the end of the gorge. There is nothing there really but an illusion of sharp descent is maintained by the upward-slanting layers of rock in the canyon walls. Thus the canoeist is left with the impression of an ever steeper and swifter plunge as he proceeds. We simply paddled smoothly through but others should still be cautious. With lower water the Ramparts can be dangerous and three parties flipped there a year ago.

JUNE 29: RADIUM CHARLES

Today we paddled seventy miles. I suppose if there is justice in the world then sometime we shall have to pay for these delightful days with some miserable ones. Nevertheless, we are sure enjoying ourselves in the meantime. When you're hot, you're hot! Actually most of the credit for today's fine progress belongs to Radium Charles.

262

Last night began so normally. We like to camp where tributaries enter the Mackenzie and yesterday we chose the one just a few miles below Fort Good Hope. A road from the fort leads down there ending with an almost level ramp where we set up camp. Not unexpectedly a few natives dropped by in the evening (suppertime) and stayed to chat. Anyway, it was not till 10:30 that everybody left and we were free to take a quick skinny-dip and pop into the tent. We wrote up the log and dozed off in the heat.

The first inkling that something strange was happening came at 2:30 in the morning when a forklift rumbled noisily into camp and sat snorting right outside our tent. This is a very disorienting experience. Suddenly there were men everywhere shouting into little CB radios, ''Bring her in, bring her in here.'' Then there was a tremendous jarring thump marking the arrival of Radium Charles. There we were with a big tug and two barges rammed into one side of our cozy nest and a forklift sitting on the other. There were hurried consultations between the parties and then the consensus blared out, ''Move the camp.'' They meant to unload right through us.

Workmen swarmed around tugging at our gear and canoe and I knew the tent was next. There was really no choice. We got out of the tent to make it easier for them. This may have been a strategic error though. Somehow, not really awake yet, we found ourselves bundled into the canoe and paddling off by 3:15, a very early start.

It was a blisteringly hot still day and by noon we had already covered fifty miles. We were too hot and tired to keep pushing however. We ate lunch drifting across the Arctic Circle, and stopped soon after for a swim. We tried to rest on the beach but it was just too hot and bright, so we ended up continuing another few hours before we stopped to swim again and camp. Imagine, swimming north of the Arctic Circle in June. We never would have believed it could be so hot. The sun sets shortly after midnight but only very briefly, and it won't get dark again until mid-August. There is hope of temporary relief though. It has been thundering all around for an hour and now storms are headed this way. Still I wonder how long these hot days can last. We shall be north of the Arctic Circle for over a month, in fact all the way to Fort Yukon, and it is hard to believe it can stay this warm.

the RESPITE

SANDERS '85 ©

JUNE 30: FRAYING AT THE EDGES

Last night's thunderstorms cooled things off nicely so everyone got some rest. This morning the wind blew strongly out of the north making progress difficult, but the latter part of the day turned hot and calm. Despite the good conditions, though, or perhaps because of them, we seem to be fraying a little at the edges. The long hours and the heat are wearing on everybody. The children are coming down with cabin fever. By the end of the day every nudge or stray comment seemed to elicit tears. Margie too is getting tired and called a halt shortly after supper. Too many hours in too small a space and it becomes hard to sit still. (Since our last shopping spree there have been extra bags and cans tucked everywhere around our feet and about the boat.) Even small things have become annoying. Tonight the passengers were irritated by the slowness with which we landed. When I angled in to shore the swift current carried us far beyond our projected landfall, making it appear that I was deliberately prolonging the night's excursion.

The final irritation for Margie came with my premature closing of the packs. This is a nightly problem. Each evening in ritualistic fashion I strap the four of them shut for the night and pile them under cover before we retire. Inevitably, however, she must then make one last foray, opening them all again on the pretext of getting out a final food item for tomorrow or putting away some extra clothes. This annoys her so and I used to feel quite sorry for her as she invariably has to go through everything to find what she wants. Now, however, I have discovered her true purpose and my sympathies have vanished. It has suddenly become clear that she is secretly engaged in rotating our belongings nightly through the packs in some obscure version of the shell game. Certainly it is true that the rest of us can no longer find a thing.

Well, the river is obviously beginning to wear on all of us. It is immensely long and we shall be glad to finish it. The terrain is changing. It's flatter now, almost boring, with more open tundra-like country. The water in the side-streams and river too has become warmer and muddier -- good for swimming perhaps, but less refreshing to drink.

JULY 1: TIMBERLINE TENTS

Today was hot and humid. It is our third day above the Arctic Circle and each one we have gone swimming. The children, in particular, play in the water for hours. They like to take a large log and sit astride it, either paddling to and fro in the shallows or riding it down a sidestream to the river. Truthfully though, there is just no relief from the sun which beats down over twenty hours a day, making eveything hotter and hotter. The temperature is always in the 80's but amazingly enough we still see melting chunks of ice here and there along the shore.

The shoreline is changing. We now canoe between mud banks which reach up a hundred or even 200 feet and there is very little rock anywhere. The river is not as fast as it was earlier and there are many mudbars, some barely submerged (we ran aground on one yesterday).

Although the travel has turned monotonous we are a little apprehensive about leaving the Mackenzie. Each time we duck into a sidestream for fresh water we are covered by mosquitoes, a bad omen for the next leg of the trip. And the poor kids! Their tent zippers are both broken now and the bugs are free to swarm in. I have been a slow learner but the lesson has finally taken hold. I will never buy or recommend a Eureka Timberline tent again, at least until they improve the zippers. They are simply not durable enough for prolonged wilderness trips. I have used their product for years and this makes three of their tents in a row whose zippers have given out. This last one lasted less than two months, leaving us with almost a thousand miles and many millions of mosquitoes to go.

JULY 2: SLOWING DOWN

It rained in the night and was still thundering this morning. It was too buggy and threatening to let the kids sleep in the canoe so we stayed in bed till late. Then this afternoon when it got windy we stopped early. In between times, after a few sprinkles, it did turn warm and sunny. The kids went wading and Tina took a quick dip but a breeze kept everyone a shade cooler than yesterday. In fact, Randy has started wearing clothes again. Both kids are rarely bothered by sunburn and Randy hardly seems to notice the bugs as he plays "au naturel", but today he covered up.

Supper was TVP ("tender vittles for paddlers;" textured vegetable protein if you prefer). It comes in four flavors: ham, beef, chicken, and hamburger, and we have used it with great success for the past two years. We mix it with rice or noodles and a cheese sauce or gravy to make a light, nutritious and cheap addition to our diets. It is also very compact; a single number ten can seems to last for weeks. The rubbery little chicken chunks are out of favor though and I am the only one who still enjoys them. Margie donated some to Sue and will dispose of the rest next time some natives come to dinner.

JULY 3: ARCTIC RED RIVER

One reason we stopped early last night was to avoid arriving in Arctic Red River after the store closed. We wanted to buy a few odds and ends such as a loaf of bread and something to mend or replace tent zippers. We hoped to breeze into town for a late breakfast this morning, but the wind was so strong early on that we stayed in camp. Then when we finally did leave we had to turn back after a mile or so to search our campsite for a misplaced Elly. It was all very frustrating but more than compensated for by the caribou we spotted soon afterwards. He was very curious and trotted right up to us for a close inspection. Then he went back to picking his way along the shore and wallowing in the mud to keep off the bugs.

Well, it took all morning to reach the town and when we did arrive it turned out that no one was there except for a Catholic Sister who was very anxious for company. She was an intriguing hostess and we spent a very enjoyable lunch with her. Among other things we learned that:

1) the ice broke on the river May 25

2) Great Bear Lake is still covered by ice

3) sunrise is January 13 but you can see it shining on the ramparts across the river after January 6

4) we are the third group down the river this year.

5) There was no summer last year. In fact, there was only one day all season when the temperature reached 80 degrees.

Also, there were no mosquitoes (they are extremely thick this year as I believe we've mentioned).

On a personal note, she was quite surprised that I had not shot the caribou. Also she gave us some clothespins to pin up the children's tent. We are hoping that the pins together with the excess mosquito netting

267

Margie has sewn across the opening will keep the worst of the bugs out.

Well, the wind was so strong this afternoon we only went a few miles, not even out of sight of town. The kids built a log cabin from driftwood logs while I set up camp and lazed around. Margie washed clothes and rigged up a clothesline, threading the rope though the shirt arms and pants legs to prevent their blowing away. The new clothespins came in handy for the socks though.

JULY 4: END OF THE MACKENZIE

Again today progress was slow. We had plans of camping somewhere along the Peel but had to be content with one more night on the Mackenzie. We were up early but a single glance at the blanket of dark clouds rolling in and the whitecaps whipping up the river convinced us to stay put awhile. Perhaps we are losing our drive. Anyway, we cooked breakfast (cocoa and Sister Matte's donuts) then went back to bed and tried again at noon. Conditions were marginally improved by then and we pried the children out of their tent. For the next couple of hours we fought the wind singing "Onward Christian Soldiers" and then switched to more patriotic material ("Yankee Doodle Dandy"- - it is July 4th). Soon the sun came out and the temperature rose from 50 degrees to over 70. At supper the kids actually went swimming.

Tonight we are just a trifle concerned about our food supply. Our Fort Norman estimates called for us completing the Peel tomorrow which we still expect to do, but just barely. We were secretly hoping to do a little better on this stretch but the weather has held us back. Indeed with its mud banks and adverse winds the Mackenzie has begun to seem endless and we are glad it's done. It is a long run from Great Slave down to Inuvik. In fact, it seems forever since we left Hay River about three weeks and a thousand miles ago.

We got out gloves and turtlenecks tonight in anticipation of the bugs tomorrow. Also we saw ice again today, piled along the shore. I wonder if we shall ever be free from it this summer.

JULY 5:   HUSKY CHANNEL

Tonight we are camped at the junction of the Peel River and the Husky Channel. The latter appears well-named. About suppertime our camp was invaded by six husky sled dogs but they are fairly shy and have done no harm. Their trapper owner showed up briefly to shoo them home, but now he is gone and for all the effect he had, he might have saved himself a trip. Actually, it was somewhat upsetting to talk with him. Tomorrow we plan to start up the Rat which, according to our map, is the stream we see 100 yards away. The trapper, however, assured us that it is not the Rat. This is a trifle disconcerting, but we have decided to ignore him. How can aerial photographs and a topographic map both be wrong! Moreover we have a trip description from a party who went that way in '65. Nevertheless, the trapper was sure we wouldn't make it. Historically, about half the attempts on this river have failed, but he was very specific. He predicted we would get lost in the lakes and he related the tragic plight of a party who tried and failed only a few weeks ago. It all sounded very strange as our maps don't even show any lakes where we are going. Anyway, he says the real Rat comes in 22 miles farther down, but as I say we are ignoring him, although with trepidation.

Well, this morning it was overcast and looked like rain but now we are all in our tents naked and dripping with sweat from the heat. The dogs have returned to patrol outside and are browsing through our belongings. For awhile today the bugs were terrible and we all wore headnets and gloves as we paddled along. The 17-mile paddle up the Peel was against a persistent but not terribly strong current. It was certainly noisy though as the eroding banks thawed and tumbled into the water all around us during the heat of the day. Occasionally in the distance we caught sight of the mountains we must cross. Ominous! A campsite was hard to find. At our first attempt Margie sank up to her knees in what we had taken for firm mud, and our present spot is very sticky along the shore.

It is late now and a large river boat just motored by. It held three canoes, six riders and a pile of gear as well as a native guide. Now we really don't know what to think. Presumably they are being motored up to Destruction City via the real Rat. They did not stop or wave hello. We still plan to follow our maps but we are having real misgivings.

JULY 6: FRUSTRATION

This was the worst day of my life, let alone the trip! First off, I have never seen the mosquitoes so bad. They were waiting for us in the morning and from 6:00 a.m. till noon we travelled in headnets, mittens, turtlenecks and rainclothes. The raincoats helped but left us gasping with the heat. The kids tried to endure but it wasn't easy. Eating their meals under the tarp helped them a little but not enough. All day we listened to the whine of mosquitoes, felt them peppering our clothes, and saw them blanketing the people and packs.

As for the travelling, in the morning it was slow but steady against the current. At least we were making progress and hopeful about our prospects. Also we saw a bear swimming across the river which was the first of the day's two highlights.

The day's first real blow came about 1:00 when the river suddenly ceased to conform to our map. I mean it. Our topographic map was dead flat wrong. Drawn from our accompanying photomaps, it showed the river following what is now an old dried-up spring overflow channel. This channel lay several feet above our present river and was absolutely dry. There was no choice of course and we continued on, following the water that we had. Instead of proceeding west then we began to swing a little south.

Two hours later the trapper's warnings were brought to mind when we entered what turned out to be the first of a series of little lakes. This was more than a little disappointing. We were deep in the Mackenzie delta. This undistinguished swamp encompasses thousands of square miles and hundreds of tiny ponds and meandering placid streams going nowhere. Our goal was to cross this swamp and reach the ridge forming the western boundary, but how to do it? The country is frustratingly impenetrable.

Well, luck was with us. While casting about the shore of our little pond for an exit, I suddenly realized where we were. Sometimes the hours spent studying topographic maps pay off and this was one such time. The entire picture seemed to click and I had Margie pass me back the map. Sure enough, of all the hundreds of little ponds, I knew for certain which was ours. That was the second and final highlight of the day. Our spirits really lifted knowing where we were, and the next four hours were exciting as we wove in and out around marshy lakes and channels certain of our course.

All our meals were in the canoe today and the last was almost pleasantly bug free. We tied up to a log in the middle of a breezy pond for supper and ate cold pea soup, cooked the night before. We had been swinging south and west across the delta to snuggle up against the ridge marking the western boundary. Now our course lay north to join the real Rat a couple of miles below the "Destruction City" of Klondike days. Trouble came though as we tried to leave our supper spot. We searched the swampy shore for an hour but failed to find the exit we knew was there. The closest thing to a channel was an almost dried-up stream completely choked by logs. More searching revealed a swampy means of circumventing the obstacle but it was with hesitation that we proceeded. The river was now a muddy ditch and depressingly small at that.

The next corner hid a jam over a hundred yards long and here there was no choice. We had to portage, stumbling and dragging though the most miserable terrain I ever hope to see. Mud, swamp, jammed-up logs, debris and alder trees made progress of any sort all but impossible. The driftwood jumble extended from shore to shore and on into the alders. There was nowhere to even step without risking a twisted ankle. To top it off I wiped out physically. When I tire it happens suddenly, without warning and with exasperating finality. It was 9:30 p.m., a long day already, and the heat and hard upstream paddling had snuck up on me unawares. Half way through the carry I was suddenly shaking with exhaustion and Margie was left with more than her share. And the mosquitoes. They were absolutely covering us and we were likewise drenched with sweat. There was no place to camp, hardly a square inch of free space existed and there was nothing for it but to continue. Everybody had to sit and wait while Daddy drank some Tang and caught his breath. With the deep mud and heavy packs no one else could load the canoe, so we had to wait there in the swamp and mosquitoes for the 15 minutes or so it took me to recoup some strength.

When we finally paddled off in seach of camp we still had half a mind to complete the remaining six miles to Destruction City and finish this awful swamp. Even at half speed I knew we could make it by 1:00 or 2:00 in the morning at the latest, and there was plenty of daylight. Then came the killer. Within a mile we reached another log jam, this one worse than the last. We searched high and low, climbing slippery 12-foot banks and clawing over little trees to peer ahead. There seems to be no way around or through or over and who knows where the end is. We drifted a half mile back to find a spot to camp and by midnight we were all in bed, but never have I been so discouraged. The bugs, the

271

mud, the log jams, all have taken their toll. If we had not by sheer chance discovered where we were this afternoon I believe we would turn back tomorrow to search for the real Rat farther down the Husky Channel. The stream here is almost dry and who knows how many log-jammed portages lay ahead. Certain of the distance though (six more miles) we intend to press ahead tomorrow.

JULY 7: DESTRUCTION CITY

Boy was yesterday awful! We were up 18 hours and working to capacity for most of them. To reiterate, no one should ever take the Rat River labeled on the map -- the channel marked there is but an overflow for the true Rat which empties into Husky Channel some 20-odd miles below its junction with the Peel. The trapper was right.

Well, the day began with us clawing up steep slippery mud banks and forcing a trail through impenetrable swamp. The irresistable force meeting the immovable object! That first portage turned out to be the big physical effort of the day and took most of the morning. The next few miles of paddling however were an emotional rollercoaster. Never, even shooting the wildest rivers, have I proceeded with such trepidation. At every turn I was almost shaking with anxiety for another such jam would surely break us, but fortunately the rest of the obstacles were more easily handled and no bad jams appeared. And then we reached the Rat! Ah, heaven! We could paddle once more.

Today then turned out to be almost a recovery day, especially when compared to yesterday. Still conditions were bad. The mosquitoes alone drove the children into tears of frustration after only a couple of hours and we all wore headnets and gloves throughout the day.

Once past Destruction City the character of the river changes abruptly. Indeed this nonexistent city (there is nothing there but a clearing) marks the end of what in any sense can be termed navigable water. We simply quit there for the night, dragging up the first little set of rapids and crawling into the tents to get away from the insects. All our information indicates that we now have a minimum of nine days of absolute misery ahead of us as we try to struggle up over the Rockies. The next 50 miles are reputed to be one continuous rapid with no canoeable stretches and rising over 1000 feet. We shall be passing through deep valleys and mountain canyons and the mosquitoes are supposed to be lying in wait at every corner with eternal vigilance. Tomorrow though we shall hit the Rat with determination. We have been mentally preparing for this all summer long. We would like to reach the top in less than nine days but in our hearts we know it will take longer. Weighed down by our big canoe, children, and heavy load we realize we can not match the speeds of those who have gone before.

We saw a lynx today. He (or she) was very close and did not scare off and Margie may have taken some excellent pictures.

JULY 8: DAY NUMBER 1

Since we left Marlborough to start this journey over two years ago, the Rockies have always loomed as our biggest obstacle. In the entire chain of mountains from Mexico to the Beaufort Sea there is no more plausible place to cross than McDougall Pass. It is less than 1100 feet high and the portage from the source of the Rat to Summit Lake (and the beginning of the Little Bell River) is no more than half a mile. Indeed, the route is an old one used by the voyageurs, the Klondikers and occasional travellers such as ourselves. And now the big push has started. If we can ascend the Rat we shall make it to Alaska. We have no doubts about our eventual success but at the moment I would say the Rat is slowly defeating us. Two days ago we paddled 31 miles, yesterday we went seven and today, well today we managed only five.

We ate breakfast in the tents again this morning to escape the bugs. Tina hates to open her eyes when she wakes up now. The first thing she sees each day are those big mosquitoe tummies hanging down, sort of pinkish from tanking up in her tent during the night.

Today's travel was paddle, wade, line, then wade and line some more. The only time we got in the canoe was to ferry across the stream. The constant in and out though is gradually cleaning the mud out of the canoe and off our clothes, at least from the waist down.

Our upstream techniques need a little brushing up, I'm afraid. We made two mistakes today. The first occurred after lunch when the kids were tired of walking along the rocky shore while we pulled the canoe up the central channel (the stream braids terribly). Anyway, we agreed to let them sit in the canoe while we lined up the next rapids. It was certainly not as steep as some of the other ones and we didn't expect their weight to make much difference. The water was too swift though and before we knew it the canoe had gotten too far out in the waves and current, and we were about to lose control. There the kids were, bobbing in the canoe at the end of a 50-foot line in the middle of the rapids. We couldn't pull the boat in sideways, the water was too strong and would swamp it. Margie had to release the stern line and help me at the bow as it was all I could do to keep from slipping back. Slowly, carefully we hauled at the line until the canoe nosed into the shallows; the kids scrambled out and we breathed a sigh of relief. After that the kids walked whether they were tired or not.

The second mistake occurred on a move we had done many times already; wade up one side of a channel, then everyone get in and ferry across to the other side where we could get out and wade again. Only this time we lost control. Before we could get across, the current swept us backwards into the previous rapid. We spun the boat around and aimed for a gravel bar half way down, landing with a crunch. We leaped out to turn the canoe again and then started wading back upstream, the water swirling around our thighs. We had to cross to the far bank from our gravel bar island but the channel proved a little too deep and swift for Margie. She was swept off her feet and just barely managed to keep her grip on the gunwale while I dragged everyone to the bank. Heaven help us if we ever both lose our balance at once while wading up this river.

Well, we were exhausted by this evening. We travelled eight hours, not a terribly long day, but conditions were really brutal. We hope we can get used to the routine and strengthen previously unused muscles. Hauling the canoe along against the current strains every muscle in our bodies as we inch our way upstream. It would help if the bugs would let up but I don't expect they will. It would be so much easier to wade and line without headnets or mittens on.

I believe we are hot on the trail of the three canoes that motored by us on the Husky Channel. We see fresh footprints and silver paint from their canoes almost everywhere we go. It gives Tina and Randy something to look for as they walk along. They have sorted out the various treads and try to keep track of which footprints they have seen. We figure the canoes are at least two days ahead of us assuming they were motored as far as Destruction City, which seems likely.

Well, eight hours to haul five miles. We are discouraged by the slow progress. Wonder what tomorrow will bring?

JULY 9: DAY NUMBER 2

The bugs are awful! And it is not just mosquitoes either. The day starts with taking down the tents. All about under the fly and hiding inside the poles are giant flies, spiders, black flies and of course the ever-present, all-encompassing, deafening, sky-darkening swarms of mosquitoes. We never take off our gloves. The thickness of the mosquitoes is truly overwhelmingly amazing. When I brush my hand slowly down my sleeve I kill flocks and even as my brushing hand descends, new swarms are landing right behind where it has passed. Incredible! I tried pulling the canoe without gloves today for awhile but it was impossible. My hand was just a burning wriggling mass of mosquitoes whenever it rested on the boat and I could not stand to look at it. The kids have the worst of it though. They trudge along the shores and through the brush where the bugs are thickest. Their clothes are coated with moving probing searching hordes of little brown bodies.

Nevertheless, today was a good day for travel. We managed six miles and for the first time I am beginning to feel that we are starting to pick the river apart. It is exhilarating work climbing a river, rapid by rapid, ferrying back and forth, seeking the best braids to follow, etc. We didn't cover that great a distance but we did come up another 200 feet which is pretty steep going. I was able to do quite a bit of poling. Poling is the quickest, most effective way (followed by lining) to ascend mild rapids and strong current, and I am sure I poled for over a mile while the others walked on shore. Unfortunately, there were all too many places where Margie and I had to get out and wade. Actually it is not really wading -- it is manhauling your load along. Many times we were out waist deep in powerful rapids. In fact, there was one terrible sweeper I had to go out chest deep to circumvent. Margie, unable to stand against the current in such deep water, clambered over the fallen trees with a rope to help tow the canoe around. Fortunately, while cold, the water is not yet too frigid to endure. By the time we reach the top, however, it shall have dropped into the 30's. Already there are snow patches on the hillsides about us and we have still another 700 feet to ascend.

For wading gear at present I am using long underwear, rainpants, wool socks and rubber boots and have experienced no real problems due to chill. Margie is attired similarly except for sneakers, which she prefers because they stay on her feet better than boots in the swift water. We like the long underwear better than pants as they dry more quickly and

FASHION PLATE

SANDERS, '84

don't bind while wet; the knees stretch better for walking and sitting. The rainpants are mosquito-proof and keep us warm. It was in the 40's and overcast this morning.

JULY 10: BARRIER RIVER

We only went four miles today. It is hard to look forward to the wading and the bugs on a cloudy day but we were off by 8:00 a.m. We were making steady progress but when we reached the Barrier River shortly after 2:00 and found the three canoes we have been trailing, we stopped to join them for the day. Any excuse to get out of the water!

There were six men there, all from Europe, and they have been having a perilous journey. They came down the Peel to reach the Rat and are now headed, as are we, to Fort Yukon in Alaska. They had many spills on the Peel and we gather two of them are lucky to be alive after one terrible accident in which a canoe and gear were totally lost. They spent a week in Fort MacPherson waiting for a replacement canoe and then hired a native to motor them to Destruction City. Since then however they have lost their two-day head start on us. One of them became sick and another twisted a knee so they have rested here recuperating. Some of the Europeans we see in the north are experts but it seems all too many are such candidates for disaster. In some ways this group is typical. They are only kids and may well be in more trouble than they realize. They are obviously inexperienced and quite unabashed by the fact that the RCMP has already flown one rescue mission on their behalf (back on the Peel). Now they have less than ten day's food with them. This would not be enough for us. On the other hand they are younger and stronger and can put three or four men on a canoe in the really bad stretches. This means they can go a little faster than us. In fact, they expect to reach McDougall Pass in only three more days while there is no way we can do it in less than five. Tomorrow they plan to let us start out an hour ahead of them so that we shall reach the upcoming canyon at about the same time. They have excellent information about the river, gleaned from their days in Fort MacPherson, and have explained they will have to help us through the canyon. Apparently it is not even possible for two men to get a regular canoe through alone so we with our two children and big load are facing a hopeless task. Very considerately they are planning to

277

help us out. Actually we are going to help them too. Margie plans to give them extra food but they have gone out hunting now and we're in bed. Tomorrow should do as well though as we expect to be together one more night.

Well, today was a short day, really only half a day for us. We think now it may actually take us the full ten days we have allowed to reach the pass -- nuts!

Tonight we are nearly level with the snow patches on the hills and we passed a big sheet of ice upon the shore this morning.

JULY 11: CANYON

The weather was perfect today, sunny and not too hot. Briefly we tried using repellent instead of headnets but it was impossible. The bugs swarmed all around and we could not open our mouths to breathe nor our eyes to see. They simply clogged our eyelids and our nostrils, and the experiment lasted only a few minutes.

It was a very tough day. There were continual rapids, many waist deep, with big boulders to pull around or wade over. Above the Barrier River the Rat runs muddy so we could not see beneath the surface. The canyon was awful and at times we were in water over our heads. It was also very uneven footing. We would be wading along and suddenly bang our knees or toes into an unseen boulder. In other places we simply stumbled off of rocks into bottomless pools. In places the rocks rolled away underfoot leaving us hanging on to alders along the steep shores. At one point we were forced to swim, one hand on the gunwale, the other pulling our way along by rocks and tree roots projecting from the canyon walls. We passed through without accident or injury however and only hope the six Europeans fared as well. It is late evening now and they still have not caught us.

The afternoon was a little easier than the morning; I poled again and the others walked along the shores. Still we are all exhausted tonight and everyone has tired feet.

Margie lost her life jacket today. She set it on a rock at lunch and then we left without it. Oh well, there is little danger in all that comes ahead.

We want a day without bugs!

JULY 12: BULLDOZER

Our canoe has seen a lot of uses this year. Back on Great Slave we used it as an ice-breaker and even as a sled. Today it was a bulldozer, rolling rocks up the Rat and grading down the streambed. We are only putting in about seven hours a day but lately our speed has picked up. I probably poled five of today's eight miles and tomorrow looks just as promising.

Putting the obstacles aside, the Rat is truly a beautiful river, following up a valley flanked by snow-streaked ridges and mountains towering into the sky. The varied rock colors and green hillsides are striking set against the deep blue sky. If it were not for the hard work and the insects the Rat would make a great trip in itself. There has been a lot written about the intense cold of the water and the need for wetsuits, but we are doing just fine in that respect. Really anyone who enjoys wading up our New England streams in the early spring will relish this river. Just expect to be wet all the time.

Well, I am very tired again tonight. Poling the loaded canoe is extremely hard work and the alternative today was mostly manhauling. This last is an exhausting activity in which the two of us stand thigh-deep in the rushing rapids and haul the canoe inch by inch up the steep incline of what at times are almost falls. This literally takes all the strength we have as we brace against the rocks and heave the boat forward, distributing the strain across our backs and shoulders and down our legs. Balance is critical and we spend long minutes crouched with the curlers foaming at the gunwales as we jockey for secure footing. A single slip portends disaster and the tension is electric on the steeper pitches. (At times it would seem doubly hard and then a backward glance would show I was dragging Margie as well as the boat.) Anyway we progressed another day without mishap. We have begun to worry about the Europeans though. A second day has passed and they are still behind us.

JULY 13: DAY 6 ON THE RAT

Today was almost a repeat of yesterday. It was cool (44 degrees) at breakfast but warmed up once the sun came over the mountains. The bugs weren't quite so bad, giving the children some relief as they walked

279

along. The kids were tired though, especially Randy, and we progressed slowly. I did less poling also which was another reason for the slower pace. The rapids were almost continual but not as big as a few days ago; slowly we are running out of water. The river is colder and clearer, but still bearable for wading. Really Margie is the only cause for concern at this point. She slightly injured an ankle wading yesterday and we stopped early tonight when it began to really bother her.

The scenery continues to be breathtakingly magnificent. There is nothing but tundra and barren snowpatched peaks around us now and only the occasional tufted toothpick or "wannabee" (scrawny shrubs that want'a be trees) to remind us of the forests farther down. We are having no problem yet collecting fuel for cooking but to be safe we are starting to carry a few twigs and sticks as well as some birch bark in the canoe. We may well have troubles making fires as we continue to close in on the pass and Summit Lake.

As far as we can tell there is only one canoe ahead of us. The Europeans said two Germans had an eight day lead on them. We see occasional silver signs of their passage on the rocks, but from their constant depth I do not believe we are gaining. There is no sign of other parties so perhaps we four (the party who turned back, the six Europeans, the two Germans and ourselves) are the only ones making the attempt to cross this year. Traditionally, only half the parties are successful which is bad news for the six Europeans who are still behind us -- we and the Germans are going to make it!

JULY 14: LOST

We are beginning to identify with Hannibal. At least he didn't have to pull his elephants over the Alps in a canoe. Today was/is really awful. First off, it was raining when we got up and it is raining now. It did clear up in between but the bugs have been simply unendurable.

We worked very hard today and only got another four miles. Now we are weary and discouraged. The worst came this afternoon when we got separated for several hours. The idea was for me to work the canoe alone up the braids while the rest of the family walked along the treeless bluff rather than be ferried back and forth across the channels. Well, it didn't work. Besides the mosquitoes, they had to cope with uneven spongy hummocks and bushes waist-high on the kids. As a result I was around the corner before they got half way along the bluff and decided to descend to the river again. For three hours they bushwhacked along the river, up and down the 50-foot banks, and finally waded several channels to reach the gravel bars and farther shore where travelling was easier. Meanwhile, I was alternately struggling to drag the canoe upstream alone, and back-tracking on foot to look for everyone else. We were all out of sight so long we became quite worried about reuniting. From now on we stay together.

Tonight we are at the Forks and even they aren't right. The map shows four streams meeting here but I have searched and can find only three. We would take the middle one without hesitation except:

a) it doesn't have much water and starts with a miserable little rapid in a gorge which we would have to portage around and

b) the silver scrapings from the Germans go up the right branch. It is hard to believe they would go the wrong way, but we shall trust our intuition and start the morning with the portage.

It is only ten more miles to the summit and today's frustrations are breeding a grim determination. Tomorrow we shall hit the river hard and not stop moving, we hope, until we have reached the top.

JULY 15: SUMMIT LAKE

We did it! Tonight we're camped at Summit Lake! It was after 6:00 by the time we struggled up the little ridge that marks the great divide. Our heavy packs were forgotten as the four of us gathered together. We stood there for a few moments and even took our headnets off, oblivious to rain and bugs. We were ecstatic as we stared west towards Alaska, listening to the wind whistle through the holes in our heads. Even the children were excited. It has been a long trip but the rest is all downhill. After a few minutes' pause to savor the scene before us, we moved on down to find a spot to camp by the lake.

Well, it was a hard day. The sky was gray and it showered almost continuously. We began by wading across Sheep Creek on the left and portaging the first 100 yards up Rat Creek to get around a little gorge with rapids. I decided to take the empty canoe up the gorge rather than portage it and ended by getting wet to the chest for my efforts. More

281

than that, I had to get Margie to help me, so she was wet too -- though only to the waist. After that it was wade, drag, paddle a few feet then jump out and wade some more. Somehow in that stretch I managed to lose my pole; in hurriedly switching from pole to paddle I must have dropped the pole in the water instead of tucking it inside the canoe. Margie feels badly about littering the countryside with our belongings but I just regret losing them as one by one they drop by the wayside; pole, life preserver, sneakers, etc.

By lunchtime most of the riffles were behind us. Then came a few miles where we actually paddled, flailing around one little corner after another against a steady current. There were a few logs to haul over and later on some beaver dams as our creek narrowed to a three-foot ditch in the grass.

Tina did a lot of paddling to help us as the current remained surprisingly strong most of the afternoon. Also she and Randy had to keep a sharp lookout for branches that might poke them on the way by. They behaved wonderfully, helping when they could and not complaining the rest of the time. They just sat in their seats or lay back on the packs in their raingear and headnets, enduring the rain and bugs and cool weather. They were still tired from yesterday and glad just to be riding in the canoe again. Also they knew we were pushing hard to be done with the Rat.

About 5:00 we reached Ogilvie Lake. The Rat had degenerated to a winding, brushy ditch by then and our long canoe could hardly make it around the corners. We elected to skip the rest of the stream and instead set off across the tundra in a southwest direction headed for the next little pond about a quarter of a mile away. There was no trail and the terrain was all muskeg so we carried the packs and then I dragged the canoe over with all the odds and ends. Crossing this last pond we began the final carry. I say "carry" though once again I dragged the canoe over the tussocky tundra. The footing was poor as we stumbled along on and between the grassy hummocks and squishing into the marsh between. It was sprinkling and the bugs were out but we were soon tempted to remove our raincoats, it was such hot sweaty work. And now we've done it. In a sense the trip is over and the rest is anticlimax, a victory lap if you will, as we coast down to the Yukon Flats.

To finish the day we paddled across the lake to a nice high and dry campsite. It is still raining but we are warm and dry in our sleeping bags with a hot meal inside us. Again today the scenery was fantastic with the snow-streaked Richardsons rising 4000 feet on either side of us.

Indeed paddling though the ditch approaching the pass was like driving along a scenic skyline road through the mountains.

We saw sign of the two Germans again today so apparently they backtracked to correct their error and are still ahead of us.

Everything is great and we are so glad to be here.

JULY 16: THE LITTLE BELL

We really feel the trip is over and that the last obstacle has been overcome. We celebrated this morning by getting out the balloons. The kids blew them up, wrote their names on them, then tossed them to the winds. Hurrah, we made it! In fact tonight we are still celebrating and Margie baked a chocolate chip cake for dessert (last night was too late and rainy for a lengthy baking session).

This morning when we arose there was the biggest bull moose we have ever seen, right in camp. He had a huge rack and was so slow to move off that everybody had a chance to get up and watch him go. The balloons were next and then a leisurely breakfast.

The work began with us portaging the gear and dragging the canoe over the tundra the mile or so to the Little Bell. Again it was hummocky going but no one cared. In fact, conditions were miserable all day long but we scarcely noticed (euphoria is great). Counting today during which it rained again -- and is still thundering -- we have gone three days now without seeing the sun.

The Little Bell is only 13 mosquito-infested miles in length but it has a few rocky rips in which our poor canoe took, I trust, the last bangs of its career. It has served us well for six hard years, over 10,000 miles, and we shall be sad to part with it when the time comes.

Tonight we are finally done with wading and are camped on the Bell. It was like a breath of fresh air to leave the ditch-like streamlet that is the Little Bell. Now the water is a clear deep green, and miraculously there are no bugs. We stopped at a gravel point beside a little rapids, caught some grayling and cooked a super supper.

Tomorrow we would like to put in about fifty miles and get down out of the mountains and perhaps into better weather. We are so looking forward to this final stretch. The last two weeks have been the most despairful we can recall. We'll never forget living all those days in our

283

ALASKA

SANDERS, '85 ©

headnets. The world is an insipid greenish-grey when viewed through a gruesome cloud of bugs from behind a smelly veil of netting. We even ate our meals in them. The only exception was Randy who is nearly impervious to bugs, sun, and weather. As often as not we would turn around to discover he had stripped down to go swimming in the Rat, but even he spent long hours staggering along in his headnet.

Randy cleaned his first fish today. He caught two grayling and before we knew it he had picked up my knife and whacked off the bigger one's head. He's certainly growing up.

The zipper on our Timberline tent is broken also now and the kids are sharing their clothespins.

JULY 17: GRIZZLY

Today was exciting. There was no wading, no getting wet and no headnets. Margie's whole day looked brighter when she could wriggle her toes in dry wool socks and not once have them go squish. All day long we had spectacular views of the Richardson Mountains as we gradually left them behind. And best of all we saw our first grizzly. He was at the water's edge eating goose grass as we paddled up behind him. We took several pictures and finally said "Hey, bear" so he would turn around, and he did. He took a good look and then ambled slowly off.

The day was cool and cloudy and we lazed along. Tina read a new book; Randy caught a really big grayling and we stopped early for supper. Really a pleasant day.

We also saw birch trees again today and a long shelf of ice on a sidestream which had somehow missed the summer sun.

JULY 18: EXPLOSION

We are surprised at how slow the current is on the Bell. There was no wind to hinder us today and still we managed only 36 miles after 10 hours of paddling. It was cold to start (32 degrees), but gradually the day warmed up and by evening we were hot.

If there is one thing that marks the experienced traveller it is caution.

Those who travel alone, depending only on themselves, must think before they act. With experience, safe patterns of action become routine. Tonight, however, we were a little careless and paid the price. First we used "mud" stones for the fireplace and secondly the big pack was placed, for convenience sake, too close to the fire. At any rate our fireplace exploded. This is not unheard of as shales frequently contain a little water and burst explosively when heated. Unfortunately, this time our bannock was flipped onto the beach, soiling its sticky top, and burning embers were scattered everywhere. Randy was barefoot at the time and blistered both his feet stepping on hot coals before he realized how widespread they were. At the same time an unnoticed coal had landed in the supper pack and soon we had a smoky blaze in there. If the flames has reached the matches in the side pocket we might have had a problem. As it was we got off easily, but it reminded us how quickly disaster can strike. I don't mind an accident such as rising water or blown down tents when the potential has been foreseen and the risk consciously assumed. But, to be caught by surprise, that is another matter. I think it was the Arctic explorer Steffansen who observed that "adventures" are for the inexperienced. How right he is.

JULY 19: THE PORCUPINE

We reached the Porcupine River this morning and the current began to pick up a little. By travelling from 7:00 a.m. to 10:00 p.m. we managed to cover fifty miles. The Porcupine is very nice and getting even better. The upper stretches were placid with muddy banks, but now gravel bars and occasional riffles are beginning to appear. The morning was cool with showers, but it soon cleared up and we have had a gorgeous evening.

It was exciting being in the high mountains the last two weeks, but we are glad to be back among the birds and little animals. On the other hand, supper was almost too much of a good thing. We ate at the foot of a cliff for shade and a peregrine "serenaded" us for two hours. They are very common among the cliffs and high rocks and their screeching can be quite annoying.

There are lots of wild flowers and the children picked a huge bouquet to adorn our supper setting. They also harvested a lot of wild onions (which were pretty tough and woody).

286

We hope that the campsites improve soon. The last three nights we have had to sleep on book-sized rocks, the only choice around.

We all desperately need baths now, but the air and water have been too cold lately to make swimming attractive. We saw another moose today.

JULY 20: WIND

It was a beautiful day today; clear, blue sky and lots of sun. The river has grown very pretty with lots of gravel bars and swift current, but still we were frustrated. The wind blew so hard out of the south and west that we simply could not travel most of the time. Instead we relaxed on a gravel bar which would have been ideal except for the flying bits of gravelly sand and silt which gritted our eyes and made breathing unpleasant; it was really blowing. In fact, we had even undertaken the precaution of overturning the empty canoe on the barren shore when the wind tried to play a little trick on us. While we were turned away it blew the boat upright into the water and sent it skittering back upstream. Ha, ha, the joke was on it. Long ago we learned to tie the canoe to the packs when nothing else is around, so 50 feet later it came up short. Cautious habits can pay off.

Tina is undergoing a transformation. Twice a day she gets out the mirror to inspect herself. She examines her teeth to see which ones need a little extra brushing and then she spends an hour or so fixing her hair. Quite a change.

It was nice to clean up and sit around for a few hours today, but now that we are getting so close to Alaska we are starting to make plans. Very soon we shall be anxious to arrive. We are certainly way ahead of schedule though, and have lots of food. I wonder whatever became of the six Europeans.

JULY 21: THE TWO GERMANS

When we left at 6:30 this morning we had hopes of a calm day. Within an hour, however, it was already blowing up from the southwest, same as yesterday. By noon there were big waves with whitecaps and clouds of dust were whipping off the mud/gravel bars. Ordinarily we would have quit for the day but Old Crow, the Yukon Territory's northernmost community, was just around the corner (8 more miles). We battled on and at 4:00, much to the relief of our aching muscles, we arrived.

Two Norwegians were there and we all camped together below town. It turned out that they were the two "Germans" from the Rat and they had only gotten in an hour before us. It was a grand evening as we swapped tales of horror about the Rat River and our ordeals. They had indeed missed the proper turn at the Forks on their first time by, and they had earlier survived a swamping in one of the many rapids.

We are in bed now and down below five ravens are playing king of the mountain on our overturned canoe. Their antics are quite amusing. The surface is very smooth and even the winners keep sliding off at the slightest jostle. What they like to do is push a wing into the other fellow's face while they are pecking at his toes. They are not the only silly birds around though. Earlier we passed a baby goose "hiding" on a steep mud bank. He had his body pressed down flat and his face was in the mud. His efforts at camouflage went for naught, however, as he was slowly sliding backwards down the slick slope, a very comical sight. His poor frantic mother was in hysterics, but dared not come too close.

We reported the probable plight of the six Europeans to the RCMP today. We also remarked on the apparent scarcity of sled dogs and learned that the town just finished shooting ninety of them. They had been running wild in packs and had begun to attack people in the street.

I saw a 40-lb. king salmon today, netted by a native. Of course, it would be illegal for any white man to do the same. Canadians thrive on the double standard, however, and this type of reverse discrimination seems to meet with their approval. The fish was huge.

Note: We heard later from the RCMP that the Europeans arrived safe and sound (but very tired and hungry) in Old Crow just four days after we left.

JULY 22: OLD CROW, DAY TWO

We did not see the sun at all today -- just clouds and wind. I guess if there is anything a traveller learns though, it is patience. Fifty and even sixty miles a day are not uncommon rates down the Porcupine, but not

288

for us. We've been struggling just to paddle 25 and today we didn't move an inch. Even the big 30-foot riverboats can't go through the ramparts below town when it gets like this. The wind was howling out of the southwest and by 6:00 a.m. the gravel bars were already trailing plumes of dusty silt hundreds of feet into the air behind them while whitecaps licked around their fronts and sides. We and the Norwegians toured Old Crow, visited the store, then spent the day eating. Pleasant, but expensive (bread is $2.50 a loaf).

Today I was asked (not for the first time) about life jackets, etc. Each traveller must really decide for himself about safety features such as life jackets, canoe covers, and wet suits. They are all good livesaving devices and it is foolish to have reservations as regards a single one of them. Still, a qualification may be in order. More than once we have met people using these devices as a substitute for expertise. These confidence-building gadgets tempted them into trouble they might have otherwise avoided. Of the lot I would only say that life jackets are required.

JULY 23: RAMPARTS

This started out to be a very promising day. We said goodbye to the two Norwegians and set out at 6:00 under sunny skies. It was cool though and by breakfast time it was growing overcast. At least it was still calm and we paddled till after lunch through occasional drizzly showers. The river showed very little current overall.

Early in the afternoon we entered the ramparts and they were beautiful; steep rock walls bounding either side of the river. The current was faster there, but we had only progressed a few miles when the wind sprang up, incredibly enough from the same westerly direction as before. It built very quickly, whistling down between the canyon walls, and the waves began mounting up over three feet tall. There was nothing for it but to stop and camp -- but where?

All morning we had been passing lovely campsites, but now the best we could find was a narrow bar of sand and boulders (no bushes) beneath the cliffs. There was no shelter and while we stood there deciding what to do it began to pour rain. We finally hunkered down behind a huge rock outcropping.

Eventually, the rain let up and now the kids are out playing in the sand. The place isn't perfect, but we seem to be okay. At least we managed to cook supper and bannock hiding behind our rock wall. The wind is still blowing, in fact, sand fills the air. It's in our eyes, clothes, packs -- everything. It's 10:00 p.m. now and we are waiting to see if the wind will let up enough to permit setting up the tents.

JULY 24: RAMPARTS, DAY TWO

What a night! The wind barely let up at all. We tried sleeping out behind the rocks for awhile, heads buried in our bags to avoid the blowing sand. Increasing rain and decreasing wind got us up around midnight to erect the tents. Two hours later though we were up again, stormlashing the tents down as the wind built up once more and threatened to blow everything away. Even then with all the flapping and uncertainty no one got much sleep. At least it's still light all night, which is a big help during such poor conditions. It really will be funny though to get farther south and see darkness and even stars. We're still above the Arctic Circle.

Well, we didn't move again today. The wind never let up, in fact, it increased and we had to take the tents down come morning. Perched on a sand/rock bar in the Ramparts as we are, with our backs to the canyon wall, there is no place to escape to. We just have to sit here eating sand. It can be pretty hard to take. Both Margie and the kids have been reduced to tears -- Margie at breakfast time. She had been looking forward to pancakes for it seemed like weeks. She bought syrup and butter at Old Crow in hopes of having a rest day soon (they are a slow meal), and this was the big day. What a disaster! Every cake became encrusted with flying sand before it had a chance to cook. We all pretended to like them crunchy, but she wasn't fooled.

We were hoping to leave for a nighttime paddle and, indeed, at 10:00 it seemed to quiet down some, so we packed up. Forget it! It's 11:00 p.m. now and the wind and rain are back, stronger than ever. We have wearily unpacked the tents again and crawled into bed. We are hoping for the best, but preparing for the worst. Tomorrow we plan to start husbanding our food. With such strong winds out of the southwest for the last five days, who knows how long it will take to reach Fort Yukon. This isn't a vacation, it's a test.

JULY 25: CANYON VILLAGE

Well, we paddled nearly sixty miles today. The wind finally died down about 3:30 a.m., but we stayed luxuriating in the stillness for another hour so it was not till almost 5:00 that we set off. The morning was cloudy, but calm, and the high rock walls of the Ramparts canyon were spectacular. There were towering cliffs of all colors: gray, black, orange, pink, green, and white. The current sped us right along and we reached the border by 7:00 a.m. WE DID IT! We are officially in Alaska now. Once more we have sneaked across a border, this time "illegal aliens" in our own land.

The wind did come up later, but with nothing like the ferocity we've grown accustomed to, and we just kept paddling. We picked up some clear, cold drinking water at Salmon Trout Creek (the Porcupine is very muddy). Then we continued on to camp at the deserted site of Canyon Village where there are only a handful of crumbling cabins left today.

This evening a gentleman from Eagle motored in to join us. He is rowing/motoring down the Porcupine and we all ate supper together. He has set up his tent inside a cabin, while we perched out on the beach. Now it is really pouring out, the worst rain we have seen in a month. Hope we don't wash away in the night!

We saw an unusual fox today. He was completely black, except for a silver-white tip on his tail.

JULY 26: CANYON VILLAGE, DAY TWO

After travelling so many long days -- really almost three full summers -- we are beginning to tire. Two years ago we might have tried to force out a few more miles in weather such as this, but when the southwest wind came up so strong on the heels of last night's storm we decided to just sit and molder on the shore for the third day in a week. The gentleman from Eagle was trapped here too and spent his time profitably dismantling the old radio tower. He stuffed the pieces into his boat and plans to erect a windmill when he gets home.

All along our goal has been to reach Alaska and at last we're here. The problem now has become where to stop and what to do. Everyone has tried to discourage us from ascending the Tanana to Fairbanks ("it can't be done'') and for once we are heedful of such advice. We are thinking about stopping at Fort Yukon. It's time to start looking for a home and job. In a month we must be living somewhere and have the kids in school. We are entering a transition phase, coming out of our trip and into an uncertain future. The next few weeks will be unsettled ones as we wrestle with our goals and ponder our choices.

Well, enough. Today in Canyon Village was excellent in many respects. The town appears to have been deserted in '63 and, while the adults sat in the sun musing on our family's future, the children had a wonderful time exploring. They found the old school and spent hours cleaning up the classroom, organizing it, and collecting books. We have a whole library for the canoe now, perhaps fifty children's books, and their summer entertainment is assured.

We saw a moose standing on a gravel bar in the middle of the river opposite us at suppertime.

JULY 27: RAIN

There seems to be two kinds of weather around here, wind and rain. Today we had both. We were in a fighting mood though, and started out at 5:00 a.m. We battled the elements till almost 3:00 and then gave up for the day. At least if we can keep this up we will reach town eventually; it is about 150 miles more and I think our food can hold out that long if we are careful.

There were showers and wind all day long and the children got pretty cold and miserable. Also, the daily little irritations seem to be building up for them. Randy fusses every day about brushing his teeth and both of them take offence at the slightest provocation. Tina hates closing up the tent in the evening with all the clothespins, but isn't satisfied with the way Randy does it. Still, they get along surprisingly well most of the time and do a lot of camp chores this year to help us.

Tonight the tents are in a cozy spot among the pines high on the bank, while our gear is stored under the canoe down below. Everyone dried out pretty well by the fire before going to bed, but we are all tired of coping with such weather. Margie is trying to estimate how many more bannocks she will need to bake this summer.

292

JULY 28: THE CROSS FOX AND THE SCARE-BEAR

We all enjoyed today. The winds, while out of the west, were tolerable and there was plenty of sunshine. In fact, the clouds cleared about 3:00 last night letting the sunlight through and, unable to restrain ourselves, we were off and paddling by 4:00. Tonight we are in the Yukon Flats with about 100 miles left to the Fort, and the country has changed significantly. The river still has current but the banks are low and muddy and the stream itself has braided into dried-up sloughs and sand bars.

While the scenery has been a little dull, the wildlife has been great. Most exciting for us was the sighting of our first cross fox. He was quite large for a fox, mottled gray, red, and black with a white tip on his plume. We also saw a beaver and two bears. The second bear was by far the boldest. We spotted him this evening on the gravel bar opposite our camp at about the same time he spotted us. When he swam the river toward us and began sneaking through the brush to camp, we decided to prepare a little surprise. I took the orange tarp and with a willow bush made a scarecrow (scare-bear?) near the tent at the top of the bank. I'd just gotten the tarp suitably settled over the man-sized bush when the bear popped up over the bank perhaps a canoe-length away. Was he surprised! The wind gave the tarp a flap and that bear was off and running. One last bit of wildlife, though, was pleasantly conspicuous by its absence -- and I don't mean the mosquitoes. We only saw two peregrine falcons all day long. They are such annoying birds. They can "skriee" and shout for an hour at a time whenever we get near their rocky eyries.

Well, we have met a couple of true Alaskans lately, and I begin to worry that with the sparse population there may not be enough shoulders in the state to carry all the chips they bear. They seem to carry an inordinate amount of peeves around, dealing mostly with the lower 48 and in particular with the federal government, but I could easily add environmentalists, the Park Service, the Sierra Club and any other number of "do-gooders". Of course, the east coast isn't perfect either. If you are not prepared to discuss the fine points of gardening or heating with wood, then you'll have trouble in New England.

Margie and I are still wrestling with our future. We find that the joy is in the doing. We've had a wonderful time getting here, but now that we have done it our thoughts are beginning to wander. One of the joys of unemployment is the world of opportunities it opens up. We're free

293

to do anything and can't wait to get started, but we aren't sure what to try.

JULY 29: WHY?

Please feel free to skip this day or to at last go directly to the last paragraph summarizing the day's activities. As we get near the end here we seem to be growing more introspective.

Tonight we are wondering why we undertook this trip. I have been rebelling at the effort needed to resolve this question. In fact, I had hoped that the reader would somehow come to know us better than we know ourselves and so draw his own conclusions. But now I believe our thoughts and personalities have been too well guarded by our daily litany of difficulties. We are still unable to discern our ultimate motivations, but we have been mulling the problem over and have reached some tentative conclusions.

Why would anyone do something like this? Well, to start with, it was a natural outgrowth of a continuing lifestyle. There was no deep philosophical motivation, simply the desire to do a "bigger and better" trip than the one before. This trip had been in the back of our minds for years and suddenly the time seemed right. Beyond this I can only try to sneak up on the question of "why" by describing some of our values and some of the rewards of such a trip.

First, we reject the theme that we see ourselves as being in conflict with nature in some elemental and competitive way. Indeed, all our effort is directed toward living in harmony with nature. Similarly, we are not trying to test ourselves with some rugged, austere lifestyle. We seek a certain simplicity to be sure, but we are more than happy to be dependent on our modern tents, sleeping bags, food stores, etc. If we were out to prove something, this trip might well be our last, whereas it is but the latest in a lifetime of trips.

If then we are not competing, why push so hard? The answer lies buried in our subconscious. We all possess a drive for accomplishment and this energy may be sublimated in a number of ways: a zest for knowledge, power, money, recognition, etc. In us it finds release in the sheer exhilaration generated by travelling alone and living close to nature. The song of the old voyageur strikes a responsive chord deep within us. So do we really travel hard? Yes and no. Yes, the hours are long, but

294

for the most part no longer than we genuinely desire. Our self-imposed timetable is determined by the distance and available days of travel, and was known to us before we even started. This trip is not a vacation in the restful sense of the word, but it is not the same as work, either.

What are the rewards? It depends on one's personality and values. First off we gain almost total personal control of our lives. No longer are we the victims of our temperamental car, balky T.V. or job frustrations. There is freedom from all the niggling rules, authorities and petty machinations of society. There is a chance to laugh at life. Step into the bush for a few months and you will return with a new perspective, a smile and a lust for life. Job, property, civilized ways will all seem scarcely worthy of the consuming sanctity with which they are generally regarded.

Then, too, there are the rewards of family. There is a whole world waiting to be discovered and enjoyed through the unclutterd eyes of our children. Look together with them at even the smallest things and see how differently they perceive. They have a perspective that we, as adults, have all too easily forgotten. Perhaps we could experience their discoveries at home, but there we seem to lack the time and patience. Out here, thrown together 24 hours a day, the bonds of family are strongly forged.

As for the joys of becoming more closely attuned to the natural world, I need scarcely say a word. Others have detailed the glories of a northern day: the morning sunrise through the predawn mist, a startlcd deer, rushing streams and scenic vistas, a crimson sunset, purpling hills in evening's hush, a crackling fire and then the late night's aurora borealis.

Well, it's getting difficult to travel long hours even though we are anxious to be finished. Today was sunny and calm -- perfect conditions. Nevertheless, the kids were restless and we needed breaks so we had long stops for breakfast and lunch. The river is still changing to more mud banks and slid-down trees. The current is fairly strong in places and we moved along at about five miles per hour.

No special animals today -- just a beaver, some bald eagles, and assorted ducks. Still we enjoy watching the eagles soar high over the treetops or the little ducks scurry into the bushes. The wildlife has always been an attraction for us on these wilderness trips. We feel the thrill of discovery on rounding a corner and seeing a moose or bear feeding just yards away.

JULY 30: NEAR THE END OF OUR JOURNEY

As we get down near the end it is becoming tough to wait out the finish. We are starting to get excited about our arrival. It will be sad to part with the canoe though. We've lived in it a long time and it is like one of the family.

It rained in the night but we managed to get up by 5:00 anyway, and for the first few hours it only drizzled so nobody got too wet. Then about 9:00 the roof fell in. It just poured for two hours and it seemed like all we did was bail. By the end everyone was sopped and cold. Really, the weather has not been that glamorous lately. In fact, now that we are well down in the Yukon Flats the scenery too has become singularly unattractive. The river winds and braids with many sloughs through the muddy countryside but the water is so low we must always stick to the main channel, which, of course, is not the shortest. Some of those sloughs would save miles, but they are nearly dry now. At least the campsites have been fairly good. We have taken to camping on top of high banks among the stunted poplar groves near the ends of points, which has been very pleasant.

Only 17 more miles to Fort Yukon! OH, JOY!

JULY 31: HOMEBREW

Only 17 miles to go and we did not make it -- unbelievable! At first it rained and we stayed in bed late. Then the wind came up, making progress slow. The cruncher though was a navigational error. First off, you can't just paddle up to Fort Yukon. It is around the corner from the Porcupine and upstream on the Yukon, past a stretch that is extremely fast. Canoeists must portage in from the shore opposite Homebrew Island (on the Porcupine) some 300 yards through the bush to Hospital Lake, on which the village lies. Anyway, about mid-afternoon Margie announced we had arrived at Homebrew. We spent an hour searching for the missing portage and only then determined we still had two more corners left to paddle. Heartbreaking. Anyway, tonight we are definitely camped on Homebrew Island. I think we must be very close to the portage and tomorrow we shall search it out before breakfast. Well, we were looking forward to getting into town today, but now we are partying

UNDER the STARS

SANDERS, '84

instead and enjoying our last night on the trail. Our glorious venture is coming to an end at last.

AUGUST 1: THE END

The end was perfect. Last night we were indeed camped exactly opposite the carry and today we portaged into town. Everything worked out so well. We sold the canoe to the first person we met and then a BLM (Bureau of Land Management) crew invited us to spend the night with them. Such luxury! There were hot showers, washer/dryers, and real beds. And supper! Apple juice and shrimp for entrees followed by fresh salad, choice of dressing, steak, baked potatoes, asparagus, mushrooms and onions, and fresh milk. Welcome to Alaska!

We have mixed emotions about being done. This trip has permeated our lives for the last three years -- winter and summer. It's something we will never forget and tonight we spent a nostalgic evening of "Remember when ...". Still, it is exciting to look ahead and know that next year's plans aren't preordained. Anything could happen and surely will. In the meantime, we are high on the trip just ended and it feels pretty good.

EPILOGUE: WHAT HAPPENED NEXT

Coming down the Porcupine to Fort Yukon we'd built up more momentum than we realized. Once you're moving it's hard to stop, and before we knew it we'd crossed the state and were out the other side.

The first step was the short flight to Fairbanks where we quickly discovered there were no teaching jobs available. A phone call to the University of Anchorage revealed that my job possibilities there had likewise shrivelled. It was too good a chance to pass up for more vacationing. We took the train down to McKinley Park where we spent eleven wonderful days hiking the backcountry and sightseeing around America's largest mountains. A phone call to the Alaska Marine Highway revealed there were exactly four walk-on spaces available for the Seattle ferry. Ah, fate. We passed on down to Anchorage, bussed to Haines (the ferry landing), and spent three days cruising down the British Columbia coast.

There was still a week before the children would have to be in school. We moved to San Francisco where I am now working as a consultant. The children are happy in their new school and we are enjoying central California. The place is full of fruitcakes and we seem to be fitting in just fine.

So, what about the trip? First off, despite the frustrations recorded in the journal, it was obviously a highlight of our lives. Would we do it again? Margie and I will almost surely, say 25 years from now, run a repeat for old time's sake. There are just too many great memories not to go again. There'll be some differences of course. Next time we'll go alone, travelling light and fast. I'm thinking about taking a 25-pound canoe and a sackful of money. We'll be older then and financially more secure. We'll carry the best equipment and some scrumptious lightweight food for variety. Most importantly, we'll do it in a single season, starting in mid-April.

And what of the immediate future? The years lie rich ahead. The wilderness is filled with trips and we shall be long enjoying them. And, in the years to come, if we should meet on some lonely trail or windswept northern shore, then stop and say hello. Become a part of our lives as now I hope we're part of yours.

> With all best wishes,
> **CARL, MARGIE, TINA and RANDY** —
> The Shepardson family —
> (not to forget Turtle and Elly, too).

299

Books available through Indiana Camp Supply, Inc., P.O. Box 344, Pittsboro, Indiana 46167. Check, money order, VISA, Mastercard and American Express accepted; please include expiration date of card. Write or call (317) 892-3307.

Commercial orders must be addressed to Stackpole Books, P.O. Box 1831, Cameron and Kelker Streets, Harrisburg, Pennsylvania 17105. For fast service use the toll free number. Call 1-800-READ NOW. For library telemarketing orders, call 1-800-LIBRARI. In Pennsylvania, call (717) 234-5041. Please call between 8:30 a.m. and 4:00 p.m. EST.

WILDERNESS MEDICINE
William W. Forgey, M.D.
An informative medical procedures manual written specifically for outdoorsmen interested in preventing, diagnosing and treating common illnesses and injuries. Emergency medical and surgical techniques are described in simple terms. Devoted to the selection of medications, both prescription and non-prescription and their use under wilderness conditions. **Paperback**, 5½ x 8½, 120 pages, photos, diagrams, illus. 0-934802-14-9 **$9.95** Canadian $12.95

"... a clear, concise guide to treating the gamut of outdoor mishaps, from insect bites and fishhook removal to more serious problems such as broken bones and heatstroke."
Sports Afield 11/84

COOKING THE WILD HARVEST
J. Wayne Fears
Over 250 recipes recommended by various agricultural universities' Cooperative Extension Service home economists. Fears combines his talents as a wildlife biologist, outdoorsman, and prize-winning outdoor writer for hints on proper field dressing and procuring. **Paperback**, 6x9, 185 pages. 0-934802-14-9 **$12.95** Canadian $15.95

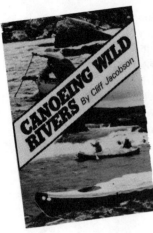

CANOEING WILD RIVERS
Cliff Jacobson
An easy reading manual, of source material, canoeing tips, advanced techniques, and gear recommendations by a weathered expert. **Paperback**, 340 pages, color photos, illus.
0-934802-17-3 **$14.95** Canadian 17.95

> *"If you've ever dreamed of canoeing Alaska's arctic rivers, or for that matter, any waterway in North America, then* **Canoeing Wild Rivers** *is the first book you should obtain."*
> Alaska Outoors 11/84

> *"This book,* **Canoeing Wild Rivers,** *by Cliff Jacobson is the one I recommend above all others ... It is not a re-hash of previous writers, but the accumulated learnings of much personal experience."*
> Verlen Kruger ['84]
> Ultimate Canoe Challenge member

HIKING
Calvin Rutstrum
A comprehensive, procedural coverage from the short urban walk to the extensive wilderness trek, with analysis of equipment, outdoor living methods, and modern hiking ethics. **Paperback**, 6x9, 125 pages, photos, illus.
0-934802-20-3 **$8.95** Canadian $11.95

BACK COUNTRY
Calvin Rutstrum
A volume of adventures, trips and events from the Northern Wilderness during the first part of this century. **Paperback**, 6x9, 255 pages, Les Kouba illus.
0-934802-11-4 **$14.95** Canadian $17.95

COOKING THE DUTCH OVEN WAY
Woody Woodruff
Written by a designer/manufacturer of dutch ovens, and a 50-year Scouter and life-long camper and hiker. Recipes for good old fashioned dishes and baker's favorites, easily prepared at home or in the north-woods. **Paperback**, 6x9, 142 pages, illus.
0-934802-01-7 **$8.95** Canadian $11.95

A TRAPPER'S LEGACY
Carl Schels
A rare glimpse of a professional trapper's life, difficulties, and dangers of existence deep in the wilderness. Forced into poverty by the Great Depression, Carl Schels decided to chase his dream of wilderness living and survived to write this story -- his legacy. **Paperback**, 5½ x 8½, 212 pages, photos.
0-934802-12-2 **$9.95** Canadian $12.95

HODIO
C.N. Day
The true story of a 19-year-old American seaman captured off the shores of Burma during a naval battle of World War II. For the 42 months in brutal prison camps of Indonesia, **HODIO** became synonymous with Prisoner of War. **Paperback**, 5½ x 8½, 216 pages.
0-934802-13-0 **$9.95** Canadian $12.95